Frank Theodore Cole

The early Genealogies of the Cole Families in America

Frank Theodore Cole

The early Genealogies of the Cole Families in America

ISBN/EAN: 9783337179403

Printed in Europe, USA, Canada, Australia, Japan

Cover: Foto ©ninafisch / pixelio.de

More available books at **www.hansebooks.com**

ANK T. CO

TABLE OF CONTENTS.

PAGE.

PREFACE.

THIS work was begun in 1871, but after some fifteen months of labor, was laid aside because of the pressure of other duties. In January 1886, it was again taken up, and the work done thus far is here presented

Following the tradition of my family, that Connecticut was the early home of my ancestors, investigation was made in that direction, and a large amount of material gathered, when the unreliability of the tradition became evident.

A study of the first four generations of all the various families of the name then followed, and the right line found. It seemed that the results of that study might be of use to some future student, if they were placed in an accessible form. The hope that this might be the case is the excuse for the first hundred pages of the text.

It is only too evident that many lines in the Salem family have been dropped. This has been from inability to trace them in the time allotted for the work. It seemed that the book must be published this spring or not for several years. This must be the excuse for the incompleteness. It is the expectation to publish some time in the future, an enlarged and revised history of the Salem family of Thomas Cole, and in anticipation thereof correspondence is solicited, with a view to making the work complete. It may not come for five years, nor for twenty-five, but if time and strength and length of days are granted, it will come.

The published matter relating to the families has been freely used, and in most cases credit given. The list of those who have aided in gathering material, and who have helped with encouraging words, is too long for insertion. Thanks are given to them all. Those who might have supplied information, but neglected to answer the letters of inquiry, are not aware how much disappointment they have caused us. We ask better treatment for the next geneologist who writes to them. The list of those who have encouraged us by their subscriptions will be found at the close of the volume.

Columbus, O., May 21, 1887. FRANK T. COLE.

INDEX No. I.

Index to those bearing the name of Cole (those dying in childhood omitted)

A.

B.

C.

D.

E.

F.

G.

H.

I.

J.

K.

L.

M.

R.

S.

T.

INDEX No. II.

Names Other than Cole, Coles, or Cowles.

A.

B.

C.

D.

E.

F.

G.

H.

I.

J.

M.

N.

O.

P.

S.

T.

V.

W.

Y.

COLES.

COWLES.

THE HARTFORD FAMILY.

SKETCH NO. I.

JAMES COLE, the first of this family in America, was b. in England, probably in Essex County. He married and was left a widower, with one little daughter, Abigail (Elizabeth[2]).

He then m. Ann Edwards, the widow of the Rev. Richard Edwards, a Puritan minister of London. She had one young son, William Edwards.

Soon after this marriage, Mr. Cole, with his wife, daughter and step-son, emigrated to New England. They may have gone direct to Newtown, now Cambridge, or they may have been of the party that settled at Mt. Wollaston, and then removed to Cambridge.

They joined the party which, under the lead of the Rev. Thomas Hooker, left Cambridge in October, 1635, for the Connecticut Valley.

After two weeks of toilsome journeying they reached the present site of the city of Hartford, and purchased land of the natives, and made their settlement.

Mr. Cole's name appears on the lists of the original settlers as given by Hinman, and by Porter, and also on the monument erected by The Ancient Burying Ground Association of Hartford, in memory of the original settlers.*

The settlers purchased of the Indian chiefs the tract of land running west from the Connecticut river six miles, east and west, and bounded on the north by Windsor, and on the south by

*Hinman. First Puritan Settlers, pp. 18, 161, 165.
Porter. Hartford in 1640, p. 8.

Wethersfield. This deed was lost, and on July 5, 1670, another was obtained from all the Indians interested.*

It is probable that the meadows had been cleared and cultivated by the Indians before this. The lands were divided among the original purchasers, as house lots, plow lands, wood lands, etc., and small house lots were granted to settlers who were not proprietors.

The original town plat occupied nearly the same space as the older part of the present city. The central part was divided into lots called two acres each, and distributed among the original proprietors, and on the border were half acre house lots granted to other settlers.† West of the town was a large stretch of land set apart as a commons for pasturage, and west of that was a very large tract of land that was afterwards divided among the proprietors.

The most distinguished families among the first settlers were located on the east side of the present Governor street; on the two sides of the Little (Farmington) river; on the Main street in front of the State House; and south of the Little river.

James Cole had the lot on the corner of two streets, called in the old records the one "The road from Moody's to the ox pasture," or "The road to Wethersfield." This is now Main street.

The other was called "The road to Wethersfield," "The Road from Wm. Hill's to the ox pasture," "The road to the ox pasture." This street was originally named Cole street, and retained that name till March 10, 1851, when it was changed to its present name of Governor street, because five Governors of the colony and State had lived thereon.‡

Adjoining Mr. Cole's lot on the north, was the lot of Thomas Judd, and next to that was the estate of George Wyllys, a Gov-

*Porter, p. 4.

†Porter, p. 18.

‡Hartford in the olden time, pp. 32, 46.
Porter, p. 20.

ernor of the olony, on which estate stood the famous Charter Oak.

Across the street to the east from Mr. Cole's was the estate of Thomas Hosmer.

The following record is found in the hand writing of John Allyn, who transcribed the names from the old town book into the records in 1665:

"The proprietors of the undivided lands in Hartford, with each of their proportions in one division, as follows, according to which proportion they payd for sayd land."

In this list is the name "James Coale, 12, 10."*

Mr. Cole was a cooper by trade, and probably had apprentices, as John King came to the colony when 16 years old, in 1645, and lived with Mr. Cole till he was of age.†

He d. in 1652. His will was as follows:

I, James Cole, of Hartford, upon the river of Connecticut, being of perfect memory and soundness of minde, doe according to my duty, (knowing the frailty of my body, and uncertainty of my life, for the preventing of distraction to myself while I live, and differency in my family when I am gathered to my fathers), make and ordaine this, my last will and testament, and do dispose of that outward estate wherewith the Lord hath of his abundant mercy blessed me, in the manner following:

Impri. I give to my deare and well beloved sonn and daughter, Daniel and Abigail Sullivane, my new dwelling house in Hartford, with all other out-housings, orchard, garden, homelott, with all the appurtanance thereto belonging, with one piece of land, being about five acres more or less, lying pennywise, within Wethersfield bounds; as also one parcel of upland, being about fower acres more or less, lying about the Wolf Pond.‡ all which fore mentioned lands and housings I give to them and their heirs forever, provided that my son Daniel and my daughter Abigail, pay yearly to my well beloved wife, Ann Cole, the just and full sum of three pounds in good current pay, during her natural life; further my will is that my wife should have an upper room at the south end of my new dwelling house during her widowhood, with free liberty of egress and regress without molestation. Further, my will is that shee my wife Ann Cole, should have the use of their fireing for her own use in every respect; and also any fruit or herbs in the orchard or garden for her owne particular spending; as also the use of the well belonging to the house. Further, if my wife desires to keep a cow, or a hogg, or some poultry for her par-

*Porter, p. 18.

†Hinman, p. 280.

‡The Wolf Pond was the name given to a lot or two lying on the east side of and about the middle of Washington street, on the south side of the Little river. Porter, p. 32.

ticular use, she providing meat for them, my will is that she shall have yard room for them where my son Daniel's cattel are usually yarded.

ITEM. I give all my cooper's tools equally to be devided between my well beloved son William Edwards, and loving cousin Henry Cole.

ITEM. I give my deare and well beloved wife, Ann Cole, all my house hold stuff of any kind undisposed of, with all my cattel and crop of corn now on the ground, with all my debts owing to me, provided that she pays all my just debts, and defray all that charge which shall be thought necessary by the overseers of this my will, for my christian burial, also I doe desire and appoint my trusty and well beloved friends, Mr. John Webster and William Gibbins, overseers of this my will, and further I doe appoint my deare and well beloved Ann Cole to be my sole executrix of this my last will and testament.

JAMES COLE.

Witnesses, JOHN WHITE,
THOMAS HOSMER.

Now, although there is no mention in the will of any son I am confident that he had a son, John. Hinman says, (page 204) that he had, and in the division of public land in November, 1674, the record says (Porter, p. 45) that John, the son of the original settler, James Cole, received 18 acres, and a year or two later in another division he received 15 and 5-8 acres. Again, in 1655, John Coal, residing on Wethersfield Lane, was admitted a freeman. Now Wethersfield Lane was where James Cole had lived (Porter, page 36). Savage says that he had a son by his first wife, named John, who probably died young, but on what he based his judgment I am unable to say.

Ann Cole, the widow of James, d. February 20, 1678 (9).

She evidently saved something from her income during her widowhood, or else had property of her own, as she sold two pieces of land, one of two acres in the west field to Mr. Lord, (old Record Book, page 134), and one of three acres in the pine field to Jonathan Gilbert, January 17, 1677(8). (Old Record Book, page 460).

She gave her house and lot to her son, William Edwards,* dur-

*William Edwards, the step-son of James Cole, was made a freeman in 1646, and resided on the north side of State Square. (Porter, p. 36.) (Goodwin, 48).

He m. Agnes Spencer, the widow of William Spencer, of Concord, about 1645, and had a son, Richard, b. May, 1647. who was the only child.

William d. in 1672, (Goodwin, p. 48). His son Richard d. April 20, 1718, leaving the lives of William and his wife, then to vest in her grandson, Richard Edwards, and his heirs forever. The estate was 103 pounds, and Richard was appointed administrator.

The children of James Cole were

i. Abigail, b. ———— She m. Daniel Sullivane, and is mentioned in her father's will. Some three years after her father's death, her husband having died, she sold her interest in her father's estate to her brother, John Cole, for £112. In that conveyance she is called Elizabeth, and is mentioned as living in the colony of New Haven.

ii. John Cole, b. ————, d. 1685.

2

John[2] Cole (*James*[1]), the only son of James Cole by his first wife, was b. in England. I am of the opinion that he came to the colony of Connecticut sometime after his father was established there. He was admitted as a freeman in 1655, three years after his father's death, and he may not have come to the colony till after that event. He is stated as living on Wethersfield Lane and that was where his father had lived. In the will of James Cole his property was left to his daughter and her husband, subject to certain life estate of the widow. Soon after his death his son-in-law also died, and in 1655 John bought the interest of his sister in the property. The sister, Abigail, (so called in her father's will) or Elizabeth (so called in the deed), had in the meantime removed to the New Haven colony. The contract of sale is a curiosity, and is given at length:

"This Indenture witnesseth that I Elizabeth Sullivant of New Haven widdow doe by these presents bargain and sell and by these have bargained and sold unto John Cole of Hartford all that my house and home lott and all the meadow and lands and accommodations belonging and appertaining unto the same. And in consideration hereof I the said John Cole doe hereby promise to pay or cause to bee payd

---

ing an estate of 1652 pounds. He was the grandfather of the celebrated Dr. Jonathan Edwards, and the progenitor of the Edwards family of Connecticut. (Hinman, p. 220,) (Savage; Goodwin, Geneological Notes, p. 48.)

to the sayd Elizabeth or her assigns the inst and full somm of fifty eight pounds in wheat and pease at 3d and 4d, that is to pay 4d wheat and 3d pease and the said prize of fifty eight pounds to be fully satisfied and payd in manner and form following that is to pay twenty nyne pounds at or before the twentieth day of Aprill next ensuing the date hereof and the other twenty nyne pounds at or before the twentieth day of Aprill 1657. And for the sure and true payment thereof we have hereunto set our hands this third day of October 1655.

With the sayd house and accommodations is also at the same prize of fifty eight pounds alowed a bedstead and a table.

ELIZABETH SULLIVANT.
JOHN COLE.

Received of the summs above specified by order from Mr. Goodyear and upon his account the summ of forty nyne pounds ten shillings. July the third (57)

HENRY WOLCOTT."

Savage says that Mr. Cole was Constable in 1657. That office was in former times a very honorable and dignified one, and was held by the reliable men of the colony.

In the oldest book of records in Hartford is given a list of his real estate for taxation. The list is as follows:

Lands belonging to John Cole.*

1. *One Parcel* of land in the Ox pasture, which he bought of John Whitting, Dea. Edward Stribling and others, containing by estimate about eight acres, abuting on the highway leading to Wethersfield on the west, on Mr. Hames meadow on the east, on Philip Davis's land on the north, and on Mr. Hopkins' Ox Pasture on the south. Recorded Jan 11, 1665.
2. *One Parcel* of land which he bought of Thomas Hosmer containing five roods, lying in the forty acres belonging to the south meadow, and is grass land, and abuts on John White's land on the north, and Thomas Selding's land on the south, and on Ben. Harbor's and a swamp on the west and on Thomas Hosmer's on the east, as appears by a writing dated July 26, 1671 Recorded February 17, 1678.
3. *One Parcel* of upland which he bought of John Wilcox containing seventeen acres, abuting on a pond in John White's swamp on the east, upon Wethersfield bounds on the south, on the highway on the west end of the Ox Pasture Lots on the west, and on G. Winter's on the north, as by deed of September 18, 1660. Recorded February 20, 1673.
4. *One Parcel* of land which he bought of Samuel Wills, abuting on the highway on the east, on Mr. Will's home lot on the north, and on Cole's house lot on the south and west, as by deed of February, 1673 containing one Rood, Recorded February 20, 1673.
5. *One Parcel* of land which he bought of James Steel, lying in the forty acres, which containeth two acres by estimation, and abuteth on the Wethersfield

*Book of Records (not numbered) pp. 541, 564.

bounds or John Cole's land on the south, on John White's on the west, on Thomas Standish's Island on the east, and on James Steel's on the north, as by deed of February 18, 1673. Recorded January 23, 1674.

6. *One Parcel* of Swamp land of five and a half acres, bought of John White abuting on John Cole's land the Wethersfield bounds on the south, on John Cole's land on the east and west, and on John White's and Thomas Wells' on the north, as by deed of February 16, 1674, and acknowledged April 9, 1675.

7. *One Parcel* of land lying on the east side of the Great River which he bought of William Edwards, containing one acre and three roods abuting on Thomas Spencer's land on the north, on lands of Nathaniel Barding's heirs on the west, on Thomas Olcott's land on the east, and on the highway from the river eastward on the south, as by deed of April 9, 1675.

8. *One Parcel* lying in long lots abuting on the highway on the north, on land of N. Rogers on the south, on the Commons on the east, and on the Farmington bounds on the west, containing eighteen acres, being six rods wide. (This was a portion of the large tract of land lying between the Commons and Farmington, which the proprietors on January 30, 1672(3), voted to have laid out in lots and divided. This division was consummated in November, 1674. The lots were laid out of different widths but were all one and one-half miles long. The town had previously voted (February 9, 1671(2), "That when any of the undevided lands shall be laid out every proprietor for himself and those he stands for shall receive his proportion of what lands shall be agreed to be laid out, according to the rule for division of lands agreed upon and entered in the town book dated January 3, 1639, of which this on the other side (James Coale 12, 10, etc.), is a copy of the proportion. In this division Lot No. 22, went to John Cole, son of James, (Porter pp. 41–43).

9. *One parcel* of land given him by the proprietors on four mile hill abuting on the highway from Farmington to Wethersfield on the east, on the land of J. Mitchel and others on the west, Philip Davis land on the north, on Joseph Smith's land on the south, containing fifteen and one half acres, 25 rods wide and 100 rods long, as laid out by James Steel and certified to January 2, 1681, and recorded the same day. (This is a lot of land that he got out of the land disposed of by the following: "At a meeting of the proprietors of the undevided lands in Hartford January 3, 1677(8). The proprietors voted................ It was also voted that the piece of land lying next Wethersfield bounds, and is an overplus after the lots are laid out, shall be laid out in five tiers of lots; the middle tier of lots shall be 20 acre lots, the tier next the town commons 10 acre lots, the others 15 acre lots; and those to whom the lots shall be given are not to sell them before they are fenced in and improved." John Cole got lot No. 3 in the third tier. (Porter pp. 45–46.)

10. *One parcel* of land which he bought of Elizabeth Sullivant, containing 3 acres and 2 roods, abuting on the highway on the south, east and west, and on the land of Thomas Judd on the north. (This was the land he bought in 1655 and was the old homestead of James Cole.)

11. *One parcel* of land bought of Elizabeth Sullivant formerly land of Mr. Hollister, containing five acres, abuting on J. Wilcox land on the east, James Cole's land on the north, and the Great river on the west. Recorded June 4, 1684.

So it will be seen that in twenty-two years he had obtained possession of over eighty acres of land.

The following from the Court Records of Hartford, refers to him:

"June 8, 1661, General Sessions. This Court. taking into consideration ye estate yt is in John Cole's improvement, yt formerly belonged too Edward Hopkins Esq., doe order that ye shal require and take into his custody and improvement, ye rent of ye house and land at Hartford from John Cole, and to be accountable for ye same, when ye Court shall call him ther' wnt.——— ——— Ye Treasurer and Willm Wadsworth aer desired to acquaint John Cole that ye Court expects him to continue in ye improvement of ye farm according to his lease, and it lieth with them to inform him that ye Court desires and is ready to encourage him in the business in the future."

This land was a large tract of meadow on the south side of the Farmington or Little river, and east of the Main street, extending towards the Great or Connecticut river.

In his will, dated August 4, 1683, are bequests as follows:

That his son John, of Farmington, should have 30 pounds payd him out of the estate, besides what he hath had, and that he should also have his wearing clothes; that his daughter Benton, and his daughter Wilson, should have five pounds apiece, also paid out of it; that his son Job, in England, should have ten pounds, if it can be conveyed to him; and that his loving wife should have six pounds a year allowed her out of his estate while she liveth, and a cow, which shall be kept also winter and summer, and she shall have her wood; and the rest of his estate shall be divided between his sons Samuel and Nathaniel, excepting the housing and home lot, and his wife consenting, that is that his son Samuel should have the home lot as wide as his own down to the ditch, and that he should have twenty bushels of apels a year for six years; and the rest of the houseing and houselot should be given to his son, Nathaniel; only his wife shall have two rooms in the house while she liveth, if she see cause to live there, and she shall have the disposal of the household stuffs; and Hannah Yeoman shall have forty shillings, and his will is that Ensign Nathaniel Stanley and Stephen Hosmore, his loving friends, would see the performance of this his will. Witness this 4 August, 1683.

STEPHEN HOSMORE, JOHN COLE.
BENJAMIN GHRIMES.

Book 4, page 237. The inventory of John Cole's estate, deceased, taken the 17th day of November, 1685, his wearing apparel and other personal estate together with the real estate was inventoried, and the amount of the inventory was 396 pounds, 18 shillings, 6 pence.

At a Court held at Hartford, March 4, 1686, the following was recorded:

"The last will and testament of John Cole was exhibited in Court, proved and ordered to be recorded, with an inventory of his estate, and this Court grants administration on the estate to same, and Nathaniel Cole, with the will annexed." (Bk. 4, p. 117.)

He died in 1685.

It is his daughter that is referred to in the curious letter of the Rev. John Whiting to the Rev. Increase Mather, dated at Hartford, October 4, 1682, and giving an account of the case of Ann Cole, supposed to have been bewitched, in 1662, by a woman who was next door neighbor, and who was afterwards executed. Mr. Cole is referred to as "a Godly man among us." The minister says that Ann recovered from her strange fits after the death of the witch. The letter, with a full account of the witch, may be found in Massachusetts Historical Collections, Fourth Series, Vol. VIII, p. 466.

The children of John Cole were:

3. i. JOHN, b.
ii. JOB, b.——— He is mentioned in his father's will as living in England. He probably always lived there.
4. iii. SAMUEL, b.——— d. 1694.
iv. MARY, b. June 27, 1654, probably d. young.
v. ANN, b.———, m. Andrew Benton, a freeman of Milford, Connecticut, who moved to Hartford, and admitted freeman there in 1664, and married Ann as his second wife. They lived on Wethersfield Lane. The proprietors voted him lot No. 3 in the first tier of lots (10 acres), in the division of 1677(8). Her children were Ebenezer, Lydia, and Hannah, who m. Edward Schofield, of Haddam. She d. 1686. Benton d. July 31, 1683, leaving an estate of 364 pounds.
vi. LYDIA, b. ——— ———, m. John Wilson, and had children John, Stebbing, Hannah and Mary. He was the son

of Robt. of Windsor, and was made freeman 1675. He d. Jan 16. 1698.

5. vii. NATHANIEL, b. ——— ———, d. in Hartford, April 28, 1700.

3

JOHN[3] COLE (*John,[2] James,[1]*) the oldest son of John and Mary ——— Cole. He settled in Farmington, and was one of the prominent men of the town. November 30, 1657, he was elected constable, which office he held for two years. The following receipt is copied from the records:

"HARTFORD, 1657.

"Received of John Cole, constable for this year in Farmington, the sum of fifteen pounds five shillings, wich is for that town's proportion in the year of his constableship. In witness of the fact, I say received this day, 30th Novembr, 15 pounds 5 shillings. JOHN CULLOCK."

In May, 1669, he was Commissioner for the town.

The children of John and Rachel Cole were:

6. i. John, b. 1665.
   ii. Rachel, b. 1668.
7. iii. Samuel, b. 1676.
8. iv. Nathaniel, b. 1678.
   v. Dorothy, b. July 3, 1681.
   vi. Lydia, b. Mar. 22, 1684. (Mar. 18, 1685.)

4

SAMUEL[3] COLE (*John,[2] James[1]*,). He was a freeman of Hartford, but the records do not show that he held any public office.

The list of his land for taxation is as follows: (Hartford Records, Book I, page 10.)

Land belonging to Samuel Cole in 1685-6:

Home place, containing one acre three roods, abuting on the highway on the south and west, and on Watson's and Nath. Cole's land on the North, on Nath'l Cole's land on the east.

The Ox Pasture of eight acres on the Wethersfield road, abuting on the highway leading to Wethersfield on the west, on Henry Ghrime's land on the south, on Phillip Davis's land on the north, and on Mr. Haines' meadow on the east.

One parcel in the south meadow, which was James Steel's, and abuts on said Steel's land north, Wethersfield bounds south, Thomas Standish's east, and Nathaniel Coale's land west. (2 a.)

One parcel in the Ox Pasture of fourteen acres, and abuts on the Wethersfield road on the east, on the bounds between Wethersfield and Hartford on the south, on Nath'l Sanford's land north, and on a highway on the west.

One parcel in the long lots containing eighteen acres, abuting on Farmington on the west, on Hartford Commons on the east, on the highway on the north, and on Rodgers' land on the south, which became his by his father's will and the division of Samuel and Nathaniel. Recorded Mar. 12, 1684.

Thus it will be seen that in the division between Samuel and Nathaniel, under their father's will, that Samuel took parcels No. 1, No 5, 14 acres of No. 3, No. 8, and one and three-quarters acres of the west part of the homestead, (on which he built his house,) while Nathaniel took the rest of the homestead and the other parcels, except No. 11. Of this I find no mention in the share of either.

His will is as follows:

"I, Samuel Cole, of Hartford, being weak in body though in perfect memory, and not knowing the day of my death doe ordayne this my last will and comit my spirit in to the hands of Jesus Christ my Redeemer and my body to a comly buriall at the discresion of my executors and after all my just debts and funeral expences are payed I dispose of what estate God has trusted me with in manner and form following:

I give to my beloved wife Mary the use of all my estate untill my children shall atayn their ages, the sonns of twenty one years and the daughter eighteen years of age.

I give to my wife a third part of all my moveable estate and to rooms in my dwelling house which she shall choose during her widowhood and a third part of all my land during her natural life.

I give to my son Samuel Cole my house and barn and house lot.

I give to my son Ickabod my land at the Ox Pasture, bounding on Goodman Davis north, and Benjamin Ghrimes south.

I give to my other two sons John and Jonathan all my land at poke hill to be equally devided between them.

My will is that my three daughters, Elizabeth, Dorothy and Hannah shall have twenty pounds apiece out of my estate.

My will is that if there any estate left it be equally devided between my children and if any fall short that each should abate according to their proportion given them and if any of them dye before they atayne the age above sayd that then the part or parts shall go to the survivors equally between them and I leave it with my executors and overseers hereafter mentioned according to their best discretion to put my sons out to trades that may be most suitable.

I desire and appoint my loving wife executrix of this my last will and when my son Samuel Cole shall atayne the age of twenty one years of age I appoint him to be joint executor with his mother and I desire my loving brother Nathaniel Cole and Samuel Kelog to be my overseers and to assist my executors according to the best of their ability.

Samuel Cole declared this to be his last will this 14 day of March, 1693, in the presence of us whose names are underwritten.

CALEB WATSON,
her mark
MARY **M** SEYMOUR."

The following entry shows the date of his death:

"An inventory of the estate of Samuel Cole, of Hartfort, deceased March 16, 1693(4), was made by Ciprian Nichols and Jacob White, May 29, 1694."

His wife was Mary ———. He died March 16, 1693.

The children of Samuel and Mary ——— Cole were:

9. i. Samuel, b. about 1673.
10. ii. Ichabod, b. ———, d. in Middletown, Apr. 4, 1711.
11. iii. John, b. ——— d. in Hartford, Mar. 1775.
12. iv. Jonathan, b. ———, d. in 1761 in Hartford.
v. Elizabeth, b. ———, m. Richard Smith, Dec. 20, 1705.
vi. Dorothy, b. ———.
vii. Hannah, b. ———.

5

NATHANIEL[3] COLE (*John,[2] James[1],*). He was born and lived all his life in Hartford. He was appointed administrator of his father's will in March, 1686, and in the division under that will he received the parcels No. 2, four and a half acres of No. 3, No. 6, No. 7, No. 9, and two and a half acres of the east half of the homestead, on which the house stood. He accumulated considerable property, as is shown by the list of land owned by him and listed for taxation. Book I, page 10. (Omitting the land that came from his father, which has been given above.)

1. *One parcel* which he received of Joseph Benton being upland, containing by estimation four acres bounded as followeth: east on the highway leading from Mr. Steel's to the West Swamp; west on land formerly belonging to John Moody; north on the highway; south on land belonging to Nathaniel Cole as by his deed February 3, 1695(6).

2. *One parcel* which he bought of Caleb Watson, containing by estimation six acres, and two roods abutting on the highway leading from George Steel's to the Great Swamp of the east; on the highway lying by Rocky Hill on the west; on land formerly Thomas Graves' on the south; and on land of George Stockings on the north, as may appear by a deed of sale dated May 3, 1680.

3. *One parcel* which he bought of Joseph Smith containing three acres, abuting on the highway leading from Geo. Steel's to the Great Swamp on the east, and on the highway leading up to Rocky Hill on the west; on Thomas Catlin's land on the north, and on land belonging to James Richards' heirs on the south, as appears by deed dated February 26, 1683.

4. *One parcel* of land which he bought of Robert Stanley, containing seven acres, abuting on the highway leading from the town to the Great Swamp on the east; on Mr. Joseph Whiting's land on the north; on Jonathan Bull's land on the south; and on the highway by Rocky Hill on the west, as appears by deed dated February 27, 1783.

5. *One parcel* of land which he bought of Andrew Benton, containing four acres, abuting on the highway leading from Geo. Steel's to the Great Swamp on the east, his own land on the south, Samuel Moody's land on the west, and on Joseph Benton's land on the north, as appears by deed dated March 6, 1684(5).

6. *One parcel* of land which he bought of Capt. Thomas Watts, and was confirmed to him by his wife's executors, lying on the east side of Rocky Hill on the west, on Phillip Davis' land on the north, on John Bidwell's land on the south, and on a highway on the east, as appears by deed dated June 22, 1685.

Thus it will be seen that he had bought between twenty-five and thirty acres of land between two highways, bounded on the east by the present Washington street (Porter, p. 20–33), toward the south part of the town. The Great Swamp was a tract of about 400 acres in the south part of the town. (Porter, p. 30.)

Omitting the five parcels which he inherited, we go on with the record:

12. *One parcel* of land which he bought of John Andrews, lying in the Ox Pasture three roods and abuts on the highway leading to Wethersfield on the west, on John White's land on the east, on sayd Coal's own land on the south, and sayd John Andrew's land on the north, and is three rods wide and forty-one rods in length, as appears by deed dated May 20, 1686.

13. *One parcel* of land which he bought of Mr. Joseph Welles, lying in the south meadow in the forty acres, containing four acres and abuts on John White's land on the north, and on the west, and on the east, and on Nathaniel Cole's own land on the south, as appears by deed April 5, 1693.

14. *One parcel* of land which he bought of John Moody, containing twelve acres, and abuts west on a highway leading from Mr. Webster's southerly to the Great Swamp, and on land formerly Mr. John Whitings and Henry Ghrimes'

on the east, and on Andrew Benton's land on the north, and on Mr. Richard's land on the south, as appears by deed dated April 25, 1793.

15. *One parcel* of land which he bought of Mrs. Susana Webster, lying in the south meadow swamp, containing an acre and a rood, and abuts on Samuel Wylly's land on the north, of land formerly of Mr. Thomas Wells on the south, on said Mrs. Webster's land on the east and west as appears by her deed dated March 18, 1694(5).

Thus by inheritance and by purchase he possessed fifteen parcels of land amounting to upwards of seventy-five acres.

He probably purchased other lands after this date, but the record has not been found.

He died April 20, 1708. His will is as follows:

"In the name of God Amen: the seventeenth day of aperill in the year of our Lord 1708 I Nathaniel Coale Of the town of Hartford in The Colony of Conn., being sick in Body but of sound and perfect rememberance (blessed be the name of the Lord for it) do constitute ordain and make this my last will and testament in manner and form following. First I commit my soul into the hand of Almighty God my Creator who gave, trusting and relying to be saved by the only and the lone merits of Jesus Christ my Redeemer, and my body to a decent and Christian burial, and for my worldly estate wherewith God has blessed me of his Mercy and goodness, I give and bequeath as follows:

To my loving and dear wife Mary Coale one third part of all my moveable estate forever (my said wife to let Ebenezer Benton have a bed out of it) and also one third part of all my real estate to improve to her use during her natural life (only my said wife is to pay one third part of the purchase money of that land I bought of Ichabod Coale), also I give my said wife the improvement of the south end of my house to live in and one third of the barn during the time she shall remain a widow, but if my said wife should marry that then she shall release her third part of the house lot and take it out in other lands.

ITEM. I give and bequeath to my loving son Nathaniel Coale all the rest of my movable estate not given to my wife, and also all my lands (except the improvement of one third part of them given as above to my said wife), also my will is that Ebenezer Benton should be maintained by my wife and my son jointly so long as my wife shall remain a widow, but if she should marry that then my son Nathaniel Coale shall take care to maintain him during his natural life, if my son Nathaniel shall live to survive him, and that my said son shall have what estate was given to maintain the said Ebenezer Benton not yet disposed of for his maintainance, and I do make and constitute my son Nathaniel Coale sole executor of this my last will and testament.

In testimony whereof I have hereunto set my hand and seal the day and year above written.

NATHANIEL COLE, Senior.

HEZEKIAH WILLIS,
JONATHAN WEBSTER.

June 7, 1708, Nathaniel Cole appointed administrator and gave bond.

July 5, 1708, inventory filed amounting to 572 pounds, 9 shillings, 8 pence. (Book 7, p. 114.)

He married November, 1676, Lydia Davis, who died 1683. October 23, 1689, he married again, Mary Benton, by whom he had no children. He died April 20, 1708.

The only child of Nathaniel and Lydia (Davis) Cole was:

13. i. Nathaniel, b. Nov. 6, 1682, d. in Hartford, April 20, 1735.

6

JOHN[4] COLE (*John*,[3] *John*,[2] *James*,[1]) born 1665, in Farmington, probably. He lived in that town all of his life. Joined the church March 15, 1693. He married a daughter of Deacon Hart.

The children of John and —— (Hart) Cole were:

i. Sarah, b ? Aug. 27, 1693.
14. ii. John, b. Mar. 15, 1695(6).

7

SAMUEL[4] COLE (*John*,[3] *John*,[2] *James*,[1]) born in Farmington, 1676.

8

NATHANIEL[4] COLE, (*John*,[3] *John*,[2] *James*,[1]) born in Farmington, 1678.

9

SAMUEL[4] COLE, (*Samuel*,[3] *John*,[2] *James*.[1]) the eldest son of Samuel and Mary Cole, was born in Hartford about 1672. He married Mary, daughter of James Kingsbury, of Plainfield, January 2, 1693.

The children of Samuel and Mary (Kingsbury) Cole were:

i. (*A son*)—ez. b. Feb. 9, 1698.
15. ii. Nathaniel, b. Aug. 18, 1701.
16. iii. [Selah (Caleb)] b. Feb. 8, 1703.
iv. [Sarah] b. Feb. 18, 1705.
v. Abigail, b. Sept. 18, 1706.
vi. Mary, b. July 10, 1707.
17. vii. Samuel, b. Feb. 7, 1710.
18. viii. Ichabod, b. Mar. [1712 ?]
ix. Dorothy, b. Nov. 27, [1714 ?]

Under his father's will he received the homestead.

10

ICHABOD[4] COLE (*Samuel,*[3] *John,*[2] *James,*[1]) born in Hartford. Moved to Middletown, Connecticut, and settled there. He married Sarah ——. He died April 4, 1711.

The children of Ichabod and Sarah —— Cole were:

19 i. Stephen, b. July 17, 1708.
ii. Rachael, b. Jan, 23, 1710.

Under his father's will he received a lot of eight acres in the ox pasture. He sold this to his uncle, Nathaniel Cole, Sr., about 1707, and moved to Middletown.

11

JOHN[4] COLE (*Samuel,*[3] *John,*[2] *James,*[1]). He was the third son of Samuel Cole, and was probably a youth when his father died in 1694. (See Jonathan for account of inherited property.) He married Elizabeth Goodwin, of Hartford, September 12, 1713. He had children:

i. Elizabeth, b. Sept. 7, 1714. Probably d. young.
ii. Jerushe, b. June 17, 1715(6,) m. Thomas Tisdale.
iii. Lydia, b. Nov. 2, 1718. Probably d. young.

He may have had others, but these are all that are recorded. He died about 1775, as on March 23, of that year, administration on his estate was granted to Capt. Aaron Bull and Barnabus Hinsdale. He is spoken of as Lieut. John Cole.

In the inventory of the estate the following land is mentioned:

16 acres in the ox pasture lot, a lot in the back lane, a pasture of 12 acres at the lower end of the back lane, and 30 acres in the west division.

The inventory amounted to £722 6s 7d. The appraisers in their report set off to the widow Rachel her dower interest in the estate,

"And the whole of the remainder to Jemima, wife of Thomas Tisdale, only child of the said deceased." (Bk. 23, p. 56.)

Therefore, his wife must have died, and he taken a second; and also his youngest and oldest daughters died young.

12

JONATHAN[4] COLE (*Samuel*,[3] *John*,[2] *James*,[1]) the fourth son of Samuel Cole. He must have been quite young when his father died in 1694, and I judge him to have been born not far from 1685.

Under the terms of his father's will, he, with his brother John, received all the land of the father not specifically disposed of by that will. This would be two acres in the south meadow, fourteen acres in the ox pasture abutting on the Wethersfield bounds, and eighteen acres in the long lots, unless Samuel had disposed of them before his death, and there is no evidence of that.

The brothers also were heirs of the one-half interest that their father had in the undivided lands of the town. This from the original proprietor James, through his son John. And they obtained a tract of land in the division of that portion of land lying east of the river, which was divided after their father's death.

This land was in the present towns of East Hartford and Manchester. On January 13, 1714(5), he conveyed to Joseph Bigelow for a consideration of twenty-seven pounds, a lot of six acres and three rods, bounded on the east by land of George Kilbourne, on the north by the highway, on the west by the land of the said Bigelow and on the south by the land of Jacob Bunce and William Goodrich. I judge this to have been on the east side of the river.

He moved onto his land on the east side of the river and I think lived there all his life.

On March 3, 1736, he and his brother John, conveyed to Ezekiel Webster "The moity or half of a certain lot of land lying and being in Hartford aforesaid, and in the second division or tier of lots from Bolton westward in the tract of land commonly called the five miles on the east side of the great river of Connecticut, which half is in quantity twenty-one acres and a half, be it more or less, the whole lot being out of the right of our honored grandfather John Cole, late of said Hartford deceased, and is bounded north and south with the land of said Ezekiel Webster and the said lyeth in common and undivided with the other half thereof now belonging to said Webster which he bought of John Cole, son of Nathaniel Cole deceased and is bounded east and west with highways."

On June 2, 1756, he sold for ninety pounds two acres of land "being part of the lot on which I dwell and is bounded north on the land of John Goodwin, south on land of Benjamin Roberts, east on land of John Hurlburt running west till it makes two acres by measure." That is two acres off the east end of his home lot.

I suppose that his oldest son became of age about 1749 or perhaps earlier, for on April 24 of that year he gave to his son Jonathan, Jr., a small lot twelve rods long by two and a half rods wide in the northwest corner of his home lot. This was presumable as a house lot.

He died about 1760, as on January 1, 1761, letters of administration on his estate were granted to his widow Mary and Jonathan Olmstead, and they gave bond in the sum of three hundred pounds. The administrators exhibited their first account May 20, 1761, and it was approved and filed.

On January 5, 1762, the administrators made a deed in which they recite their authority specially granted by the general assembly of the colony and the advise of the Probate court of Hartford, Connecticut, in the matter, and convey for £24 7s 6d to John Hurlburt, "one parcel of land belonging to the estate of Jonathan Cole deceased, being in Hartford aforesaid, on the east side of the great river, being about six and a quarter acres, bounded as follows: North by land of John Hurlburt, south by land of Benjamin Roberts, east by land of John Hurlburt and west partly by land of Mary Cole, now the wife of John Kendall and partly on land of Hannah Cole."

The widow died in July, 1763, probably, as administration on her estate was granted August 1, 1763, to Deacon Wm. Whiting, who gave bond in the sum of £100.

The children of Jonathan and Mary Cole were:

20. i. Jonathan, b. ———

ii. Mary, b. ——— ——— m. John Kendall, of East Hartford. She was referred to in a deed of January 5, 1762. Kendall bought land of Samuel Flagg, in East Hartford, June 1, 1789. In the papers of the Rev. Dr. Williams, of Hartford, it is noted that "old Mr. Kendall d. in June, 1806."

iii. Hannah, b. ——— ———.

21. iv. David (?), b. ———

And perhaps others.

13

NATHANIEL[4] COLE (*Nathaniel,*[3] *John,*[2] *James,*[1]) the only son of Nathaniel and Lydia (Davis) Cole, was born in Hartford, November

6, 1882. He was administrator of his father's estate, and it is probable lived quietly in Hartford all his life. He married Elizabeth Knight, daughter of George Knight, June 12, 1707. He died August 20, 1735.

Their only child was:

22. X i. John, b. February 15, 1708.

14

JOHN[5] COLE (*John,*[4] *John,*[3] *John,*[2] *James,*[1]). He was born in Farmington, March 15, 1796. He probably lived there all of his life.

In the family of Charles L. Cole, of Cullman, Alabama, there is an old deed and also a note of hand that probably refer to him. They are as follows:

A Deed from David Bull to John Cole of Kensington, Town of Farmington, County of Hartford, Colony of Ct., dated Apr. 5 in the ninth year of his magisty's reign A. D. 1736. Received for record Apr. 8 1736 in Book 5 folio 684.
Signed, JOHN HOOKER, Register.

A Note of Hand given to John Cole of Kensington, for fifteen pounds, current bills of Public Credit of the said Colony or neighboring Provinces.
Dated Feb. 12, 1733. Signed, WILLIAM SCOVILLE.

These papers refer to him or to his father, but I think to him. His children were:

26. i. John, b.———
Probably others.

15

NATHANIEL[5] COLE (*Samuel,*[4] *Samuel,*[3] *John,*[2] *James,*[1]) born August 18, 1701.

16

(SELAH or CALEB) COLE (*Samuel*,[4] *Samuel*,[3] *John*,[2] *James*,[1]) born February 8, 1703.

17

SAMUEL[5] COLE (*Samuel*,[4] *Samuel*,[3] *John*,[2] *James*,[1]) born Februruary 7, 1710.

18

ICHABOD[5] COLE (*Samuel*,[4] *Samuel*,[3] *John*,[2] *James*,[1]) born March, 1712.

19

STEPHEN[5] COLE (*Ichabod*,[4] *Samuel*,[3] *John*,[2] *James*,[1]) born in Middletown, Connecticut, July 17, 1708. His father died when the boy was three years old. I think he is the one of the same name who lived in Farmington in 1761, and served as appraiser of the estate of Mathew Cole in that year, but possibly not.

20

JONATHAN[5] COLE (*Jonathan*,[4] *Samuel*,[3] *John*,[2] *James*,[1]). Probably the oldest child of Jonathan and Mary Cole. Born—— —— On April 24, 1749, his father deeded him à small lot for a house, off his own home lot in east Hartford. The only other mention of him in the records is on June 29, 1756, when he sold a tract of three roods of land, about forty rods east of the South Meeting house, to Capt. Daniel Goodwin, of Hartford. This land is described as follows: "Bounded south on a highway that leads to the meadow;

west partly on the town bound and partly on Widow Grosse's land, and east on said Goodwin's land, and north on John Skinner Jr.'s land."

I suspect that about this time he removed from the town.

21

DAVID[5] COLE (*Jonathan,*[4] *Samuel,*[3] *John,*[2] *James,*[1]). He was probably a son of Jonathan and Mary Cole. On September 12, 1751, he was a witness to a deed from Caleb Olmstead to Jonathan Cole. He married Hannah —— about 1753. In the Hartford Probate Records, book 20, p. 187, appears an entry that shows that on October 7, 1769, Hannah, wife of David Cole, was appointed guardian of her children, Samuel, aged fourteen, and David, aged thirteen. The record recites that David Cole, Sr., had not been heard from for nearly seven years.

The children then were:

27. i. Samuel, b. —— 1755.
28. ii. David, b. —— 1756.

22

JOHN[5] COLE (*Nathaniel,*[4] *Nathaniel,*[3] *John,*[2] *James,*[1]) the only child of Nathaniel and Elizabeth (Knight) Cole, was born in Hartford, February 15, 1708. He inherited a handsome estate from his father. I think he became a physician and practiced in Hartford, but I am not sure.

26

JOHN[6] COLE (*John,*[5] *John,*[4] *John,*[3] *John,*[2] *James,*[1]). He was probably born in Farmington, Connecticut, and lived there or in some other Connecticut town. Very little is known about him.

His children were:

30. i. John, b. —— ——.
31. ii. Gideon, b. —— ——.
32. iii. Ezekiel, b. —— ——.

30

JOHN[7] COLE (*John,*[6] *John,*[5] *John,*[4] *John,*[3] *John,*[2] *James,*[1]). He was born in Connecticut. He moved to Rome, Oneida county, New York, where he lived and died. There is a tradition in the family that there was a long gun handed down from father to son, and that when it came to this son he caused it to be cut off.

He left two sons:

33. i. Ichabod, b. —— ——.
34. ii. William, b. —— ——.

31

GIDEON[7] COLE (*John,*[6] *John,*[5] *John,*[4] *John,*[3] *John,*[2] *James,*[1]). He was born in Farmington, Connecticut, May 15, 1751. He married September 25, 1777, Chloe ——. She was born October 15, 1756. Mr. Cole moved from Connecticut to Clinton, Oneida county, New York, and in 1814 from there to Prattsburg, Steuben county. It is said that at this time he was offered the tract of land on which the city of Rochester was afterwards located, but he refused to settle in a swamp and preferred the hills of Steuben. He raised a large family of children, who became "men and women of excellent and superior qualities of mind and heart, and made very useful and influential citizens." He died in Prattsburg, September, 1826.

His children were:

i. Anna, b. Sept. 25, 1778, m. Benj. Wood; d. in Chili, N. Y. She had five children.

35. ii. Henderson, b. Apr. 8, 1780, d. in Elkhart, Ind., Sept. 9, 1851.

iii. Nancy, b. Oct. 19, 1781, m. Israel Gardner; d. in Prattsburg. She had two children.

iv. Betsy, b. Jan. 30, 1783. She m. Sept. 12, 1800, Timothy Barnes who was b. Jan. 30, 1780. She d. 1807, in Jerusalem, N. Y. Her children were: 1. Betsy Ann, b. Feb. 25, 1802, d. Nov. 15, 1807. 2. Leverett Munson, b. Aug. 10, 1803, d. Feb. 25, 1813. 3. Amy Maria, b. Jan. 8, 1805, who m.——— Stanton and moved to Rochester, Peoria Co., Ill., where she d. Nov. 24, 1850. She had two sons and two daughters.

v. Amanda, b. Sept. 25, 1784, m. Joel (Rufus?) Stanton, d. in Pulteny, N. Y. She had two children.

vi. Emily, b. Jan. 29, 1786, m. David Parmalee, and 2nd, Anson Bull. d. in Vernon, N.Y. Had three children.

vii. Almira, b. Jan. 17, 1791. She m. Nov. 7, 1808, Timothy Barnes, the husband of her sister Betsy, deceased, and d. in Prattsburg, Aug. 26, 1820. Their children were: 1. Eliza, b. Feb 3, 1810, m. (1) Chauncy Messenger, and had two sons; she m. (2) Jacob Ross and went to Scandanavia, Republic Co., Kan., about 1870, where she d. in Aug., 1884. 2. Erastus, b. Aug. 5, 1811, m. Eliza Eddy, Feb. 24, 1846; he lives in Barnes, Pa., and has three daughters; his only son d. Sept. 11, 1881, aged 31. 3. Timothy Munson, b. May 16, 1813, and d. Nov. 29, 1820. 4. Leverett, b. Jan. 30, 1815, m. Sept. 6, 1840, Adeline Sperry, and had four sons and one daughter. For fifty years he has lived at Chester, O. 5. Asa Harmon, b. Jan. 2, 1817, m. Sept. 13, 1840, Lettetia Force, and had six sons and two daughters. He lived in Kingsville, O., for four years, and all the rest of his life at Barnes, Pa. He d. Jan. 21, 1875. 6. Chloe Amanda, b. Nov. 11, 1818, m. True Greeley in 1838. She had two daughters and one son, and resides in Tiskalwa, Ill.

36. viii. Horace, b. July 1, 1792, d. in Roscoe, Ill., in 1862.

ix. Rhoda, b. Apr. 29, 1795, m. John Bramble. Had six children.

37. x. Hiram G., b. Mar. 4, 1798, d. in Prattsburg, Feb. 26, 1847.

xi. Chloe, b. Mar. 24, 1800, m. Theron Lindsey, d. in 1873, in Milford, Oakland Co., Mich. Her children were: Fletcher, Harmon, Charles, Lydia, Sarah.

xii. Harmon, b. May 29, 1802, d. 1825, while a young man; unmarried.

32

EZEKIEL[7] COLE (*John,*[6] *John,*[5] *John,*[4] *John,*[3] *John,*[2] *James*[1]).

33

ICHABOD[8] COLE (*John,*[7] *John,*[6] *John,*[5] *John,*[4] *John,*[3] *John,*[2] *James*[1]).

34

WILLIAM[8] COLE (*John,*[7] *John,*[6] *John,*[5] *John,*[4] *John,*[3] *John,*[2] *James*[1]).

35

HENDERSON[8] COLE (*Gideon,*[7] *John,*[6] *John,*[5] *John,*[4] *John,*[3] *John,*[2] *James,*[1]) born in Litchfield, (?) Connecticut, April 8, 1780, died near Elkhart, Indiana, September 29, 1851. He married Betsy Parmalee, who was born in Connecticut, December 1, 1783, and died near Elkhart, December 15, 1870. The families of both moved to Oneida county, New York, and they were married just before or just after the removal, July 4, 1807. From Oneida county they removed to Ontario county and settled on that part that was afterwards set off to Yates county. They lived in the town of Italy (P. O. Italy Hill) till 1838, when they removed to Elkhart, Indiana, where they spent the rest of their lives. Mr. Cole for a time held a commission as Justice of the Peace in New York State. He was a farmer all his life.

His children were:

38. i. Truman, b. Apr. 9. 1810.
39. ii. Orin, b. Oct. 10, 1811.
iii. Phile Ann, b. Sept. 16, 1813. She m. Nathan Harris, in Yates Co., N. Y. They removed to Elkhart Co., Ind., where Mr. Harris d. in 1838, leaving two sons: 1. Dwight M. Harris, now in the employ of the L. S. & M. S. R'y in Elkhart; and 2. Charles C. Harris, a passenger conductor on the L. S. & M. S. R'y, living in Elkhart. After the death of her husband, Mrs. Harris, with her children, returned to Yates Co., where she m. Albert Covert. They removed in a year or two to Elkhart Co., where he soon d. She now lives with her son Charles. By her second husband she had one daughter: 3. Susan, who has been twice married and is now living in Kansas.
iv. David P., b. Oct. 17, 1815, d. unmarried.
v. Chloe E., b. Dec. 16, 1817, m. in Yates Co., N. Y., Leonard Dinehart, now a very successful farmer, living near Elkhart, Ind. They had four sons, three of whom are living, and six daughters, all living.
40. vi. Reuben B., b. Aug. 26, 1819.
vii. Betsy Almira, b. Feb. 28, 1821. She m. David Meader, a widowed farmer with three children, residing near Elkhart. She had several children, only two of whom are now living: 1. Myron E. Meader, an att'y at law and real estate dealer at Goshen, Ind.; and 2. Ella C. Meader, wife of Lawrence W. Campbell, M. D., of Ada, O.
41. viii. Gideon Henderson, b. Mar. 7, 1823.
42. ix. Myron E., b. Jan. 1, 1829.

36

Horace[8] Cole (*Gideon,*[7] *John,*[6] *John,*[5] *John,*[4] *John,*[3] *John,*[2] *James,*[1]) the second son and eighth child of Gideon and Chloe ——— Cole, was born in Oneida county, New York, July 1, 1792. He married in Westmoreland, Oneida county, in 1813,

Abi Frisbie, daughter of Joseph and Diantha (Mott) Frisbie. He went with the family to Steuben county in 1814, where he lived till 1830, when he removed to Westfield, Chautauqua county, where he lived several years. He then removed to Roscoe, Winnebago county, Illinois, where he died in 1862. His widow is still living, ninety-one years of age, "a woman of great vigor, mental and physical, an earnest, warm-hearted Christian, attending Divine service with great regularity, and also the social meetings of the Society, and still interests herself in matters of general welfare."

The children of Horace and Abi Ann Cole were:

i. Abi Ann, b. Jan. 14, 1815. She m. Amos Tuttle in Northeast Pa., Nov., 1833. Her children were: 1. Aurelia Diantha, b. Aug. 1839, d. Feb., 1846. 2. Harmon B., b. June 10, 1845; grad. at Beloit College and Chicago Theological Seminary, 1873. 3. Elbert, b. Mar. 4, 1848; resides in Algona, Ia. 4. Amos Elliott, b. May 1, 1851; resides in Worthington, Minn. 5. Lillie E., b. Nov. 19, 1853, m. Apr. 28, 1880, E. W. Hobart, of Roscoe, Ill.

ii. Horace Frisbie, b. Oct. 7, 1816, d. Feb. 1, 1836.

43. iii. Hiram Beckley, b. Aug. 30, 1818. He is a farmer, and resides in New Milford, Winnebago co., Ill.

44 iv. Seth Beach, b. Dec. 25, 1820.

v. Theodore Goodwin, b. Jan. 25, 1823. He was educated as a physician, and spent some three years on the west coast of Africa, as a medical missionary, from 1851. On his return he settled in Wis. and there d. in 1856. He m. in Africa, M. B. Aldrich. He was a successful physician and minister.

vi. Gideon Harmon, b. Jan. 16, 1825, killed by a falling tree at age of sixteen.

45. vii. Edwin Dwight, b. Aug. 7, 1827.

viii. Sarah Jane, b. July 22, 1830. m. Nov. 12, 1856, the Rev. W. H. Burnard, a native of England, b. Mar. 7, 1829, educated at Knox College, Ill., and Lane Theo. Sem., Cincinnati, O., and lives in Algona, Ia., where Mr. B. has been pastor of the Congregational Church for many years. Children: 1. Sarah Catherine, b. Jan. 10, 1858; 2. Horace William. b. July

12, 1863; 3. Julia Elizabeth, b. Sept. 8, 1866; 4. Edwin Theodore, b. Jan. 21, 1868.

ix. Nancy Elizabeth, b. Jan. 9, 1832, d. while at school in Prattsburg, 1852.

x. Chloe L., b. June 9, 1835, d. young.

xi. William Adair, b. July 3, 1838, d. young, in 1846.

37

HIRAM G.[8] COLE (*Gideon,*[7] *John,*[6] *John,*[5] *John,*[4] *John,*[3] *John,*[2] *James,*[1]) born March 4, 1798. He moved with his father to Prattsburg, New York, and always lived there. He held several civil offices. He died February 26, 1847, aged 49. He married February 6, 1820, Flora Frisbie, of Vernon, Oneida county, who died August 2, 1861.

Their children were:

46. i. Charles L., b. Mar. 13, 1821.

ii. Aurelia T., b. May 4, 1827, m. Dewitt C. Ainsworth, of Prattsburg, who d. in Mar., 1847. She afterwards m. the Rev. John Knapp, of Prattsburg.

47. iii. Eli F., b. Oct. 1, 1832.

38

TRUMAN[9] COLE (*Henderson,*[8] *Gideon,*[7] *John,*[6] *John,*[5] *John,*[4] *John,*[3] *John,*[2] *James,*[1]) born in Vernon, Oneida county, New York, April 9, 1810. He is a merchant and farmer in Sandusky, Cattaraugus county, New York. He married Octavia Gillett, in Pulteny, Steuben county, November 3, 1830, and in October, 1831, moved to Centerville, bought wild land, and cleared and improved it till he had a fine farm. In April, 1852, he sold and moved to Yorkshire Village, in Cattaraugus county, and after farming for seven years, was fourteen years engaged in merchandising, and since then has been living retired from active business.

His children were:

48. i. Harmon E, b, Nov. 11, 1832, d. Sept. 26, 1880.
49. ii. Martin L., b. Sept. 11, 1834.
iii. Electa, b. in Centerville, N. Y., Apr. 28, 1838, m. Jan. 27, 1857, Samuel C. Durfey. He d. Apr. 30, 1876. On June 5, 1882, she m. Daniel Howlit, and lives in Sandusky, N. Y. She has no children.
iv. Chauncy G., b. June 7, 1851, at Centerville, d. Mar. 31, 1855, at Yorkshire.

39

ORIN[9] COLE (*Henderson,*[8] *Gideon,*[7] *John,*[6] *John,*[5] *John,*[4] *John,*[3] *John,*[2] *James,*[1]) b. October 10, 1811. He is a carpenter and farmer in Highland, Oakland county, Michigan. He was married there, to ——— a widow with several children. His wife died ——.

His children were:

51. i. Hiram (twin), b. —— ——
ii. (girl) " b. —— ——

40

REUBEN B.[9] COLE (*Henderson,*[8] *Gideon,*[7] *John,*[6] *John,*[5] *John,*[4] *John,*[3] *John,*[2] *James,*[1]) born in Yates county, New York, August 26, 1819. He lives in Berrien Springs, Berrien county, Michigan. He married Sarah Erwin, who died —— ——.

Their children were:

54. i. Charles H., b. —— ——, resides in Eureka Springs, Ark.

55. ii. J. Oscar, b. —— —— A passenger conductor on the Chicago & Atlantic R. R., in Ill.
56. iii. Frank, b. —— —— A mason by trade; married and living in Mo.
iv. (A daughter), b. —— ——
v. (A daughter), b. —— —— d. young.

In —— —— he married Sally Ann Leonard, a cousin of his first wife.

Their children were:

57. vi. Horatio, b. —— —— He is m. and lives in Oregon.
58. vii. Hascall, b. —— ——, now living at home.

41

[Gideon] Henderson[9] Cole (*Henderson,*[8] *Gideon,*[7] *John,*[6] *John,*[5] *John,*[4] *John,*[3] *John,*[2] *James,*[1]) born in Yates county, New York, March 7, 1823. He has dropped the first name and is known as Henderson Cole. He moved to Colorado in 1868; returned to Indiana in 1870; went to Kansas, 1879. He is now a carpenter and wagon maker, although he has been engaged in several lines of business, in Elk Falls, Elk county, Kansas.

He married in Prattsburg, New York, Alzina L. Sears, 1853, who died in Colorado, December 28, 1868.

Their children were:

59. i. Erastus B., Apr 23, 1856, a druggist in Elk Falls; married.
ii. Minnie B., b. Feb. 9, 1859, m. M. M. Kennedy, and resides in Liberty, Jackson Co., Mich.

42

Myron E.[9] Cole (*Henderson,*[8] *Gideon,*[7] *John,*[6] *John,*[5] *John,*[4] *John,*[3] *John,*[2] *James,*[1]) born in Italy, Yates county, New York,

January 1, 1829. Removed to Elkhart county, Indiana, with the family when nine years of age. He was twenty-two when his father died. He spent several years of his young manhood in school teaching, after which he entered the employ of the M. S. & N. I. R. R., first as clerk to a station agent, and afterwards was agent at Elkhart, from May 1, 1857, to May 1, 1859. In October of that year he was elected Recorder of Elkhart county, serving as such to general acceptance for a term of four years.

In the Spring of 1864 he entered the First National Bank of Elkhart, as book-keeper, remaining three years. Some years later he again took the same position, and held it for nearly twelve years.

In the summer of 1858 he married Mrs. Orrilla L. Potter, a sister of his brother Henderson's first wife. They are still living in Elkhart.

They have one daughter:

i. Jessie W., b. —— —— m. Albert W. Emery, a locomotive engineer on the L. S. & M. S. R. R. She resides in Elkhart and has one son (now fourteen months old), Myron Cole Emery.

43

HIRAM BECKLEY[9] COLE (*Horace,*[8] *Gideon,*[7] *John,*[6] *John,*[5] *John,*[4] *John,*[3] *John,*[2] *James,*[1]) born in Steuben county, New York. He married Sylvia Beardsley November 14, 1852, in Raymond, Racine county, Wisconsin. He now resides in New Milford, Winnebago county, Illinois, and is a farmer.

His children are:

60. i. Frank H., b. Apr. 5, 1855.
    ii. Emma N., b. Sept. 27, 1856. Is unmarried.
61. iii. William J., b. June 19, 1859. Is unmarried.

SETH BEACH[9] COLE (*Horace,[8] Gideon,[7] John,[6] John,[5] John,[4] John,[3] John,[2] James,[1]*) the fourth child and third son of Horace and Abi A. Cole, was born in Prattsburg, Steuben county, New York, December 25, 1820. He received the degree of M. A. at Union College in 1846, and represented Steuben county in the State Legislature in 1855–56. He was Principal of the Franklin Academy, Prattsburg, nine years.

In 1856 he was a member of the National Republican Convention that met at Philadelphia and nominated John C. Fremont for the Presidency, and he was also an active member of the Kansas Aid Committee, of New York. After that he was a resident of Brooklyn, and a lawyer by profession, having been admitted to the bar in 1855.

He was a delegate to the National Republican Convention at Chicago that nominated Abraham Lincoln in 1860.

In 1867 he took up his residence at Nyack, Rockland county, where he has been District Attorney, Judge and Surrogate. He is an elder in the Presbyterian Church, and has several times represented the Presbytery of Hudson in the General Assembly.

In 1845 he married Ann Eliza, daughter of the Rev. J. W. French, at Albion, New York. Her brothers are Rev. E. W. French, D. D., of Jersey City, and the Rev. J. Clement French, D. D., of Newark, New Jersey. She was a graduate and valedictorian of LeRoy University, Leroy, New York.

Their children are:

62. i. Edward H., b. in Prattsburg, Oct. 13, 1847.
ii. Emma F., b. in Brooklyn, Oct. 6, 1860.

45

EDWIN DWIGHT[9] COLE (*Horace*,[8] *Gideon*,[7] *John*,[6] *John*,[5] *John*,[4] *John*,[3] *John*,[2] *James*,[1]) born in Steuben county, New York, August 7, 1827. He now lives in Roscoe, Illinois, and is a farmer. He never married.

46

CHARLES L.[9] COLE (*Hiram G.*,[8] *Gideon*,[7] *John*,[6] *John*,[5] *John*,[4] *John*,[3] *John*,[2] *James*,[1]) born in Prattsburg, Steuben county, New York, March 13, 1821. In 1856 he moved to Pine Run, Genesee county, Michigan. In 1881 he moved to Cullman, Alabama. He has been justice of the peace for over twenty years, postmaster for two or more terms, and has held various county offices. He married December 5, 1843, Clara M. Andrews, formerly of Arlington, Bennington county, Vermont.

Their children were:

63. i. Hiram Dewitt, b. Oct. 29, 1844.
ii. Clara, b. May 19, 1851, d. Aug. 5, 1856.

47

ELI T.[9] COLE (*Hiram G.*,[8] *Gideon*,[7] *John*,[6] *John*,[5] *John*,[4] *John*,[3] *John*,[2] *James*,[1]) born in Prattsburg, New York, October 1, 1832. Moved to Iowa in 1857, thence to Eureka, Winnebago county, Wisconsin, and then to Oshkosh, Wisconsin. He married Mary Foster, September 12, 1855.

They have two children:

i. Ellen M., b. Sept. 12, 1862, m. Feb. 18, 1881, to ———
ii. Flora F., b. Sept. 24, 1872, d. Jan. 12, 1881.

48

Harmon G.[10] Cole (*Truman,[9] Henderson,[8] Gideon,[7] John,[6] John,[5] John,[4] John,[3] John,[2] James,[1]*) born November 11, 1832, in Centerville, New York. He removed to Iowa and married there, January 21, 1856, Ann L. Hatfield. He was a farmer near Osage, Mitchell county, and died September 26, 1880. His widow still lives at Osage, Iowa.

His children were:

i. Arthur J., b. —— ——. Resides at Westport, Dak.
ii. Myron, b. —— ——. Resides in California.

49

Martin L.[10] Cole (*Truman,[9] Henderson,[8] Gideon,[7] John,[6] John,[5] John,[4] John,[3] John,[2] James,[1]*) born September 11, 1834, at Centerville, New York. He is now a merchant and postmaster at Elton, New York. He married Mary J. Chamberlain, June 6, 1865.

His children are:

i. Myrtle, b. —— ——
ii. Milton, b. —— ——

59

Erastus B.[10] Cole (*G. H.,[9] Henderson,[8] Gideon,[7] John,[6] John,[5] John,[4] John,[3] John,[2] James,[1]*) the only son of G. Henderson and Alzina (Sears) Cole, was born April 23, 1856. Soon after he became of age he engaged in hotel business in Indiana, with success. In 1880 he went to Elk Falls, Elk county, Kansas, and for three years kept a hotel there. In 1883 he opened a drug store, to which he now devotes his time. He also, with his father, owns a large ranch devoted to the raising of thoroughbred stock. He is one of the popular and leading young men of Elk county.

He married January 1, 1883, Anna R. Haynes, daughter of Col. Haynes, of Fremont, Ohio. They have no children.

60

FRANK H.[10] COLE (*Hiram B.*,[9] *Horace*,[8] *Gideon*,[7] *John*,[6] *John*,[5] *John*,[4] *John*,[3] *John*,[2] *James*,[1]) the oldest child of Hiram B. and Sylvia (Beardsley) Cole, born April 5, 1855. He married, January, 1883, Minnie Kennedy, and is a farmer in Alexandria, Hanson county, Dakota.

His children are:

i. Edith, b. —— ——
ii. Frank Edgar, b. —— —— d. aged five months.

62

EDWARD H.[10] COLE (*Seth B.*,[9] *Horace*,[8] *Gideon*,[7] *John*,[6] *John*,[5] *John*,[4] *John*,[3] *John*,[2] *James*,[1]) born in Prattsburg, Steuben county, New York, October 13, 1847. Graduated at Williams College, in the class of 1869. Was admitted to the bar in —— and is now an attorney at law and a magistrate at Nyack, Rockland county, New York. He married Carrie, daughter of the Rev. Mr. Chamberlin, of Brooklyn.

63

Hiram Dewitt[10] Cole (*Charles E.*,[9] *Hiram G.*,[8] *Gideon*,[7] *John*,[6] *John*,[5] *John*,[4] *John*,[3] *John*,[2] *James*,[1]) the only son of Charles L. and Clara (Andrews) Cole, was born in Prattsburg, New York, October 29, 1844. He moved with his father to Pine Run, Michigan, in 1856, where he married, May 21, 1871. In 1881 he went with his father to Cullman, Alabama.

His children are:

i. Charles Hiram, b. Mar. 12, 1872, d. ——
ii. Charles Dewitt, b. 1874.
iii. Clinton T., b. 1876.

I

Henry Cole. He is mentioned as at Sandwich, Massachusetts, in 1643. He went from there to Hartford, Connecticut, where he married, December 10, 1646, Sarah Rusco, daughter of William Rusco, of Hartford, who came from Billerica, Essex county, England, in the Increase in 1635, to Cambridge, and thence removed to Hartford.

They removed to Middletown, and there lived for many years, when he removed to Wallingford, and died in 1676. His widow died in Saybrooke, in January, 1688.

James,[1] the cooper of Hartford, mentions him in his will as his cousin, and gives him one-half his cooper's tools. The term cousin was then used for nephew frequently, and it is probable that this was the relationship Henry bore to James.

His lands were recorded June 9, 1654 (book I, p. 11), and he is on the list of householders and proprietors of Middletown, March 22, 1670, and is rated at £115.

Children:

2. i. Henry, b. Sept. 20, 1647.
3. ii. James, b. Feb. 8. 1649, d. Dec. 22, 1721.
4. iii. John, b. Feb. 14, 1652.
5. iv. William, b. Apr. 25, 1653.
v. Sarah, b. Oct. 22, 1654, d. probably before 1688.
6. vi. Samuel, b. Sept. 10, 1656.
vii. Mary, b. June 11, 1658, m. —— —— Richard Goodale, of Middletown.
viii. Joanna, b. Aug. 1, 1661, m. Jan. 19, 1681, Aaron Goff, of Wethersfield. Her children were:
  (i.) Solomon Goff, b. Feb. 7, 1685.
  (ii.) Aaron Goff, b. Mar. 10, 1689.
  (iii.) Gershorn Goff, b. Mar. 12, 1691.
  (iv.) Samuel Goff, b. Apr. 30, 1698.
  No others recorded in Wethersfield.

ix. Abigail, b. Oct. 28, 1661, m.—— —— John Stephens, of Killingworth, and lived there in 1688.
x. Rebecca, b. Apr. 5, 1667. Unmarried in 1688.

2

HENRY[2] COLE (*Henry*,[1]) the oldest son of Henry and Sarah (Rusco) Cole, born in Middletown, Connecticut, September 20, 1647. "In 1868 he was living in Wethersfield," says Savage, but I am inclined to think that he is the Henry who is mentioned by Savage as being at Boston, and who married Mary —— and had

Ann, b. Nov. 9 (bapt. 13), 1687.
7. Henry, b. Jan. 2 (bapt. 6), 1689.
Mary, b. Dec. — (bapt. 14), 1690.

And perhaps others.

3

JAMES[2] COLE (*Henry*[1]). Born in Middletown, Connecticut, February 8, 1649. Died December 22, 1721. In 1688 he was living in Wallingford.

4

JOHN[2] COLE (*Henry*,[1]) born in Middletown, Connecticut, February 14, 1652. "In 1688 he was at Boston," says Savage. He married Mary, daughter of Capt. John Gallop (son of John of Dorchester, 1630), of Stonnington Connecticut, and his wife, Hannah (Lake) Gallop. Gallop was one of the captains killed in the great Narragansett swamp fight, December 14, 1675, the hardest battle of King Phillip's war.

His children were:

9. i. Samuel, b. 16, bapt. 21 of Sept., 1684.
10. ii. Thomas, b. 23, bapt. 25 of Apr. 1686.
iii. Mary, b. May 9, 1668, bapt. Mar. 9, 1690.

Was he the Boston schoolmaster?

5

WILLIAM[2] COLE (*Henry*,[1]) born at Middletown, April 25, 1653. In 1688 he lived at Wallingford. Could he have been William of Boston who married Martha ——— and had

i. William, b. Apr. 14, bapt. July 24, 1687, d. soon.
ii. Martha (twin), b. 7, bapt. 10 Feb., 1689, d. soon.
11. iii. William " " " "
iv. Martha (twin), bapt. Nov. 16, 1690.
v. Mary " " " "

6

SAMUEL[2] COLE (*Henry*,[1]) born in Middletown, Connecticut, September 10, 1656. He married September 25, 1679, Lydia ——— He was in Wethersfield in 1688.

His children were:

12. i. Joseph, b. Sept. 12, 1681.
ii. Lydia, b. Jan. 18, 1684.

JOSEPH[3] COLE (*Samuel,*[2] *Henry,*[1]) born in Wethersfield, Connecticut, September 12, 1681. He married Abigail, daughter of Serg. Jonathan Riley, January 13, 1709.

His children recorded in Wethersfield were:

i. John, b. June 13, 1710.

The following belong to the families of Henry[2] or Samuel.[2]

Sarah Cole and David Collins, married in Wethersfield, November 11, 1742.

Children:

i. Abigail Collins, b. Dec. 4, 1742.
ii. Lucy Collins, b. Dec. 5, 1745.
iii. Josiah Collins, b. July 26, 1748, d. Nov. 22, 1749.
iv. Josiah Collins, b. Sept. 26, 1750.

Lucy Cole and David Lowry, of Wethersfield, married April 21, 1771:

Children:

i. Lucy Lowry, b. July 26, 1771.
ii. Mary Lowry, b. Dec. 1, 1778.

Martha Cole and Jonathan Boardman, married in Wethersfield, June 13, 1754.

Children:

i. Abigail, b. Oct. 22, 1755.
ii. Mercy, b. Aug. 2, 1757.

THE PLYMOUTH FAMILY.

JAMES COLE.[1] One of the families that came from England to Plymouth was that of James Cole. I have not been able to find anything concerning him previous to 1634, but he probably had a family with him when he came to the settlement. He was the first settler on the eminence known as "Burial Hill." The first mention of him in the Plymouth Colony Records is in the list of freemen of 1633, where the name is spelled Coale ("Ply. Col. Rec. I-4.) In the tax list of May 27, 1634, his rate is put down at 9d. There are many at that rate, but none lower.

On January 2, 1636, a grant of seven acres to him is recorded, same to belong to his dwelling and not to be sold.

His name is found in the list of freemen for the year 1637, and in that year he was one of the men pressed for service against the Pequots, but the levy was not called upon. There is a record concerning him, dated July 2, 1638, in which he is styled a "saylor," but in September of the same year he is called "inn-keeper," and it is probable that between those dates he opened the "Ordinary," which he kept for thirty years, although no license is recorded.

In September, 1640, the following order was passed:

"James Cole of Plymouth is prohibited to draw any wine or strong water until the next term of the General Court, and not then without special license from the court."

No reason is given for the passing of this order, and the privilege of selling liquors was given to another person until 1645, when, on account of the inconvenience to travelers in having no liquor sold at the inn, the above order was rescinded (Do, vi. 153. viii. 79.)

During this interval he was several times fined for selling. In September, 1641, he obtained from the court fifty acres of upland, at Lakenham Meadow, together with some meadow to be laid out on view. That year and the following he was appointed highway Surveyor, also again in 1651 and 1652. In October, 1642, he obtained a further grant of land. The next year his name, together with those of his oldest two sons, appears on the list of those able to bear arms. In 1644 he was chosen constable. There is a record of a suit for slander preferred by him against Thomas Pope in 1647, but the case was dropped on the defendant Pope admitting the charge and paying the costs. In 1654 his boat was pressed for an expedition against the Dutch, but the plan was abandoned. On October 2, 1650, he was presented by the Grand Jury for assault and battery, but was acquitted.

Between 1641 and 1666 he appears as participant in nine civil suits, only two, however, as defendant, in one of those cases being sued as surety for £3 10s, and confessed judgment in 22 bushels of Indian corn; and in the other the verdict was for him, and the plaintiff paid the costs. Six of the other cases were for debt and he recovered judgment in all but one. The seventh case was the slander suit above referred to.

On June 7, 1657, the court granted to him ten pounds for the repair of his inn.

"The court having given unto James Cole of Plymouth the sum of ten pounds towards repairing the house he now liveth in, so that it may be fitted for an Ordinary, for the entertainment of strangers" (Do. iii-166.)

He is several times recorded as serving on grand, petit and coroners' juries, and is twice fined for selling liquor to the Indians. In June, 1662, he received a grant of land at Saconett neck. In 1665 he received one share (30 acres,) on the west side of the Namassett river. (Do. iv. 94). Probably about 1670 he gave up his business to his son James, as in that year the excise tax of James Cole, Jr. was remitted, he being a new beginner. His name appears on the list of freemen for 1670, and Savage says that he was living in 1688, very aged.

His wife was Mary ——, she was living in March, 1660.

Children:

2. i. James, b. about 1625 d. ——
3. ii. Hugh, b. about 1627, d. ——
4. iii. John, b. —— d. 1677.
iv. Mary, b. —— m. John Almy, he was a son of William Almy of Plymouth, 1643. After his marriage to Mary Cole he moved to Portsmouth, R. I. He was Capt. in King Phillip's war, and died in 1676.

2

JAMES[2] COLE (*James*[1]). The oldest son of James Cole, the Plymouth inn-keeper was probably born in England and came to the colony when a boy with his father. The date of his birth was probably about 1625, as he is on the list of those able to bear arms in 1643, together with his younger brother Hugh.

He married December 23, 1652, Mary Tilson, at Scituate, and there his oldest child was born.

Deane says that he soon removed from Scituate to York, Maine, and perhaps in 1654 to Kennebec, for among the inhabitants of Kennebec who took the oath of fealty to Plymouth colony, May 23, 1654, was James Cole.

If he did go to Maine, he returned, for in 1656 he was chosen surveyor of highways for Plymouth. He held that office again in 1678 and 1685.

In May, 1665, he was presented by the Grand Jury, and fined 3s. 4d., for striking Robert Rawson; but the record states that the court, considering the great provocation given, and the generally peaceful character of the defendant, remitted the fine. (Col. Rec. iv–88).

In October of that same year he was one of the appraisers of the estate of Nicholas Miller, alias Hodge, and his name appears on the record several times as serving on petit and coroners' juries. About the beginning of 1670 he took his father's business, as inn-keeper, and in June of that year his excise tax was abated by the court, as he was a new beginner. In 1673, his tax was abated one-half, and in 1677 remitted altogether.

His name appears in the freeman's list of 1670

The children of James, Jr. and Mary (Tilson) Cole, were:

i. Mary, b. in Scituate, Dec. 3, 1653. She m. John Laythrop, (the youngest son of the Rev. John Laythrop, the first minister of Scituate, (1635), and afterwords of Barnstable, 1639, where he d. Nov. 8, 1653,) b. at Barnstable Feb. 9, 1645, m. at Plymouth, Jan. 3, 1672, d. Sept. 17, 1727. Their children were:

- (i.) John Laythrope, b. Aug. 5, 1673.
- (ii.) Mary Laythrope, b. Oct. 27, 1675.
- (iii.) Martha Laythrope, b. Nov. 11, 1677.
- (iv.) Elizabeth Laythrope, b. Sept. 16, 1679.
- (v.) James Laythrope, b. July 3, 1681.
- (vi.) Hannah Laythrope, b. Mar. 13, 1683.
- (vii.) Jonathan Laythrope, b. Nov. 14, 1684.
- (viii.) Barnabas Laythrope, b. Oct. 22, 1686.
- (ix.) Abigail Laythrope, b. Apr. 23, 1689.
- (x.) Experience Laythrope, b. Jan. 7, 1692.

and perhaps others.

5. ii. Ephraim, b. probably while his father lived in York or in the Kennebec region.

6. iii. Nathaniel, b. —— —— in Me. probably.

3

HUGH[2] COLE (*James*[1]), the second son of James and Mary Cole, was born probably about 1626, as he is found on the list of able-bodied men in 1643, and those lists generally included the men from sixteen to sixty.

He married June 8, 1655, Mary, the daughter of Richard Foxwell.*

In 1657 he took the oath of fidelity. He was on the grand jury in 1666, and was surveyor the following year. The following entry occurs on the records under date of July 2, 1667:

"The Court have granted unto Hugh Cole respecting his father's grant being an ancient freeman, and his own grant six score acres of land between Mattapoinset River and the eastern bound of Ackshenoh."

And on October 30 of the same year:

"The sum of fifty shillings is ordered to be paid Samuel Jackson by Hugh Cole, for taking up his boat which went adrift."

He was a witness to the will of Nathaniel Warren, Sr., of Plymouth, June 29, 1667. In 1668 he was appointed administrator of the estate of his father-in-law, and is mentioned in the will dated April 7, 1668. Between this date and 1671 he must have moved to Swansey, R. I., for in June, 1671, he was elected a Selectman of that town, which office he held in '71, '72, '75, '85, '86. In 1673 he was elected a deputy to the general court, and re-elected in '74, '75, '80, '81, '83, '84, '85, '86, '89.

The following letter written by him is found in Winsor's History of Duxbury, page 103. The addresses had been destroyed:

SWANSEA, April 1, 1671.

Much Honored Sir:

Yours I receaved this first of Aprill, whereby I perceave you desire to know what posture the Indians are in. I do not finde them to continue in a posture of war as they have been. I went to Mount hope the last second day one purpose to see there proceedings and was at manie of their houses but saw nothing as intending to war, but asking them what was ye reason ye kept togather at Mount hope, the[y] answered it was to see Phillips child burried and did intend to returne home as soone as the child was burried, and I have seene sum return but yet the greatest part of them are togather and the give the reason because the wind blowd soe agaynst them yt they cannot get home with there canowes, not els, but rest yours to command in what I am able.

HUGH COLE.

* Richard Foxwell came with Winthrop and was admitted freeman in 1631. He moved to Situate, R. I., in 1634, and m. Ann Shelly. He was one of the church in Situate under the Rev. John Laythrope. He d. about 1668. His children (recorded in Barnstable) were: i. Mary, b. Aug. 17, 1635, m. Hugh Cole. ii. Martha, b. Mar. 24, 1638, m. Sam'l Bacon, May 9, 1699. iii. Ruth, b. Mar. 25, 1641. iv. John, b.—— d. Sept. 21, 1646.

In 1667 King Phillip conveyed to Hugh Cole and four others five hundred acres of land at Mettaposset, on the west side of the river, now known as Cole's river from this proprietor. (Hist. Gen. Reg. XII, 171.)

On February 7, 1671, the freemen of Swansey voted that all lots and divisions of land hereafter granted shall be proportioned according to these ranks, the first rank to have three acres, the second two, and the third one.

This ranking was to be done by commissioners, and in the first report Hugh Cole and his brother John were placed in the second rank. This did not satisfy them, and after the excitement of King Phillip's War was over, in 1681, the town voted that Serg. Hugh Cole and several others, and their heirs forever, should be admitted to the privileges of the first rank. (John had previously died.)

Hugh Cole was a great friend of King Phillip's, and it is reported that on the breaking out of the war in 1675, among the first men captured were two of his sons. They were taken to Mount Hope and immediately released by King Phillip on account of his friendship for their father, and with the warning to leave that country, as he was unable to restrain his young men. They reported to their father, and the whole family immediately started for a place of safety. Before they had been gone an hour the house was burned. (Register, XII, 169.)

Mr. Cole probably served in the war and attained the rank of Sergeant. In 1669 he was one of the committee to run the line between Swansey and Mount Hope, and on July 4, 1673, the following record appears:

"Mr. John Allin and Hugh Cole both of the town of Swansey the Colonie of New Plymouth aforesaid, doe complain against Phillip, allias Metacomber, in an action on the case to the damage of two hundred pounds, for refusing to perform covenants and agreements expressed in a deed given under the said Phillip's hand, to the said Mr. Allin and Hugh Cole their heirs and assigns for the use of the town of Swansey aforesaid. The said Phillip being required thereunto before the Governor and Assistants by the said Allin and Cole, the said Phillip did engage to come before the Governor of New Plymouth or some of his Assistants, and then and there acknowledge the true and absolute sale of the said premises expressed in said deed, according to the true meaning thereof."

This suit was afterwards withdrawn without trial. He served very frequently on juries. Mr. Cole was a shipwright by trade.

The children of Hugh and Mary (Foxwell) Cole were:

7. i. James, b. Nov. 8, 1655.
8. ii. Hugh, b. Mar. 8, 1658.
9. iii. John, b. Mar. 16, 1660.
iv. Martha, b. Apr. 14, 1662.
v. Anna, b. Oct. 14, 1664, m. Wm. Sailsbury, of Swansey.
vi. Ruth, b. Jan. 8, 1666.
10. vii. Joseph, b. May 15, 1668.

On Jan. 1, 1689, he married Elizabeth, the widow of Joseph Cook,* and in 1698, as his third wife, the widow Mary Morton.

4

JOHN[2] COLE (*James*[1]), the third son of James and Mary Cole, was born ——. He served on a Jury at Plymouth in 1668, and a year or two later removed to Swansey with his brother Hugh. He was constable of Swansey in 1673, and served on a coroner's jury in 1676. He died early in 1677, as the court, on June 7 of that year, makes the following order in reference to his estate:

"In reference to the estate of John Cole, deceased, the Court does order: That for as much as the estate is small, and four small children to bring up, that the whole personal estate be settled on his widow for the bringing up of his children, and the profits of the land till the children become of age; and in case there shall be necessity thereof for the bringing up of the children, that then some of the land shall be sold, by the advise and leave of the court, and in case any lands shall be

* Elizabeth Litter was the daughter of Thomas Litter, of Plymouth, who came over from London in 1635, at the age of twenty-three, and died in 1684. He left one son and three daughters, the second of whom, Elizabeth, m. Oct. 1655, Wm. Shurtleff, who was struck by lightning June 23, 1663. By him she had three sons. On Nov. 18, 1669, she m. Joseph Cook, the youngest son of Francis, who came over in the Mayflower in 1620. He was b. in Holland and came over in the Ann, in 1623, with his mother and brother. He d. 1676, and Jan. 1, 1689, she m. Hugh Cole, who survived her.

left, then it be disposed of to the two sons according to law, they paying some small legacies to the daughters as the Court shall order." (Ply. Col. Rec., V, 234.)

His wife was —— —— m. ——

Children:

11. i. ——— (son.)
12. ii. ——— (son.)
iii. ——— (daughter.)
iv. ——— (daughter.)

5

Ephraim[3] Cole (*James,*[2] *James,*[1]) born probably in Maine, when his father was living there about 1652–4.

Admitted freeman at Plymouth, June 3, 1690. Was one of those who subscribed twenty pounds per year, for seven years, towards maintaining a school in Plymouth, provided it was settled within forty rods of the old meeting house, 1705. (Mass. Hist. Col. 2nd Series iv–87.)

6

Nathaniel[3] Cole (*James,*[2] *James,*[1]) born —— ——. In 1679 the town of Duxbury granted him twenty-six acres east of Swansey river.

He married Sarah ———.

In 1690 he, with others, hired the Duxbury Commons of the town. It was proposed to divide the Commons in 1703, but it was deferred on the petition of many citizens, of whom he was one. On September 12, 1707, a division was made, and he and two sons received shares, as they did in the division of 1712. In the division of May 10, 1748, shares were granted to the heirs of Nathaniel Cole, to Jabez Cole, and to Ephraim Cole.

His children were:

i. Rebecca. b. Sept. 21, 1680.
ii. Mary, b. Nov. 13, 1682.
13. iii. Nathaniel, b. Oct. 11, 1685.
14. iv. Ephraim, b. June 14, 1688.

7

JAMES[3] COLE (*Hugh,*[2] *James,*[1]) the oldest child of Hugh and Mary (Foxwell) Cole, was born in Plymouth November 8, 1655, and went with the family to Swansey, where he was admitted to the third rank October 1, 1672, ([2]Bayliss, v–95), and admitted as freeman November 12, 1680. He was chosen constable in 1682. Was commissioned as Ensign of the militia company June 4, 1686. In December 25, 1689, he was commissioned as Lieutenant—all the officers moving up one step. There seems to have been considerable trouble in the company, which was the burden of a letter from John Walley, of Rehoboth, to Thomas Hinckley, Esq., August 13, 1689. It would seem that Lieutenant Cole, as candidate of the young men, was elected Captain over the head of the old Captain, Brown, who was given the second place, and great trouble ensued. Mr. Walley says: "Cole has sought the place beyond measure." Another letter of Walley's dated April 16, 1690, says the trouble was settled by a new election, in which Brown was chosen Captain and Cole Lieutenant. He was Deputy in 1689 and 1690. In March, 1704, Colonel Benjamin Church raised a force to go against the Eastern Indians, and Mr. Cole was one of his Captains. (Bayliss, part v. p. 125).

8

HUGH[3] COLE (*Hugh,*[2] *James,*[1]) born in Plymouth, March 8, 1658. Moved to Swansey with the family. He was admitted to the third rank of citizens October 1, 1672, and admitted freeman November 12, 1680. Served on jury in Swansey August 21, 1681.

9

JOHN[3] COLE (*Hugh,*[2] *James,*[1]) born in Plymouth March 16, 1660. Was on jury August 9, 1681, and again on August 21.

10

JOSEPH[3] COLE (*Hugh,*[2] *James,*[1]) the youngest of the seven children of Hugh and Mary (Foxwell) Cole, was born in Plymouth May 15, 1668.

13

NATHANIEL[4] COLE (*Nathaniel,*[3] *James,*[2] *James,*[1]) born in Duxbury October 11, 1685. Received grant of land in the division of the Commons lands of the town in 1707, 1712, and 1748.

He married August 4, 1714, Abigail, daughter of Samuel and Triephosa (Pastridge) West, who was born September 26, 1682.

His children were:

15. i. Jabez, b. ——— ———.

14

EPHRAIM[4] COLE (*Nathaniel,*[3] *James,*[2] *James,*[1]) born in Duxbury June 14, 1688. He received grants of land in the divisions of the Commons land of the town in 1707, 1712 and 1748. He married March 2, 1724, Susanna Waste. In 1753 he removed to North Yarmouth.

His children were:

16. i. Job, b. March 20, 1725.
17. ii. Noah, b. March 26, 1727.
iii. Rebecca, b. Nov. 28, 1729.
18. iv. Ebenezer, b. Oct. 28, 1732.
v. Ruth, b. May 8, 1735.
vi. Eunice, b. Feb. 12, 1740.

15

JABEZ[5] COLE (*Nathaniel,*[4] *Nathaniel,*[3] *James,*[2] *James,*[1]) born —— ——. He received a share in the division of the Commons lands of Duxbury in 1748. He married Grace Kean, August 23, 1744, and in 1750 removed to Pembroke.

His children were:

i. West, b. ———, 1745.

NOTES.

Anna Mason, fifth child of Major John Mason, conqueror of the Pequots, born June, 1650, at Saybrooke, Conn., married Captain John Brown, of Swansey, November 8, 1672.

Her eldest child, John Brown, born April 28, 1675, married *Abigail Cole*, of Swansey, July 2, 1696. He was called Captain John, and died in Swansey about 1752.

Colonel B. Cole, of Providence, (1821), was of this family.

COLES IN PROVIDENCE.

GREGORY—On Freeman list of 1655.

JOHN—An Attorney at Law.

1757—One of committee to audit accounts of Capt. Olney, and all charges relating to Shurleys & Pepperell's Reg.

1765—Signer of protest against taxing.

1767—Deputy from Providence and Speaker. Postmaster at Providence, 1769–1772.

1772—The Church of England Society of Providence petitioned for appointment of him, with others, to conduct a lottery to raise $1,000 to build steeple, and other repairs; granted.

1772—Summoned as a witness in the investigation of the burning of the Guspee. His deposition of the little he knew about it may be seen in R. I. Colonial Records, Vol. VII, p. 170.

May, 1773—On committee of correspondence.

1775—On " to issue bills of credit.

1776—On " " " " " "

1776—On behalf of Protestant Episcopal Church of Providence, petitions Court for power to exchange certain lands.

Oct. 1776—On committee to revise and establish a Prize Court. He was appointed Judge Advocate of same.

Oct. 1778—Repaid money advanced on November 29, 30, 1777, £23–19–04.

Oct. 1779—Notice that his office is vacant by his death.

His son *John, Jr.*:

1775—Lieutenant in Captain Wm. Taylor's Company.

Nov. 1776— " " " Royzel Smith's Company.

Dec. 1777— " " " James Albrough's Company of Col. Stanton's Regulars.

In February, 1791, Miss Elizabeth Cole and Miss Abigail Cole were living in Providence.

COLES IN WARREN.

THOMAS.—Deputy from Warren 1757, 1758 and 1759.

EBENEZER.—Deputy from Warren 1760, 1762, 1770. May,

1777: Bill of sixteen shillings for victualling sixteen soldiers, who were on guard at Warren, allowed.

CURTIS.—Chosen Ensign, vice Smith Bowen, promoted in the company of militia of Warren, 1774. Major of regiment of militia, Bristol County, 1784.

ICHABOD.—Lieutenant of second company of Warren militia, 1784. Deputy from Warren, May, 1792, on Town committee, 1795.

ALLEN.—Ensign of first company of Warren militia, 1784.

JOHN.—In May, 1758, petitions with others in regard to the redemption of certain counterfeit bills, the government having confiscated the property of the counterfeiters. Deputy from Warren April, 1751.

THE EASTHAM FAMILY.

About the beginning of the second decade of the existence of the Plymouth colony, there came from England three young men, brothers, named John, Job and Daniel Cole. I suspect that they came over with William Collier, a merchant of London, about 1633. Their father is unknown. Whether they were brothers of James, the inn-keeper of Plymouth, I know not, but I judge that they were not.

John died at Plymouth in December, 1637, and in his will, proved January 2, 1638, he mentions by name, "Master Collier's men," his brothers Job and Daniel, and his sister Rebecca, wife of Job. He was probably unmarried.

I

JOB COLE, the eldest of the three brothers, married May 16, 1634, Rebecca Collier.*

On July 2, 1638, forty-eight acres of land were granted to him at Green Harbor, in that part of Duxbury, that was afterwards included in Marshfield. On October 2, 1650, he sold that to Thomas Chillingsworth for a calf and twenty shillings.

He was propounded as freeman in 1639, and admitted October 7 of the following year, and the next year (1641) was chosen Constable of Duxbury.

**William Collier*, a merchant adventurer, of London, came to the colony in 1633. He was assistant twenty-eight years between 1634 and 1665, and was one of the two plenipotentiaries at the first meeting of the United Colonies in 1643. He was among the first purchasers of Dartmouth, 1652, and died 1670. He left four daughters: i. Sarah, b —— ——, m. 15, 1634, Love Brewster, son of Elder Wm. Brewster. ii. Rebecca, b. —— ——, m. Job Cole. iii. Mary, b. —— ——, m. April 1, 1635, Thomas Prince, afterwards Governor. She was his second wife. iv. Elizabeth, b. —— ——, m. Nov. 2, 1637, Constant Southworth.

In 1642 he removed to Yarmouth, as his name is found on the list of able-bodied men of that town for 1643. He removed to Nawset, where he was constable in 1648, and the same year to Eastham, from which town he was chosen deputy the same year. He sold his house and land at "Morton's Hole," in Nawset, to Christopher Wordsworth for £17. He was again chosen deputy in 1654, and was excise man in 1661. His name occurs on the freeman's list of 1670, but is not on that of 1695; therefore, he died between those dates. His widow, Rebecca, died December, 1698, aged 88.

Their children were:

3. i. John, b. —— ——.
4. ii. Job, b. —— ——.
5. iii. Daniel, b. —— ——.
iv. Rebecca, b. Aug. 26, 1654.

2

Daniel Cole. (————). The younger brother of Job, and probably came over with him when they were both young men. The first mention of him is April 6, 1640, when fifty acres of upland were granted him. His name appears on the list of able-bodied men of Yarmouth for 1643. In June, 1644, he was propounded for freeman and was admitted and sworn in June, 1645. In 1648 he was one of the jury that tried Alice Bishop for infanticide. He afterwards removed to Eastham. In 1652 he was chosen deputy for that town and was re-elected in 1654, 1657, 1661, 1666, 1667, 1668, 1669, 1670, 1671, 1672 and 1673. Constable in 1664 and Selectman 1668, 1670, 1671, 1672, 1681. In 1662 he was appointed to take account of liquors, shot, lead and powder imported. Two deeds are recorded, both in 1649, and both of land which he sold in Nawset; also, one of fifty acres and meadow, at Marshfield, June 9, 1650. (Reg. VI-41-44). On freeman list of 1670 and of 1695. He died December 21, 1694, aged 80. He married Ruth ———, who died December 15, 1694, aged 69.

Their children were:

6. i. John, b. July 15, 1644.
7. ii. Timothy, b. Sept. 4, (15) 1646.
iii. Hepsebah, b. April 16, 1649, m. Daniel Doane, of Eastham, and had a son, Constant Doane, b. Mar. 7, 1670.
iv. Ruth, b. April 15, 1651, m. John, oldest son of John and Abigail Young, of Eastham, (b. in Plymouth, Nov. 16, 1649).
8. v. Israel, b. Jan. 8, 1653.
9. vi. James, b. Nov. 3, (30) 1655.
10. vii. Mary, b. Mar. 10, 1658, m. May 26, 1681, Joshua Hopkins, of Eastham.
11. viii. William, b. Sept. 15, 1663.

3

JOHN[2] COLE (*Job*,[1]) born in ——— ———. He married November 21, 1667, Elizabeth Keiler. On freeman list of 1695.

4

JOB[2] COLE (*Job*[1]).

5

DANIEL[2] COLE (*Job*,[1]) born in ———. On June 5, 1672, he was fined ten shillings for cursing. On freeman list of 1695. I think he is the one who married Ruth ———, and had

12. i. Thomas, b. —— ——. On freeman list in 1695.
ii. Hester, b. —— ——.

6

JOHN[2] COLE (*Daniel,*[1]) born in Yarmouth, July 16, 1644. He lived in Eastham and married Ruth, daughter of Nicholas Snow, December 12, 1666. He was at Groton in 1672, but probably returned, driven out by Indians, as he is on the freeman list of 1695. His wife died June 27, 1717. He died June 6, 1725.

The children of John and Ruth (Snow) Cole were:

i. Ruth, b. Mar. 11, 1668, m. Wm. Twining, brother of Stephen, son of William, and grandson of William, Mar. 26, 1689. She had children:
- (i.) Elizabeth Twining; b. Aug. 25, 1690.
- (ii.) Thankfull " b. Jan. 11, 1697.
- (iii.) Ruth " b. Aug. 27, 1699.
- (iv.) Hannah " b. April 2, 1702.
- (v.) William " b. Sept. 2, 1704.
- (vi.) Barnabus " b. Sept. 29, 1705.
- (vii.) Mercy " b. Feb. 20, 1708.

13. ii. John. b. Mar. 6, 1670.
iii. Hepsebah, b. June 20, 1672.
iv. Hannah, b. Mar. 27, 1675, d. June 11, 1677.
14. v. Joseph, b. June 11, 1677.
vi. Mary, b. Oct. 27, 1679.
vii. Sarah, b. June 10, 1682.

7

TIMOTHY[2] COLE (*Daniel,*[1]) the second son of Daniel and Ruth Cole, was born in Yarmouth, September 4, 1646. The only mention that I find of him is as follows: 1676, suit of Thomas Baxter for debt of three pounds vs. Timothy Cole, of Eastham. Verdict for the plaintiff for three pounds, two shillings, and costs. On freeman list of 1695.

8

Israel[2] Cole (*Daniel*,[1]) the third son and fifth child of Daniel and Ruth Cole, was born in Eastham January 8, 1653. He married April 24, 1674, Mary, widow of James Rodgers, of Duxbury, and daughter of Thomas[2] and Mary Paine, of Eastham. (Reg. 22–62). He was admitted as freeman of Eastham June 24, 1690, the Court being held at Barnstable. He was living in 1695, as his name is on freeman list.

The children of Israel and Mary (Rodgers) Cole were:

i. Hannah, b. June 28, 1685.
15. ii. Israel, b. June 28, 1685. (Reg. vi–41.)

9

James[2] Cole (*Daniel*,[1]) the third son of Daniel and Ruth Cole, was born in Eastham, November 3, 1655.

10

Mary[2] Cole (*Daniel*,[1]) the seventh child of Daniel and Ruth Cole, was born in Eastham, March 10, 1658. She married May 26, 1681, Joshua Hopkins, of Eastham, born June, 1657, and son of Giles and Catherine (Welden) Hopkins. (Giles came in the Mayflower with his father, Stephen, and his mother.)

Her children were:

i. John, b. April 16, 1683, d. June 24, 1700.
ii. Abigail, b. March 9, 1686.
iii. Elisha, b. Dec. 17, 1688. Lived in Eastham, a wealthy man.
iv. Lydia, b. April 1, 1692.
v. Mary, b. Jan. 20, 1695.
vi. Joshua, b. Feb. 20, 1698.

vii. Hannah, b. March 25, 1700, m. Dec. 13, 1721, Ebenezer Paine, (b. June 17, 1692, d. 1733).
viii. Phebe, b. March 11, 1702, m. Bixby, and removed to the State of New York.

11

William[2] Cole (*Daniel,*[1]) the fourth son and eighth and youngest child of Daniel and Ruth Cole, was born in Eastham, September 15, 1663. He lived in Eastham, and December 2, 1686, he married Hannah, daughter of Stephen and Susanna (Deane) Snow, born January 2, 1667, died June 23, 1737.

Their children were:

16 i. Elisha, b. June 26, 1689.
17 ii. Daniel, b. Oct. 4, 1691.
iii. Hannah, b. Dec. 16, 1693.
iv. Jane, b. Jan. 4, 1695.

13

John[3] Cole (*John,*[2] *Daniel,*[1]) born (in Eastham?) March 6, 1670. Married Mary ———. He died December 13, 1746. His wife died February 17, 1731-2.

Their children were:

18. i. Jonathan, b. Oct. 4, 1694.
19. ii. John, b. Oct. 14, 1696.
iii. Mary, b. Aug. 25, 1698.
20. iv. James, b. Oct. 23, 1700.
21. v. Nathan, b. Jan. 21, 1703.
22. vi. Joshua, b. Mar. 20, 1705.
23. vii. Moses, b. July 22, 1707.
viii. Phoebe, b. Oct. 29, 1709.
ix. Thankful, b. Oct. 20, 1712, d. young.
24. x. Joseph, b. Oct. 13, 1714.
xi. Thankful, b. Oct. 19, 1716.

These remain of this family to be followed out:

THIRD GENERATION.

The children of John,[2] (*Job*[1]).
The children of Job[2] (*Job*[1]).
No. 12. Thomas,[3] (*Daniel*,[2] *Job*[1]).
No. 14. Joseph,[3] (*John*,[2] *Daniel*[1]).
The children of Timothy,[2] (*Daniel*[1]).
No. 15. Israel,[3] (*Israel*,[2] *Daniel*[1]).
The children of James,[2] (*Daniel*[1]).
No. 16. Elisha,[3] (*William*,[2] *Daniel*[1]).
No. 17. Daniel,[3] (*William*,[2] *Daniel*[1]).

FOURTH GENERATION.

Nos. 18–24. The seven sons of John[3], (*John*,[2] *Daniel*[1]).

NOTES ON THE FAMILY OF CHAS. J. COLE, ESQ., HARTFORD, CONN.

——— COLE.

Moved from Cape Cod region (near the sea) to Chatham, a village of East Hampton, Conn. He brought with him sons:

2. Marcus, aged about fifteen when he came to Chatham.
3. Ebenezer.

2. MARCUS.[2] Ensign in French war and Revolution.

4. Abner.
5. Hendrick. (?)
6. Marcus.

3. EBENEZER.[2]

4. ABNER[3], (*Marcus*,[2] ———,[1]) Lieutenant in Revolution, Paymaster and Quartermaster.

7. Abner, father of Charles J.
Three daughters.

5. HENDRICK,[3] (*Marcus*,[2]———.[1])

8. John.
9. Ozius.
10. Harvey.

6. MARCUS.[3]

11. Horace,
12. Samuel,
13. Daniel,
14. Edmund,

All of them left Chatham, most of them going West.

EDWIN HALSEY COLE, born in Chatham, Conn., April 18, 1827. Graduated at Wesleyan University in 1851. Taught in Armenia, N. Y., in 1852 and High School in Collinsville, Conn., in 1854–6, and in Bristol, Conn. In 1856 retired on account of ill health and moved to Cromwell, Conn., where he died July 16, 1859. He married November, 1852, Julia A. Marvin, of Tolland, Conn. Children: Hattie Julia, born May 17, 1856.—*Weyleyan Alumni Record.*

THE CHARLESTOWN FAMILY

OF ISAAC COLE.

ISAAC COLE. In 1634 there sailed from Sandwich, County Kent, England, in the ship Hercules, 200 tons, John Witherby master, one Isaac Cole, of Sandwich, a carpenter, and his wife, Joan, with their two children. They had a certificate from Mr. Thomas Warren, Rector of St. Peter's, Sandwich, dated March 14, 1632, showing their conformity to the rules of the Church of England, and that he had taken the oath of allegiance. (Reg. 15–28.) He first settled in Boston, and the births of two or more children are recorded there.

He moved over to Charlestown, and was admitted with his wife to the Church there on September 7, 1638.

He took the Freeman's oath March 14, 1639.

He obtained one lot of land in a division of land east of the East Spring, in Charlestown, on August 26, 1636, and bought another at the same time.

He died June 10, 1674.

His possessions in Charlestown, as given in Charlestown Land Records, page 66, were:

1. One dwelling-house with a garden plat, situated in the east field, abutting south upon Wapping street, north on Michael Baston; bounded on the east by William Quick, and on the west by the common.

2. One milch common. (Commons for cow.)

3. One acre of meadow, by estimation, more or less, lying in the high field, abutting north on Mystic river; bounded on the east by Thomas Custer, and on the west by James Hayden.

4. Ten acres of wood land, more or less, situated in Mystic field, abutting northeast upon Walter Palmer; southwest upon Edward Gibbens and Seth Tweetsir; bounded on the northwest by Abraham Pratt, and on the southwest by William Batchelor. (Sold to Mr. Thomas Allen-*Greene*.)

5. Twenty-three acres, more or less, situated in Waterfield, abutting northwest upon Mrs. Ann Higginson, southeast upon James Thompson; bounded on the southwest by Abraham Pratt, and on the northeast by William Batchelor.

His children were:

i. Elizabeth, b. in England.
2. ii. Isaac, b. in England, d. in Woburn, June 10, 1674.
3. iii. Abraham, b. Oct. 3, 1636 (bapt. in Charlestown Sept. 14, 1638.)
iv. Mary, b. ———, 1638 (bapt. in Charlestown Jan. 20, 1639.
4. v. Jacob, b. July 16, 1641 (bapt. in Charlestown July 18, d. in Charlestown 1678.

2

Isaac[2] Cole (*Isaac*[1]). He was born in England, I presume, as his father brought two children with him to this country, and his birth is not recorded in Charlestown.

He settled in Woburn, and the town granted him a lot of land in the center, fifty poles, bounded by the highway (High street) on the east, and by the highway to the burying place on the north. April 25, 1662.

He married Jane, widow of James Britton, February 1, 1659. He was one of the eight members of the Woburn Church, presented to the grand jury in October, 1671, for refusing to commune with the Church, on the ground of certain alleged scruples of conscience, and whose case was commended by the Court for the consideration of a council of neighboring churches to assemble March, 1672, before the Court for final decision. But what was the decision of the Court or council is not known.

He was Constable of the town of Woburn in 1662. He is mentioned by Hutchinson (page 206) as being tried on the charge of refusing, as Constable, to publish the King's letter. He was acquitted. He died June 10, 1674, and his widow died March 10, 1687. They had no children.

3

ABRAHAM[2] COLE (*Isaac*[1]). His birth is found on the Boston records as of October 3, 1636. Baptized in Charlestown September 14, 1638.

4

JACOB[2] COLE (*Isaac*[1]). He was born in Charlestown July 16, 1641, and was baptized two days later. He married October 12, 1669, Sarah, daughter of John Train, who came over in the Susan and Ellen, in 1635, at twenty-five, from London. She was born January 31, 1647, and joined the First Church of Charlestown April 16, 1676, and when a widow was admonished by the Church for intemperance. (May 10, 1696.) She was for the same reason excluded from the communion at a later day, but was restored in July, 1704.

Mr. Cole was a member of Captain Moseley's company, that gathered October 9, 1675, on Dedham Plains, and engaged in the great Narragansett fight. He was wounded in this battle. He died in 1678, of smallpox, and some or all of his children died at the same time.

In 1733 his heirs were among those who received a share in the Narragansett lands. I think that the shares of the Charlestown soldiers were assigned in the present town of Templeton, Mass.

His children were:

i. Sarah, b. ——— (bapt. April 23, 1676).
ii. Abigail, b. ——— (bapt. April 23, 1676).
iii. Hannah, b. ——— (bapt. April 23, 1676).
iv. Jacob, born Feb., 1677 (bapt. Feb. 18, 1677).

The Charlestown Family

OF RICE COLE.

Rise (*or Ryce*) Cole came from England in 1630, and settled at Charlestown. He was one of the few who did not remove from Charlestown to Boston. He and his wife, Arrold, were of those dismissed from the Boston Church in October, 1632, to form the first Church of Charlestown, and their names appear on the covenant signed November 14, 1632. (Reg. 23–190.)

He was admitted Freeman April 1, 1633, and appears on the list of proprietors of October 13, 1634, and in a division in January, 1635, he obtaining four acres. He was a witness of the will of Daniel Shepherdson, blacksmith, of Charlestown, May 16, 1644. He died May 15, 1646.

His possessions in Charlestown, as shown by the land records, page 59, were:

1. One dwelling-house with a garden plat situated in the middle row, abutting southwest upon the street way, northeast upon the back street, bounded on the northwest by William Johnson, and on the southeast by the mill way.
2. Two acres of arable land, by estimation, more or less, situated in the east field, abutting southwest upon Long way, northeast upon the swamp; bounded on the southwest by William Brakenburg, and on the northwest by Daniel Shepherdson and Samuel Carter.
3. Two acres of swamp, by estimation, more or less, lying in the east field; bounded on the east by Samuel Carter, on the west by Edward Convers, on the south by Capt. Robert Sedgwick, and on the north by Robert Cutler and William Palmer.
4. Milch cow commons, three and a quarter.
5. Four acres of arable land, by estimation, more or less, situated in the line field, abutting southwest upon the Cambridge line, northeast upon the common; bounded on the southéast by John Penticost, and on the northwest by William Frothingham.
6. Five acres of woodland, by estimation, more or less, situated in the Mystic field.
7. Four acres of meadow, by estimation, more or less, situated in Mystic marshes, abutting west upon the North River, east upon the woodland; bound :d on the south by William Brakenburg, on the north by Samuel Carter.

Wheelwright party, and had, evidently, with. others, petitioned the general court in their behalf, as there is on the records an acknowledgment as follows:

"WHEREAS, I joyned in prefering to ye court a writing called a remonstrance or petition, I acknowledge it was ill done and unwarrantably, as transgressing therein ye rule of due honor to authority and of modesty and submission in private persons, and therefore I desire my name may be put out of it."

This was signed by twenty-four persons, of whom he was one.

The court, on November 27, 1637, eight months later, passed an order disarming all the followers of Wheelwright.

In February, 1638, the Ancient and Honorable Artillery Company was founded, and he was one of the charter members.

He received a large allotment of land in Rumney Marsh (now Chelsea) in 1637–38, and in May, 1658, some 400 acres at Nonotuck. He also owned a tract of pasture land on the west side of Beacon Hill. (Winsor, Vol. II, page 47.) He was a selectman of Boston from 1653 to 1657 inclusive, and sealer of weights and measures in 1654.

His second wife having died, he married, October 16, 1660, Ann, widow of Captain Robert Keayne. He died in February, 1667, probably, as his will was probated the 13th of that month. His will is given in full:

P. 249. Will of Samuel Cole, of Boston.

I, Samuel Cole, of Boston, do declare that to be my last will. * * *

I give unto my dauughter, Eliz. Weeden, that land of mine at Rumney marsh, which at present her husband and she lives upon and have done for some years past, which is the sixth part of my land, the residue whereof I sold to Cornet Hassey, as appeareth by the deed made unto him, as also all the marsh ground that I have at Hogg Island, which is six acres or thereabouts, be it more or less, all of which land my said daughter and her husband shall enjoy during their life; and my will is: That after their decease, it shall be equally divided among all their children.

I give to my daughter Mary's children, which she had by Edmund Jackson, viz.: Elisha and Elizabeth, a house lot in Boston, near the brick kilns abutting on the street, bounded on the north by George Nowell's lott, and on the south side by John Scenter and Elizabeth Gross, their house and lots.

To my grand-child, Sarah Scenter, a colt, which is now in the possession of her husband, Sarah Scenter.

I give besides what formerly is expressed unto my daughter, Eliz. Weeden, the sum of £20, which is due unto me from John Scenter, to be laid out towards the building of a house, upon land formerly exprest at Rumney marsh.

Unto my son John Cole's children £10, to be equally divided among them, and unto my daughter Eliz. Weeden's children £10 also, to be also equally divided amongst them, which £20 is due me by Elizabeth Gross.

I give my land at Manaticott, bought of Clement Cole, and given him by the town, how much and where it lies the deed expresses, unto my grand-child, Samuel Cole, the eldest son of my son John Cole.

To the old Church of Boston, 20s.

Whereas, I promised to give 20s. to Harvard College, and some part of it paid in woodenware by Elzer to Mr. Danforth, and what else I know not, my will is that the residue be duly paid, together with 20s. more, which I give to said college.

For the remainder of my estate at my decease, whether in household goods, debts due, wearing apparel, or otherwise, I give to my son John Cole, and my daughter Eliz. Weeden, to be divided betwixt them, which said John and Elizabeth I make joint executors of this, my last will and testament. But if my said son, John Cole, shall refuse to be an executor to my said will, and upon any pretense whatever shall wrangle with his sister, and not agree peaceably, according to the true intent and meaning of this, my last will, then that my daughter Elizabeth shall be sole executrix, and I give only to my son, John Cole, a legacy of 20s.

I give to my grand-child, Samuel Royall, 40s. as a legacy towards building of a house, which should have been formerly expressed.

I confirm the deed of gift made my son, John Cole, of the one-half of my house in Boston, which is mine in possession until my decease.

This will was taken from the mouth of the aforesaid testator and read before him, who owned it to be his last will and testament, December 21, 1666, in the presence of us whose names are underwritten.

This also the testator further desired at the same time, namely: That James Everell and Goodman Search, the weaver, should be pleased to be overseers, and gives either of them 20s. SAMUEL COLE.

ELIAS MAVERICKE.

ARON ✕ WAY.

JOHN SENTER.

February 13. Maverick and Way deposed.

Inventory of the estate of Samuel Cole, at Winnesimet, deceased, taken by us. Amount, £156 .15 .02.

May 2, 1666. John Cole and Elizabeth Weeden deposed.

The following refers to him:

In answer to petition of Capt. Ed Johnson the court judgeth it meete to confirme Capt. Johnson grant according to the limitation respecting him and Mr. Samuell Cole, according to court's order Oct. 18, 1659, being now laid out as p. platt on file; and considering that Mr. Cole was an adventures in the publicke stocke, and hath binn long out of his money, beene at great charges and cosses in this buisnes, hath approoved himself respective and servicable to this court, the-court judgeth it meete to grannt Mr. Samuell Cole three hundred more acres inn any place free from former grannts.

1659. Nov., 650 acres land granted to Mrs. Anna Cole, widow of Capt. Robert Koyne, which the next year was laid out at Sawheaganucke, on w. side Meremack Rive.

1659. 400 acres to Samuel Cole, of B., w. side M. Rive at Nacooke.

His children were probably by his first wife, and born in England. They were: (but perhaps in different order.)

i. Elizabeth, b. —— ——. She m. Edward Weeden, of Boston, who had come over in the Susan and Ellen from London in 1635, when 22 years of age. They were m. probably in 1643, and went to live on her father's land at Rumney marsh (Chelsea). She was a joint executor of her father's will, and the principal legatee. Her children were:
- (i.) Samuel Weeden, b. Aug., 1644.
- (ii.) John Weeden, b. —— ——. Lived in Boston; m. Ruth ———. Had dau. Sarah, b. Nov. 16, 1687. Wife joined Mather's Church in 1691.
- (iii.) Edward Weeden, b. —— ——. A soldier of Moseley's Co. in the great Narragansett fight; m. Jane ——, and had Dorothy, b. April 22, 1687, and Edward, b. July 3, 1688.
- (iv.) Elizabeth Weeden, b. —— ——, m. about 1673 Sampson Cole (perhaps her first cousin).
- (v.) Hannah Weeden. b. —— ——.
- (vi.) Mary Weeden, b. —— ——. She m. John Scenter. Had John, b. Aug. 8, 1682, and Jonathan, Feb. 8, 1685. She d. 1685.

ii. Mary, b. —— ——, m. Jan. 7, 1653, ——— Jackson. (Savage says she was a widow at that time.) She d. March 11, 1660. Her children were:
- (i.) Edmund Jackson, b. Oct. 30, 1654; d. young.
- (ii.) Elizabeth Jackson, b, Feb. 11, 1657.
- (iii.) Elisha Jackson, b. Feb. 12, 1659.

2. iii. John, b. —— ——.

2

JOHN[2] COLE (*Samuel*[1]). The only son of Samuel Cole, the innkeeper, was born in England and brought over by his father in childhood. He married December 30, 1651, Susanna Hutchinson (b. November 15, 1633). She was the seventh child of William and Ann (Marbry) Hutchinson, who came to Boston in the ship Griffin, September 18, 1635. Mr. Hutchinson was driven from Boston in 1630, and went to Rhode Island, where he was its first Governor, and died at Newport in 1642.

Mrs. Hutchinson removed to the New Netherlands, and was killed in 1643 by the Indians. Several of her children were also killed, and Susanna was taken by the Indians to their villages.

After some three years she was ransomed by the Dutch at Albany, and returned to her friends in Boston. She is mentioned in the will of Samuel Hutchinson, of Boston, April 7, 1667.

He removed before 1664 to the Narragansett country, to look after the Hutchinson lands, where the jurisdiction of Connecticut appointed him a magistrate. He died in 1707, and his wife Susanna and son William administered on his estate.

He is probably the John Cole of Wickford, who petitioned Connecticut to take jurisdiction, May 4, 1668, and as Connecticut officer had obstructed the Rhode Island officers, and was captured and taken to Providence, and released on bail July 15, 1670. On June 28, 1682, he was appointed a Conservator of the Peace for Kingston, R. I.

His children were:

3. i. Samuel, b. March 24, 1656.
ii. Mary, b. Oct. 6, 1658.
iii. John, b. Jan. 23, 1660; d. same month.
iv. Ann, b. March 7, 1661.
4. v. John, b. Jan. 17, 1666.
vi. Hannah, b. Dec. 17, 1668.
5. vii. William, b. July 13, 1671.
6. viii. Elisha, b. ——.

3

SAMUEL[3] COLE (*John,[2] Samuel[1]*). The oldest son of John and Susanna (Hutchinson) Cole, born in Boston, March 24, 1656.

4

JOHN[3] COLE (*John,[2] Samuel[1]*). The fifth child of John and Susanna (Hutchinson) Cole, was born January 17, ·1666.

5

WILLIAM[3] COLE (*John,[2] Samuel[1]*). The third son of John and Susanna (Hutchinson) Cole, was born July 13, 1671. He removed with the family to Kingston, Rhode Island, and in 1707 was co-administrator on his father's estate. His will was made September 22, 1727, and probated September 18, 1734.

His children were:

i. John.
ii. Samuel.
iii. Joseph.
iv. Benjamin.
v. Wignal.
vi. Mary Dickinson.
vii. Ann.
viii. Hannah.
ix. Susanna.

6

ELISHA COLE (*John,[2] Samuel[1]*). Born ——— ——. He lived in Kingston, Rhode Island. He died in 1729, in London, whither he had gone on a law suit. He married Elizabeth ——. His children were (though not, perhaps, in order given here):

i. Thomas, b. —— ——; d. —— 1722.
ii. John, b. —— ——.
iii. Edward, b. —— ——.
iv. Susanna, b. —— ——.
v. Ann, b. —— ——.
vi. Elizabeth, b. —— ——.
vii. Abigail, b. —— ——.

His wife and the six last named children were baptized in 1725, by Dr. McSparran, missionary of the London Society for Propagating the Gospel. He was deputy from Kingston in 1709, 1713, 1715, 1717, and from North Kingston in 1725. In 1722 he was assistant.

He was engaged in a suit with Stephen Northup over the right of flowage of land by the pond of his grist mill, and was beaten in 1726, and the dam torn out. The town ordered it rebuilt, and the mill continued.

EDWARD[4] COLE (*Elisha,*[3] *John,*[2] *Samuel*[1]), the third son of Elisha Cole, was born —— ——. In April, 1745, he was admitted a freeman from North Kingston. He was lieutenant of Captain Munford's Rhode Island company against Louisburg in 1745, and was appointed Captain on death of his commander and wrote home to the Governor on November 29, 1745, as in February, 1746, the general court directed the Governor to reply. He was also captain of a company in the attempt on Quebec in 1746.

In September, 1746, he was appointed a committee to establish a battery on Goat Island. He signed the petition to the King against bills of credit, dated September, 1750.

On March 6, 1755, the Government of Rhode Island voted to aid the expedition against Crown Point with three companies, and appointed him Captain of one of them, the First of Colonel Christopher Harris' regiment.

He was promoted to be Lieutenant Colonel, and commanded the regiment in the battle near Lake George, in which the French under Baron Dieskau were beaten. He was very favorably mentioned in the dispatches of his commander, Sir William Johnson. He moved to Newport, and engaged in the tanning business with George Rome.

When the troubles with the mother country begun he was suspected of favoring the royal cause. In 1775 he presented a petition to the General Assembly reciting that he desired to go to Carlisle, Pa., on business, and stating that as doubts were entertained of his loyalty, he was prepared to make and sign a declaration approving the course of the patriots in assembling an army before Boston, and affirming that he desired to go solely on private business, and asking a safe conduct from the Government. At the same time he presented a written declaration of approval of the acts of the patriots, and promised his assistance if it should be necessary. The court gave him permission to go, and ordered his declaration published in a Providence paper.

He probably never returned. If he did he soon left again, for in 1776 the Sheriff of Newport county was ordered to take possession of his tanyard, and an accounting of the partnership was ordered. References show that he was then absent from Rhode Island, and that his estate was nfiscated. In May, 1784, permission was given to his creditors to bring suit and subject his confiscated estate to the payment.

NORTH KINGSTON, R. I.

JOHN.—Admitted freeman May, 1726. Another of same name (or an error in record) admitted May, 1721.

WILLIAM.—Admitted freeman 1759.

HUTCHINSON.—Lieutenant in Third Company of North Kingston Militia, 1784.

SCITUATE, R. I.

HUGH.—Admitted freeman in May, 1758.

JOHN.—In May, 1785, ordered sued for trouble with his accounts as collector of assessments for raising recruits for town.

FOSTER, R. I.

JOHN.—Lieutenant of Second Company of Foster Militia 1784.

RICHARD.—Ensign of Second Company of Foster Militia 1784.

THE LONG ISLAND FAMILY

OF COLES.

I

ROBERT COLE. The name is frequently spelled with an "s" in the old records. He came in the fleet with Winthrop in 1630, and was one of those who desired to be admitted freeman October 19, 1630, and he was admitted May 18, 1631.

In 1632 it was ordered that two delegates be sent from each of the plantations to advise the Governor and assistants in regard to the raising of revenue, and he was one of the two sent from Roxbury. His drinking habits were opposed to the ideas of the Puritans, and he was several times fined. At length the following order was passed:

March 4, 1633. The court orders that Robert Coles, for drunkenness by him committed at Roxbury, shall be disfranchised, weare about his necke and soe to hange upon his outward garment a D made of redd clothe and sett upon white; to contynue this for a yeare, and not to leave it off at any tyme when he comes amongst company, under penalty of XLs. for the first offense, and V pounds for the second, and after to be punished by the court as they think meete; also he is to weare the D outwards, and is enjoyned to appear at the next general court, and to contynue thise until it be ended.

The same month he went with the party under John Winthrop, Jr., to occupy Agawam (Ipswich), and begin the settlement of that town. He did not remain there long, and he may be the man mentioned in the will of Samuel Fuller, the elder, of Plymouth, July 30, 1633, as then residing with him in Plymouth.

Savage says of him that he reformed his habits. He was one of the twelve men who joined Roger Williams in the settlement of Providence, in October, 1638. His lot in the division of the land was bounded west by the present Main street, east by Hope street, and on one other side by Meeting House street. (Annals of Providence, 33.) He was one of the founders of the first Church of Providence, March 16, 1639. (Arnold's Rhode Island, 107.) He was one of the seventeen who purchased the Pautuxet meadows, and he made his home there.

Three others were appointed with him as a committee to arbitrate disputes and to make rules of government, and their report was the compact signed by all the settlers. He became a friend of Samuel Gorton when he came to Providence, driven from Massachusetts by the intolerance of the authorities of that colony, and gave him part of his land. The actions of Gorton and his followers were such, however, as to cause the older settlers to wish to be free from them, and he, with four others, in September, 1642, appeared before the general court at Boston and yielded themselves up to the Massachusetts colony, which accepted jurisdiction and appointed them magistrates. (Arnold, 468.)

In the formal complaints of the Indians to the Plymouth colony in September, 1652, the seventh article is as follows:

"7th. Ninigrett bought a mastiff dog of Robert Cole, and gave 40 shillings for him, which dog ran home to Robert Cole, who killed the said dog; wherefore, Ninigrett requires 40s. of said Cole."

The commissioners found the charge true, and promised to write Mr. Cole to return the money. (Ply. Col. Rec. X., 375.) He died before October, 1654, as on October 18 of that year the town council distributed his property in the way he should have made his will.

The following orders refer to his estate:

WARWICK, RHODE ISLAND, June 11, 1656.

The town council having formerly disposed of the estate of Robert Cole, late deceased, and having allotted out the portions of the children, ordered that the lands and meadows, together with the pasturage on the south side of the Pautuxet river and the north line bound of Warwick bound is allotted out for security of

Nathaniel Cole, Robert Cole, and Sarah Cole, their portions amounting to the sum of six score pounds.

Further ordered, that the mill of Warwick being a part of the estate of Robert Cole, late deceased, is allotted out for security of Daniel Cole, his portion being £50.

He married Mary ———. After his death she married Mathias Harvey, and removed to Oyster Bay, Long Island, where she died.

The children of Robert and Mary Cole were:

2. i. John, b. —— ——.
3. ii. Daniel, b. —— ——.
4. iii. Nathaniel, b. —— ——.
5. iv. Robert, b. —— ——.
v. Ann, b. —— ——; m. Henry Townsend (probably b. in England, and a son of Thomas Townsend of Lynn, 1639, and d. 1677). He was a freeman of Warwick, 1655, and settled at Oyster Bay, L. I. He was probably a Quaker.
vi. Elizabeth, b. —— ——; married John Townsend, brother of above freeman of Warwick, 1655, and removed to Oyster Bay, L. I., at same time with his brother, where he d. 1669. Their children were (but perhaps in different order):
(i.) John.
(ii.) Thomas.
(iii.) Elizabeth.
(iv.) James.
(v.) Sarah.
(vi.) Ann.
(vii.) George.
(viii.) Daniel.
(ix.) Rose, married John Wicks, Jr.
vii. Sarah, b. —— ——.

2

JOHN[2] COLES (*Robert*[1]). Born —— ——. He owned land in Matinecock, Long Island. He probably died early in life, as his widow, Ann, on the eve of her marriage with William Lynes, deeded half of her property to her son, Solomon, she having a life interest in the estate. January 1, 1683.

Children:

6. i. Solomon.

3

DANIEL[2] COLES (*Robert*[1]). Born ——— ———; died November 9, 1692. He is said by Savage to have moved from Warwick to Oyster Bay, Long Island, at the same time with his mother, step-father, and brothers-in-law. He married ———.

His children were:

7. i. Samuel, b. ——— ———.
8. ii. Benjamin, b. ——— ———.
9. iii. Joseph. b. June 29, 1717.
   iv. Susanna, b. ——— ———; m. Joseph Latting.
   v. Sarah, b. ——— ———; m. Ichabod Hopkins.
   vi. Dinah, b. ——— ———; m. Derick Albertson.
   vii. Mary, b. ——— ———; m. George Downing.
   viii. Ann, b. ——— ———; d. unmarried.

4

NATHANIEL[2] COLES (*Robert*[1]). He removed with his mother and brothers-in-law to Oyster Bay, Long Island. He afterwards lived in Hempstead, where he married, August 30, 1667, Martha Jackson. She died December 17, 1668, leaving one child.

10. i. Nathaniel, b. Aug. 24, 1668.

Mr. Coles married as his second wife Deborah ———. Their children were (perhaps not in this order):

11. ii. Caleb.
12. iii. Harvey.
    iv. Martha.

5

ROBERT[2] COLES (*Robert*[1]). Mentioned in order of town council of Warwick, Rhode Island, 1656, relative to his father's estate. He married Mercy, daughter of Nicholas and Ann Wright.

Their children were:

13. i. Nathan, b. March 18, 1672.
ii. Tamor, b. —— ——; m. Nathaniel Carpenter.
14. iii. John, b. —— ——.
15. iv. Charles, b. —— ——.
16. v. Robert, b. —— ——.
vi. Mercy, b. —— ——; m. William Carpenter.
vii. Mary, b. —— ——; m. William Thorneycraft.

6

SOLOMON[3] COLE (*John,[2] Robert[1]*). On January 1, 1683, his widowed mother, on the eve of her marriage to William Lynes, deeded to him a half interest in the estate at Matinecook.

7

SAMUEL[3] COLES (*Daniel,[2] Robert[1]*).

8

BENJAMIN[3] COLES (*Daniel,[2] Robert[1]*).

9

JOSEPH[3] COLES (*Daniel,[2] Robert[1]*). The youngest son of Daniel Coles, was born in Oyster Bay, Long Island, June 29, 1713. He married Abigail, daughter of Daniel Hopkins (son of Ichabod above mentioned). She was born April 9, 1718.

His children were:

20. i. Benjamin, b. April 6, 1738.
No other sons; perhaps daughters.

10

NATHANIEL[3] COLES (*Nathaniel,*[2] *Robert*[1]). The only child of Nathaniel Coles by his first wife, Martha Jackson, was born in Oyster Bay, Long Island, August 24, 1668. He married Rose, eldest daughter of John and Mary Wright. He died September 8, 1705.

His only child was:

21. i. Wright, b. Sept. 20, 1704; d. Feb. 23, 1765.

11

CALEB[3] COLES (*Nathaniel,*[2] *Robert*[1]). Son by second wife, Deborah ——, born —— ——. His father deeded to him and his brother Harvey lands at Duck Pond, in Oyster Bay, and also in other parts of the town, December 16, 1694. The brothers conveyed these lands to their half-brother, Nathaniel, March 29, 1704, and probably emigrated to some new region.

12

HARVEY[3] COLES (*Nathaniel,*[2] *Robert*[1]). [See above.]

13

NATHAN[3] COLES (*Robert,*[2] *Robert*[1]). The eldest child of Robert and Mercy (Wright) Cole, born at Oyster Bay, March 18, 1672. He married February 21, 1691, Rachael Hopkins.

14

JOHN[3] COLES (*Robert,*[2] *Robert*[1]).

15

CHARLES[3] COLES (*Robert,*[2] *Robert*[1]).

16

ROBERT[3] COLES (*Robert,*[2] *Robert*[1]).

20

BENJAMIN[4] COLES (*Joseph,*[3] *Daniel,*[2] *Robert*[1]). The only son of Joseph Coles, was born on the paternal estate, a little south of Glen Cove, Long Island, April 6, 1738. After attending the common school in his native village, he was sent to Hempstead, where he studied the languages under the Rev. Samuel Seabury, the rector of the church there. He pursued classical studies afterwards at New Haven, and finished at King's College, New York, although it is believed that he did not graduate.

After being licensed to preach, he spent some time among the different churches of Long Island, and was first chosen pastor of the Baptist Church of New Haven, where he was for several years. From thence he removed to New Jersey, and settled in the church at Hopewell, but the revolution breaking out, his patriotic feelings led him to accept the place of chaplain in the American army.

At the dawn of peace he returned to his estate at Oyster Bay, and was soon after called to take charge of the church there, which had been without a pastor more than thirty years. He discharged his pastoral duties with fidelity and usefulness, till within a few years of his death, devoting a portion of his time to the business of classical instruction. He married Mary, daughter of Derick Albertson, September 16, 1760. She was born February 24, 1741, and died February 8, 1812.

Their children were:

i. Rachael, b. —— ——; m. James Hill, and lived near Trenton, N. J. Her children were:
- (i.) Benjamin, b, —— ——.
- (ii.) Samuel, b. —— ——.
- (iii.) Elizabeth, b. —— ——; m. Enos Titus. Lived in New Jersey.
- (iv.) Mary, b. —— ——; m. April 29, 1802, Benjamin, son of Sylvanus Townsend, of Oyster Bay.

22. ii. James, b. March 15, 1763.

iii. Charity, b. —— ——.

23. iv. Benjamin, b. —— ——, and became a Baptist minister. (Thompson's Hist. of Long Island, I., 498.)

21

WRIGHT[4] COLES (*Nathaniel,*[3] *Nathaniel,*[2] *Robert*[1]). The only son of Nathaniel and Rose (Wright) Coles, was born in Oyster Bay, September 20, 1704, and died February 23, 1765. He married Sarah Birdsall, who died May 18, 1799.

Their children:

24. i. Nathaniel, b. Aug. 23, 1734.

ii. Rosanna, b. —— ——.

25. iii. Freelove, b. —— ——.

iv. Martha, b. —— ——.

22

JAMES[5] COLES (*Benjamin,*[4] *Joseph,*[3] *Daniel,*[2] *Robert*[1]). Born March 15, 1763; married Amy, youngest daughter of Ananias Downing, June 9, 1784. He died March 15, 1825. His widow d. May 21, 1840.

Their children were:

i. Abigail, b. June 26, 1785; m. (1) James Bennett, of New York, and (2) Stephen Craft, of Glen Cove.

ii. Joseph, b. Feb. 17, 1787; m. Sarah, daughter of James Carpenter. He was a merchant in New York City, where he d. Feb. 8, 1824.

iii. Deborah, b. Sept. 8, 1791; m. James Benedict, a native of Conn., who had settled in New York City. He was several times a member of the Assembly, and was a stanch friend of DeWitt Clinton. He was for several years Maj. Gen. of Artillery in N. Y. He d. at Tarrytown, in Westchester county.

iv. George D., b. June 9, 1795. He m. Phebe, daughter of James Carpenter. He was commonly known as Col. Coles, and in 1840 was living on the ancestral estate at Glen Cove.

24

NATHANIEL[5] COLES (*Wright,*[4] *Nathaniel,*[3] *Nathaniel,*[2] *Robert*[1]). He was born in Oyster Bay, August 23, 1734, and married Hannah, daughter of John Butler, who was the owner of three-fifths of the Island of Dosoris. Mr. Cole, about 1765, purchased the other two-fifths of Dosoris, and it has ever since been the residence of the Coles family. He was a man of great enterprise, and for several years held a commission in the peace. He died January 7, 1814. His wife born September 13, 1738, and died in her ninetieth year, January 17, 1828. In 1783, on the return of peace, Mr. Coles roasted an entire ox, and invited the neighborhood to partake of it.

His children were:

i. John Butler, b. Dec. 31, 1760; was for a long time a leading merchant of New York City. He was alderman, and a member of both branches of the Legislature. He d. Jan. 2, 1827, leaving a large estate to his sons, *John B.* and *William Coles.*

ii. Nathaniel, b. March 23, 1763. He is better known

as Gen. Coles. He resided on West Island, and superintended two large mills erected by himself and his brother, John B., between the islands. He d. in March, 1824, leaving two sons, *Nathaniel* and *Butler Coles*, and several daughters.

iii. Wright, b. —— ——.
iv. Oliver, b. —— ——.
v. Sarah, b. —— ——.
vi. Elizabeth, —— ——.
vii. Charlotte, b. —— ——.
viii. Mary, b. —— ——.
ix. Freelove, b. —— ——.

COWLES.

There was in Hartford and then in Farmington, Connecticut, in the early days of the colony, one John Cole, a farmer, by some thought to have been a brother of James, the cooper. To distinguish himself and his family from the family of James, he varied the spelling of his name. In the Farmington records the name is spelled Coles, Colles, and finally in 1682, Cowles. It is also found spelled Cowle, Coule, Coules, but the family generally adopted the spelling given at the head of this article.

I

John Cowles, Farmington, Connecticut, 1652. About 1664 he removed to Hatfield, where he was admitted freeman 1666, and died 1675. His widow, Hannah, died in Hartford in 1684, where she made her will 1680.

The children were:

2. i. John, b. about 1641.

ii. Hannah, b. about 1644; m. Caleb Stanley, 1665, son of Timothy and Elizabeth Stanley, who came from England to Cambridge in 1634, and to Hartford in 1635. Caleb was admitted as freeman 1665; was sergeant 1669, and captain later. His wife Hannah d. Feb. 7, 1690, aged 44. Her children were:
   (i.) Hannah, b. Oct. 13, 1666.
   (ii.) Elizabeth, b. Oct. 24, 1669; m. Wm. Pitkin, 2d.
   (iii.) Caleb, b. Sept. 6, 1674.

iii. Sarah, bapt. Feb. 7, 1646; m. 1664, Nathaniel Goodwin, of Hartford, second son of Ozias Goodwin, an early settler of Hartford. Nathaniel was admitted a freeman 1662. Children:
   (i.) Nathaniel, b. July, 1665.
   (ii.) Sarah, b. April, 1668.

(iii.) John, bapt. May 10, 1672. Sarah, the wife, d. May 8, 1676.

iv. Mary, b. —— ——; m. (Nehemiah?) Dickenson, eighth child of Nathaniel, of Wethersfield, and Hadley, b. 1644, and d. 1723. He removed to Hadley with his father in 1659, and lived and died there. Freeman 1690. Children:

(i.) Nehemiah, b. 1672.
(ii.) William, b. 1675.
(iii.) John, b. 1676; d. soon.
(iv.) Mary (twin), b. 1676.
(v.) John (twin), b. 1676; d. soon.
(vi.) Sarah, b. 1680.
(vii.) Samuel, b. 1682.
(viii.) Hannah, b. 1684.
(ix.) Ester, b. 1687.
(x.) Nathaniel, b. 1689.
(xi.) Israel, b. 1691.
(xii.) Abigail, b. 1693.
(xiii.) Ebenezer, b. 1696.
(xiv.) Rebecca, b. 1699.

v. Elizabeth, b. —— ——; m. 1675, Richard Lyman, son of Richard of Winsor, and grandson of Richard of Roxbury, who came with Eliot in the Lion. He lived at Northampton, and in 1696 removed to Lebanon. Their children were:

(i.) Samuel, b. 1676.
(ii.) Richard, b. 1678.
(iii.) John, b. 1680.
(iv.) Isaac, b. 1682.
(v.) Jonathan, b. 1684.
(vi.) Elizabeth, b. 1686.
(vii.) David, b. 1688.
(viii.) Josiah, b. —— ——.
(ix.) Ann, b. 1695.

3. vi. Samuel, b. —— ——.

vii. Ester, b. —— ——; m. 1669, Thomas Bull, of Farmington, son of Thomas of Cambridge and Hartford, who came over in the Hopewell in 1635. Ester d. in 1691, aged 42. Children:

(i.) John, b. 1671.
(ii.) Samuel, b. 1676.
(iii.) Susannah, b. 1679.
(iv.) Jonathan, b. May, 1682.
(v.) Sarah, b. 1684.
(vi.) Daniel, b. 1687.

2

JOHN[2] COWLES (*John*[1]). The eldest child of John and Hannah Cowles, born about 1641. Removed to Hatfield, and was admitted freeman February 8, 1678, and died May 12, 1711, aged 70. He married November 22, 1668, Deborah, daughter of Robert Bartlett, of Hartford, who had come over with Eliot in the Lion in 1632.

His children were:

i. Hannah, b. Nov. 14, 1668; d. unmarried Dec. 25, 1711.
4. ii. Jonathan, b. Jan. 26, 1671.
5. iii. Samuel, b. May 27, 1673.
iv. John, b. June 15, 1676; d. June 18, 1690.
v. Abigail, b. Feb. 1, 1679; d. Dec. 8, 1690.
vi. Sarah, b. June 5, 1681; m. Joseph Bust. (He was probably son of David of Northampton, b. Sept. 26, 1673.)
vii. Mary, b. Nov. 3, 1683; d. unmarried 1742.
viii. Ester, b. April 14, 1686; m. May 25, 1713, Nathaniel Dickenson, son of Samuel of Hatfield, b. Feb. 10, 1672; d. Nov. 24. 1741. She d. 1750. Children:
  (i.) Eunice, b. July 17, 1714; m. Thomas Baker.
  (ii.) Gideon, b. April 27, 1716.
  (iii.) Joseph, b. Aug. 30, 1719; m. Submit ———; d. 1747.
  (iv.) Meriam, b. ——— ———; m. Simeon Morton.

3

SAMUEL[2] COWLES (*John*[1]). The sixth child and second son of John and Hannah Cowles, born ——— ———. He married June 14, 1661, Abigail, daughter of Timothy Stanley, who, with his wife Elizabeth, came to New England in May, 1634, and removed to Hartford the next year. His son Caleb married Hannah Cowles, a sister of Samuel's.

Their children were:

6. i. Samuel, b. March 17, 1662.
ii. Abigail, b. Jan., 1664.
iii. Hannah, b. Dec. 10, 1664.
7. iv. Timothy, b. Nov. 4, 1666.
v. Sarah, b. Dec. 25, 1668.
8. vi. John, b. Jan. 28, 1671.
9. vii. Nathaniel, b. Feb. 11, 1673.
10. viii. Isaac, b. March 28, 1675.
11. ix. Joseph, b. June 18, 1677.
x. Elizabeth, b. March 17, 1680.
12. xi. Caleb, b. June 20, 1682.

4

JONATHAN[3] COWLES (*John,*[2] *John*[1]). The second child and oldest son of John and Deborah (Bartlett) Cowles, born in Hatfield, Massachusetts, January 26, 1671; died July 1, 1756. He married January 21, 1697, Prudence Frary (probably a daughter of John, born September 17, 1669, whose father, Sampson, was killed at Deerfield by the Indians, February 29, 1704). She died July 1, 1756.

Their children were:

i. Abigail, b. May 24, 1698.
13. ii. John, b. Dec. 27, 1700.
14. iii. Jonathan, b. June 30, 1703.
15. iv. Timothy, b. April 9, 1706.
v. Kesiah, b. Sept. 6, 1708; m. Ebenezer Cowles.
16. vi. Nathaniel, b. March 21, 1711.
17. vii. Eleazer, b. Sept. 18, 1713.
18. viii. Elisha, b. April 19, 1716.
ix. Eunice, b. Aug. 18, 1719.
x. Abia, b. Oct. 27, 1722; d. May 10, 1727.

5

SAMUEL[3] COWLES (*John,*[2] *John*[1]). The third child and second son of John and Deborah (Bartlett) Cowles, born in Hatfield,

May 27, 1673; died from injuries received from a fall from a cart, August 16, 1750. He married in 1698, Sarah Hubbard, born November 12, 1662, daughter of John and Mary (Merriam?) Hubbard. The latter was a son of George of Wethersfield, Mitford, and Guilford, Connecticut, and came to Hadley from Wethersfield in 1660.

His children were:

i. Mary, b. March 16, 1698; m. March 23, 1720, John Amsden. He moved from Hatfield to Deerfield, and was drowned there, 1742. Children:
   (i.) John, b. Feb. 16, 1721; resided in Deerfield.
   (ii.) Isaac, b. Sept. 27, 1722; Conway, 1770.
   (iii.) Elizabeth, b. Sept. 27, 1724; d. unmarried.
   (iv.) Violet, b. Sept. 14, 1726; m. Jonathan Bardwell.
   (v.) Oliver, b. 1728; slain by Indians, Aug. 26, 1746.
   (vi.) Elisha, b. 1733; Conway, 1770.
   (vii.) Mary, b. 1735; m. Aaron Phelps, of Belchertown.
   (viii.) Simeon, b. 1737; slain by Indians, Aug. 26, 1746.
   (ix.) Eunice, b. 1739; m. ——— Chamberlan, of Sunderland.
   (x.) Asahel, b. —— ——; resided in Ashfield, 1770.

ii. Sarah, b. Oct. 12, 1703; m. Timothy Cowles.

19. iii. Samuel, b. March 12, 1706.

iv. Elizabeth, b. June 28, 1708; m. Charles Hoar.

20. v. Ebenezer, b. Dec. 18, 1710.

vi. A son, b. Jan. 21, 1713; d. aged one week.

vii. A daughter, b. Jan. 21, 1713; d. aged one day.

6

SAMUEL[3] COWLES (*Samuel,*[2] *John*[1]). The oldest child of Samuel and Abigail (Stanley) Cowles, of Farmington, born March 17, 1662. He married ——— ———. He and his wife joined the church in Farmington May 25, 1690.

His children were:

20*a*. i. Thomas, bapt. June 1, 1690.
ii. Rachael, bapt. June 1, 1690.
20*b*. iii. Samuel, bapt. May 25, 1692.
20*c*. iv. John, bapt. Aug. 26, 1694.

7

TIMOTHY[3] COWLES (*Samuel*,[2] *John*[1]). The fourth child and second son of Samuel and Abigail (Stanley) Cowles, born in Farmington, November 4, 1666.

8

JOHN[3] COWLES (*Samuel*,[2] *John*[1]). Third son of Samuel and Abigail (Stanley) Cowles, born in Farmington, January 28, 1671.

9

NATHANIEL[3] COWLES (*Samuel*,[2] *John*[1]). Fourth son of Samuel and Abigail (Stanley) Cowles, born in Farmington, February 11, 1673.

10

ISAAC[3] COWLES (*Samuel*,[2] *John*[1]). The fifth son of Samuel and Abigail (Stanley) Cowles, born in Farmington, March 28, 1675. He married ——— ———. He and his wife joined the church in Farmington August 11, 1696.

His children were:

i. Mary, bapt. May 2, 1697.

11

JOSEPH[3] COWLES (*Samuel,[2] John[1]*). The sixth son of Samuel and Abigail (Stanley) Cowles, born in Farmington, June 18, 1677.

12

CALEB[3] COWLES (*Samuel,[2] John[1]*). The seventh son of Samuel and Abigail (Stanley) Cowles, born June 20, 1682.

We now follow down the Massachusetts line of John[2].

13

JOHN[4] COWLES (*Jonathan,[3] John,[2] John[1]*). The second child and oldest son of Jonathan and Prudence (Frary) Cowles, born in Hatfield, December 27, 1700; died in Amherst between June and November, 1735. He married Mary ———, who died in Belchertown, 1795, aged 88.

His children were:

21. i. Israel, b. Sept. 28, 1726.
 ii. Abia, b. Dec. 22, 1729; m. March 3, 1752, Gideon Hannun, of Belchertown.
22. iii. John, b. July 28, 1731.
 iv. Martha, b. Nov. 14, 1734; m. Dec. 12, 1754, Stephen Crowfoot, of Belchertown, son of Samuel and Mary (Warner) Crowfoot, of Hadley, b. April 13, 1695.
 v. Mary, bapt. Oct. 3, 1742.

14

JONATHAN[4] COWLES (*Jonathan,[3] John,[2] John[1]*). The second son of Jonathan and Prudence (Frary) Cowles, born in Hatfield, June 30, 1703, and died in Amherst May 14, 1776, aged 73. He married June 13, 1732, Sarah Gaylord, who died February 2, 1790. She was the fourth child of Samuel and Mary (Dickenson) Gaylord, of Hadley, and was born February 1, 1709.

Their children were:

i. Sarah, b. Dec. 29, 1732; m. Abraham Kellogg, Dec. 7, 1758, and d. Oct. 26, 1819. He was a son of Nathaniel and Sarah (Preston) Kellogg, and was b. 1719. He lived at Amherst, but removed before his death to Leverett. Their children were:
- (i.) Sybil, b. Sept. 24, 1761; m. Oct. 6, 1785, Enos Graves, of Leverett.
- (ii.) Sarah, bapt. April 15, 1764.
- (iii.) Samuel, bapt. May 20, 1770; m. Hannah Marsh, and removed to Waterbury, Vt.
- (iv.) Abraham, bapt. Dec. 13, 1772.

23. ii. Oliver, b. July 15, 1735.
iii. Jerusha, b. May 5, 1737; m. Oliver Barrett, of Leverett.
iv. Jonathan, b. Aug. 2, 1739; d. unmarried in Amherst, March 14, 1772, aged 32.
24. v. David, b. Aug. 11, 1741.
25. vi. Josiah, b. March 20, 1744.
26. vii. Eleazer, b. Oct. 18, 1746.
27. viii. Reuben, b. July 22, 1749.
28. ix. Enos, b. May 5, 1752.
29. x. Simeon, b. Oct. 24, 1755.

15

TIMOTHY[4] COWLES (*Jonathan,*[3] *John,*[2] *John*[1]). The third son of Jonathan and Prudence (Frary) Cowles, born April 9, 1706. Lived in Hatfield, and died about 1788. He married his cousin Sarah, daughter of Samuel Cowles.

Their children were:

i. Sarah, b. Sept. 7, 1740; m. Peter Train.
30. ii. Timothy, b. Dec. 25, 1741.

16

NATHANIEL[4] COWLES (*Jonathan,*[3] *John,*[2] *John*[1]). The fourth son of Jonathan and Prudence (Frary) Cowles, born March 21, 1711. He married Anna, daughter of Peter and Mary (Hubbard) Montague, of South Hadley, born October 31, 1718. He lived n Hatfield for a time, and then removed to Belchertown, where he died about 1761.

His children were:

[Allow 31–33 for his sons.]

17

ELEAZER[4] COWLES (*Jonathan,*[3] *John,*[2] *John*[1]). The fifth son of Jonathan and Deborah (Bartlett) Cowles, born in Hatfield, September 18, 1713. He married December 6, 1739, Martha Graves, and resided in Hatfield, where he died.

He had no children.

18

ELISHA[4] COWLES (*Jonathan,*[3] *John,*[2] *John*[1]). The sixth son of Jonathan and Prudence (Frary) Cowles, was born in Hatfield, April 19, 1716, and died there about 1770. He married ——.

His children were:

34. i. Abner, b. May 26, 1749.
35. ii. Justin, b. —— ——.
iii. Lucy, b. June 4, 1753.
36. iv. Elijah, b. —— ——.
v. Prudence, b. —— ——.

19

SAMUEL[4] COWLES (*Samuel,*[3] *John,*[2] *John*[1]). The third child and oldest son of Samuel and Sarah (Hubbard) Cowles, born in Hatfield, March 12, 1706. He married Abigail ——, and resided in Coventry, Burlington, Harwinton, Simsburg, and Norfolk, Connecticut, dying in the latter place in 1762.

His children were:

20

Ebenezer[4] Cowles (*Jonathan,*[3] *John,*[2] *John*[1]). The fifth child and second son of Samuel and Sarah (Hubbard) Cowles, born in Hatfield, December 18, 1710. He married his cousin Kezia, daughter of Jonathan Cowles, and died in Hatfield, October 28, 1800.

His children were:

21

Israel[5] Cowles (*John,*[4] *Jonathan,*[3] *John,*[2] *John*[1]). The oldest child of John and Mary Cowles, of Amherst, born September 28, 1726; married Lydia Bardwell, and removed to Belchertown, and died there in 1797.

His children were:

22

John[5] Cowles (*John,*[4] *Jonathan,*[3] *John,*[2] *John*[1]). The second and youngest son of John and Mary Cowles, of Amherst, born July 28, 1731; married September 24, 1757, Hannah Bardwell, and removed to Belchertown, and died there.

23

OLIVER[5] COWLES (*Jonathan,*[4] *Jonathan,*[3] *John,*[2] *John*[1]). Oldest son of Jonathan and Sarah (Gaylord) Cowles, of Amherst, born July 15, 1735; died in Amherst January 23, 1799. He married October 27, 1762, Irene, daughter of Nathan and Thankful (Warner) Dickenson, of Amherst. She was born July 13, 1743, and died March 28, 1834, aged 90.

His children were:

i. Levi, b. April 24, 1764; m. (1) Dec. 25, 1805, Rebecca, widow of Elijah Hastings; she d. Nov., 1826, aged 63; (2) Submit, widow of Enoch Bangs, and daughter of John Eastman. He resided in Amherst, and d. there Aug. 22, 1829.

ii. Oliver, b. Oct. 27, 1765; m. (1) Jan. 29, 1792, Lois, daughter of Simeon Clark; (2) Jan. 16, 1806, Ruth Lindsay; (3) 1832, Submit, widow of his brother Levi; he d. in Amherst April 1, 1850.

iii. Rufus, b. Dec. 16, 1767; m. (1) Mary Putnam: (2) Sarah, widow of Solomon Boltwood, of Amherst, and daughter of Robert Benney. He graduated at Dartmouth College, 1792, and was a physician in New Salem and Amherst, and d. in Amherst Nov. 22, 1837.

iv. Chester, b. Aug. 14, 1770; m. (1) March 3, 1796, Abigail, daughter of Levi Dickenson, of Granby; (2) April 25, 1811, Sally Wade, of Chicopee. He was a physician, and d. in Amherst Feb. 25, 1842.

v. Jonathan, b. Oct. 24, 1755; d. Sept. 19, 1777.

24

DAVID[5] COWLES (*Jonathan,*[4] *Jonathan,*[3] *John,*[2] *John*[1]). The third son of Jonathan and Sarah (Gaylord) Cowles, born August 11, 1741; died November 18, 1817. He lived in Amherst, and married Sarah, oldest child of Joseph and Sarah (Ingram) Eastman, of Amherst, born January 28, 1744; died August 14, 1815.

Their children were:

i. David, b. Dec. 20, 1773; m. Sally Wheelock, of Leverett, and d. May 23, 1814. He had no children.
ii. Sally, b. July 23, 1775; m. Rev. Ichabod Draper, of Amherst, and d. in Michigan Aug. 3, 1848.
iii. Joseph, b. May 29, 1777; m. Sept., 1801, Beniah Walkup, and d. in Amherst.
iv. Silas, b. Nov. 4, 1779; m. Dec. 22, 1805, Zilpha Shumway, and d. in Hadley.
v. Jonathan, b. Dec. 2, 1781; m. April 16, 1807, Ester, daughter of Elias Graves, of Sunderland, and lived in Amherst.

25

JOSIAH[5] COWLES (*Jonathan,[4] Jonathan,[3] John,[2] John[1]*). Fourth son of Jonathan and Sarah (Gaylord) Cowles, born in Amherst, March 20, 1744; m. (1) Christian ——; (2) Widow Mary Marsh, and resided in Leverett.

26

ELEAZER[5] COWLES (*Jonathan[4], Jonathan,[3] John,[2] John[1]*). The fifth son of Jonathan and Sarah (Gaylord) Cowles, born in Amherst, October 18, 1746; died there July 19, 1795. He married December 5, 1771, Hannah, daughter of Azariah and Eunice (Stoughton) Cowles, born December 24, 1750; died October 5, 1821.

Their children were:

i. Hannah, b. Nov. 10, 1772; m. June 5, 1797, Israel Scott, of Whately, and d. in Hadley, April 20, 1827.
ii. Eunice, b. Oct. 1, 1775; d. Sept. 5, 1777.
iii. Irene, b. May 8, 1777; m. Jan. 8, 1801, Israel Thayer.
iv. John, b. Dec. 20, 1779; m. Nov. 24, 1799, Deborah Warner, and d. in New Haven.
v. Eunice, b. April 22, 1782; m. —— Day.

vi. Eleazer, b. July 25, 1784; m. Sept. 5, 1810, Sybil Montague, and d. in Amherst, 1849.
vii. Stoughton, b. Jan. 3, 1788; m. —— Osburn, and resided in Parishville, N. Y.

27

REUBEN[5] COWLES (*Jonathan*,[4] *Jonathan*,[3] *John*,[2] *John*[1]). The sixth son of Jonathan and Sarah (Gaylord) Cowles, born in Amherst, July 22, 1749; died there March 13, 1824. He married November 26, 1778, Betsy Rice.

Their children were:

i. Elizabeth, bapt. Jan. 7, 1780; m. Samuel Church.
ii. Reuben, bapt. Jan. 6, 1782; d. young.
iii. Lavina, bapt. June 6, 1784; m. Nov. 23, 1812, Zabina Cowles.
iv. William, bapt. Oct. 14, 1787.
v. Jerua, bapt. Feb. 26, 1792; m. John Randolph.
vi. Reuben, bapt. July 27, 1794.
vii. Sylvester, bapt. April 23, 1797; m. Sophronia Mason, of Cummington.
viii. Solomon, bapt. Sept. 15, 1799.
ix. Wealthy, bapt. Sept. 12, 1802; m. —— Turnbull.

28

ENOS[5] COWLES (*Jonathan*,[4] *Jonathan*,[3] *John*,[2] *John*[1]). The seventh son of Jonathan and Sarah (Gaylord) Cowles, born in Amherst, May 5, 1752; married January 28, 1779, Dorcas Goodrich, and died in Amherst, January 21, 1825.

He had no children.

29

SIMEON[5] COWLES (*Jonathan*,[4] *Jonathan*,[3] *John*,[2] *John*[1]). The eighth son of Jonathan and Sarah (Gaylord) Cowles, was born in Amherst, October 24, 1755, and died there July 8, 1831. He married February 12, 1778, Sarah, daughter of Reuben Dickenson, a captain of an Amherst company in the Revolutionary war. She was born February 12, 1757, and died April 20, 1814.

Their children were:

i. Simeon, b. Jan. 11, 1779; m. Nov. 10, 1805, Charlotte, daughter of Gideon Stetson. He moved to Goshen, and died.
ii. Child, b. Oct. 26, 1780; d. in infancy.
iii. Jerusha, b. March 4, 1782; m. Noah Smith.
iv. Orinda, b. Jan. 21, 1784; m. Chester Marshall.
v. Azabah, b. April 12, 1786; m. Timothy Baker, and d. in Springfield, May 28, 1828.
vi. Zebina, b. April 10, 1789; m. Nov. 23, 1812, Lavina Cowles, his cousin, and removed to New Haven and Lincoln, Vt.
vii. Moses, b. July 10, 1791; m. Nov. 10, 1814, Chloe, daughter of Ebenezer Dickenson; resided in Amherst.
viii. Aaron, b. Oct. 23, 1793; m. Ruth Sanders, and resided in Springfield.
ix. Sally, b. Oct. 14, 1796; m. Nov. 26, 1829, Joseph Spear, of Sunderland.
x. Eli, b. Jan. 1, 1800; m. Melinda Ball, of Holden, and d. Jan., 1844.

30

TIMOTHY[5] COWLES (*Timothy*,[4] *Jonathan*,[3] *John*,[2] *John*[1]). The only son of Timothy and Sarah (Cowles) Cowles, born in Hatfield, December 25, 1741.

[31–33 for children of Nathaniel[4].]

34

ABNER[5] COWLES (*Elisha*,[4] *Jonathan*,[3] *John*,[2] *John*[1]). Oldest son of Elisha, born in Hatfield, May 26, 1749.

35

JUSTIN[5] COWLES (*Elisha,*[4] *Jonathan,*[3] *John,*[2] *John*[1]). Second son of Elisha, born in Hatfield, ——, 1751 (?).

36

ELIJAH[5] COWLES (*Elisha,*[4] *Jonathan,*[3] *John,*[2] *John*[1]). Youngest son of Elisha, born in Hatfield, ——, 1755 (?).

---

37 Etc.

[Children of Samuel[4] and Ebenezer[4].]

The Salem Family.

I

Thomas Cole. He was at Salem in 1649–50, and is recorded as a husbandman.

There was a Thomas Cole who came in the Mary and John, March 24, 1633, and was an original proprietor of Hampton, and is mentioned as there in 1638. Whether he is identical with the subject of our sketch I know not. He married Ann ——.

His will is dated December 15, 1678, and was proved April 27, 1679. His widow Ann made her will November 1, 1679, and it was proved May 2, 1681.

Their children were:

2. i. Abraham, b. —— ——, 16—, the eldest son.
3. ii. John, b. —— ——, 164–.

2

Abraham[2] Cole (*Thomas*[1]). The eldest son of Abraham and Ann Cole, born —— ——. He was one of the inhabitants of Salem who protested against imposts in 1668. He married in Salem June 11, 1670, Sarah Davis. Savage says that he removed to Hampton, and there took the freeman's oath in 1678, and afterwards returned to Salem. In 1692 his wife Sarah was accused of witchcraft and imprisoned, but fortunately not brought to trial. She was liberated on bail furnished by her husband January 14, 1693. He was a tailor, and resided in Salem.

They had five children:

i. Samuel, b. May 11, 1670; d. June, 1670.
ii. Sarah, b. Aug. 29, 1672; living in 1715.

iii. Abraham, b. Jan. 6, 1674; d. young (?).
iv. Isaac, b. June 6, 1677; d. young (?).
v. Elizabeth, b. —— ——, 16—; m. ——— Jeffords; d. before 1715, leaving two children:
(i.) Samuel Jeffords. (ii.) Sarah Jeffords.
4. vi. Samuel, b. May 19, 1687, in Salem.
5. vii. Thomas, b. —— ——, 16—. He was living in 1715; he m. Mary Petey in Salem, June 10, 1710.

3

JOHN[2] COLE (*Thomas*[1]). The second son of Thomas and Ann Cole, born 164–. He was one of the inhabitants of Salem who protested against imposts in 1668. He married (1) Mary Knight (probably daughter of William), May 28, 1667, who died before 1675. He married (2) between 1675 and 1686, Sarah Alsbee. He was a cooper by trade, and lived in Salem till about 1675, when he removed to Malden, and about 1684 to Lynn, where he died October 8, 1703, intestate. Sarah, wife of John Cole, of Lynn, was tried for witchcraft at Charlestown, and acquitted February 1, 1693. He made a will October 5, 1703, which is endorsed "Will not perfect," and was not proved. It had but two witnesses. His son, Samuel Cole, of Boxford, was appointed administrator of the estate of his widowed mother, Sarah Cole, of Bradford, May 25, 1741.

Their children were:

6. i. John, b. May 18, 1668, in Salem.
ii. Thomas, b. Nov., 1669, in Salem; d. in 1669.
iii. Mary, b. Sept. 1, 1671, in Salem; living in 1703.
iv. Hannah, b. Dec. 12, 1674; living in 1703.
7. v. Samuel, b. Dec. 27, 1687, in Lynn; removed to Boxford.
vi. Anna, b. Aug. 5, 1690, in Lynn; m. ——— Sessions before 1728.

4

SAMUEL[3] COLE (*Abraham*,[2] *Thomas*[1]). The sixth child of Abraham and Sarah (Davis) Cole, was born in Salem, May 19, 1687, and probably lived there all of his life. His estate was settled there in 1733. He married Elizabeth ——.

Their children were:

i. Elizabeth, b. April 15, 1712; d. June 26, 1713.

ii. Ruth, b. Feb. 10, 1714; m. about 1738, Thomas Peabody, Jr., of Boxford. He was b. July 14, 1715, and lived in Boxford till 1757, when he removed to Lunenburg, Worcester county, where they probably died. Their children were:

- (i.) Jonathan, b. Nov. 16, 1736; married and lived in Brattleboro, Vt. Had three sons.
- (ii.) Samuel, b. March 4, 1741.
- (iii.) Ephraim, b. 1742; d. 1803. He m. Sarah Hutchinson, who died in 1816, aged 66. They lived in Wilton, N. H., and had three sons and five daughters.
- (iv.) Elizabeth, b. Jan. 5, 1744; m. March 3, 1778, Isaac Sanderson.
- (v.) Thomas, b. 1746; m. June 10, 1771, Hannah Ritter.
- (vi.) Phineas, b. April 20, 1749; d. Nov. 21, 1749.
- (vii.) Phineas, b. 1751; m. Lois Clapp; lived in New Salem, Mass.
- (viii.) Amos, b. April 13, 1753; lived in Northfield, Vt.
- (ix.) Moses, b. Jan. 28, 1755; m. Betty Jackman Nov. 26, 1778; d. in 1842; lived in Jaffrey, N. H., and Wethersfield, Vt.

iii. Abraham, b. —— ——, 171(6); living in 1733; d. before 1743.

iv. Abigail, b. —— ——, 171(8); m. Increase Whiston, of Andover; living in 1743.

v. Samuel, b. —— ——, 17(20). He was living in 1743, probably in Methuen, as one Samuel Cole, of Methuen, married Mary Peabody, of Boxford, May 26, 1748.

5

Thomas[3] Cole (*Abraham,[2] Thomas*[1]). The seventh and youngest child of Abraham and Sarah (Davis) Cole, born 16(89) in Salem, Massachusetts. He married Mary Petey, in Salem, June 10, 1710, and was living in 1715.

6

John[3] Cole (*John,[2] Thomas*[1]). The eldest child of John and Mary (Knight) Cole was born in Salem, May 18, 1668. He married Mary, probably daughter of Daniel and Mary Eaton. He moved from Salem to Lynn with his father, and in 1721 removed to Boxford. He resided in the west parish of Boxford, and was chosen surveyor of highways there in 1726. He died intestate, "very suddenly," February 5, 1737, in Boxford, aged 68 years. His name appears on the tax list of Boxford 1721–36. His eldest son, Jonathan, was appointed administrator July 15, 1737. His widow, Mary, died in Boxford, October 7, 1746, aged 78.

Their children were:

9. i. Jonathan, b. 1696; d. in Westmoreland, N. H., April 6, 1780.

ii. Hepzibah, b. —— ——; m. Ebenezer Sherwin, of Boxford, Sept. 21, 1726; removed to Dunstable in 1747.

iii. Mary, b. —— ——; *non compos;* lived in Boxford many years; died very old; never married.

10. iv. Daniel, b. June 20, 1703, in Lynn; was at Boxford in 1725; living in 1788.

v. Hannah, b. —— ——; m. Daniel Eaton, of "Winsor," in Boxford, Dec. 19, 1727; living in 1738.

7

Samuel[3] Cole (*John,[2] Thomas*[1]). The fifth child of John Cole, by his second wife, Sarah, born in Lynn, December 27, 1687. He removed to Boxford from Lynn in 1717, where he died January 20, 1765. He was a farmer in the west parish of Boxford, and was taxed in Boxford from 1717 to 1749. He married Susanna —— in 171–. She died July 29, 1785, aged 95.

Their children were:

11. i. Samuel, b. —— ——.
12. ii. John, b. —— ——.
iii. Rebecca, b. —— ——; m. Andrew Bradford, June 16, 1743, and d. before 1762.
iv. Susanna, b. —— ——; m. Andrew Bixby, Nov. 4, 1746. They settled in Amherst, N. H.; she was living in 1762.
v. Mary, b. —— ——; m. John Hovey, Jr., Jan. 11, 1757; she was living in 1762.

8

SAMUEL[4] COLE (*Samuel,[3] Abraham,[2] Thomas[1]*). Born about 1720. He probably moved to Methuen, and married Mary Peabody, of Boxford, May 26, 1748.

9

JONATHAN[4] COLE (*John,[3] John,[2] Thomas[1]*). The eldest son of John and Mary (Eaton) Cole, born —— ——, 1696, probably in Lynn. Moved with the family to Boxford in 1721, and married there April 8, 1724, Judith Bowen. He was dismissed from the First Church in Boxford to help form the Second Church in Boxford in 1736, and his wife was dismissed from and to the same churches the following winter. He was chosen tithingman March 9, 1742, and was taxed from 1721 to 1744. He was dismissed to the Church in Harvard, "where he now dwells," the Church records say, June 7, 1747, having removed thither in 1745.

On going to Harvard he bought a farm of sixty-five acres, on the north side of "Pine Hill Brook," from Joseph Darby, paying therefor £410.

Although they lived in Boxford for a score of years, no births of children are recorded there.

The baptisms of their first children down to 1736, are to be found in the Bradford Church records. The following are found in the records of the Second Church in Boxford:

Jedediah, baptized March 13, 1737.

Hannah, baptized May 27, 1739.

John, baptized June 21, 1741.

Mary, baptized October 2, 1743.

His wife died in Harvard in November, 1746. He died in Westmoreland, New Hampshire, April 6, 1780.

His children were:

i. Martha, b. —— ——, 1726; d. in Harvard Nov., 1746.

13. ii. Jonathan, b. —— ——, 1730; d. in Westmoreland, N. H., Sept. 13, 1813.

iii. Judith, b. —— ——, 1735; d. in Harvard, Oct., 1746.

14. iv. Abijah, b. —— ——; d. in Harvard, 1768.

v. Jedediah, bapt. March 13, 1737. (I think that this is the same as No. 4.)

vi. Hannah, bapt. May 27, 1739.

15. vii. John, b. June 17, bapt. 21st, 1741; d. in Westmoreland, N. H., April 13, 1786.

viii. Mary (Mathew)(?) bapt. Oct. 2, 1743; d. Oct., 1746.

10

DANIEL[4] COLE (*John,*[3] *John,*[2] *Thomas*[1]). The fourth child and second son of John and Mary (Eaton) Cole, born in Lynn, June 20, 1703, and went with the family to Boxford in 1721. His name appears on the tax lists of Boxford in 1724 and 1725. He probably removed from town soon after.

11

SAMUEL[4] COLE (*Samuel,*[3] *John,*[2] *Thomas*[1]). The first child of Samuel and Susanna Cole, born in Lynn, probably. He married Bethiah Hardy, of Bradford, October 5, 1738. He resided in Boxfield, and died in 1805.

His children were:

16. i. Daniel, b. Dec. 10, 1739.
17. ii. Benjamin, b. Nov. 8, 1741.
18. iii. Solomon, b. April 1, 1743.
19. iv. Phineas, b. Nov. 20, 1744; d. in Pelham, N. H.
v. Mercy, b. Aug. 3, 1746; m. ——— Emmerson; was living in 1793.
vi. Martha, b. Oct. 12, 1748; m. Daniel Silver, of Salem, N. H., Jan. 10, 1778. She was living in 1793.
vii. Rebecca, b. June 5, 1750; m. Thomas Morse, Jr., of Bradford, July 20, 1771; living in 1793.
20. viii. Eliphalet, b. May 23, 1752; m. Ruth Marsh, of Pelham, N. H., (pub.) July 29, 1775; living in 1793.
21. ix. Samuel, b. March 3, 1754; living in 1793.
x. Margaret, b. Feb. 27, 1756; m. Benj. Spofford, Sept. 18, 1784; living in 1793.
xi. Jesse (twin), b. Jan. 5, 1758; d. June 9, 1762.
xii. David (twin), b. Jan. 5, 1758; d. June 11, 1762.
xiii. Bethiah, b. July, 1760; d. June 12, 1762.
22. xiv. Simeon, b. July, 1762.
xv. Bethiah, b. June, 1764; m. Stephen Blood, of Oxford, Nov., 1784; living in 1793.

12

JOHN[4] COLE (*Samuel,*[3] *John,*[2] *Thomas*[1]). The second son of Samuel and Susanna Cole, born probably in Lynn, and taken to Boxford when a child. He married (1) Abigail Brown, April 14, 1746. She died March 8, 1747, aged 23. He married (2) Eunice Spofford, in December, 1748, and resided in Boxford till about 1763, when he removed to Amherst, New Hampshire. He was prominent in town and church affairs; was a soldier in Captain

Josiah Crosby's company of Colonel Nichols' regiment in the Rhode Island campaign of 1777.

His children born in Boxford were:

i. Abigail, b. Feb. 5, 1750.
ii. Hannah, b. Oct. 7, 1751.
iii. John, b. June 27, 1753; a soldier of the Revolution, and killed at Bunker Hill, June 17, 1775.
24. iv. Nathan, b. —— ——; bapt. Feb. 23, 1755.
v. Priscilla, b. —— ——; bapt. Dec. 12, 1756.

13

JONATHAN[5] COLE (*Jonathan,*[4] *John,*[3] *John,*[2] *Thomas*[1]). The oldest son of Jonathan and Judith (Bowen) Cole, was born in 1730. He was one of the early settlers of the town of Westmoreland, New Hampshire, and one of those to whom the charter of 1752 was granted. He settled on the "Canoe Meadow," in the south part of town, on the same farm where his descendants now live. He was for many years one of the most prominent men in the town in certain affairs, particularly in those pertaining to the church. The following is a transcript of some of the entries in the town records in which he is mentioned:

July 16, 1661. Chairman of proprietors' meeting and one of a committee to lay out the divisions of the town.

May 21, 1770. Chairman of a committee to rectify mistakes in the proprietors' book, and to decide all disputes of line between party and party to look all undivided lands belonging to the proprietors and report.

January 26, 1777. Chairman of a committee to settle with the proprietors and any others who may have claims.

May 26, 1779. One of a committee to price all undivided lands and dispose of the same and make a return.

December 12, 1775. One of a committee chosen to instruct the representative.

March 23, 1776. One of seven highway surveyors. On the same date he was chosen one of a committee to determine a site for a meeting-house, which was to be removed. (The committee reported the site on Park Hill.)

April 10, 1776. One of a committee of three to hire preaching.

March 12, 1777. One of committee of three to settle with selectmen at the close of the year, and one of a committee of five as committee of inspection.

April 14, 1777. He was moderator of a special town meeting, and on same day was chairman of a committee for the settlement of claims.

May 25, 1777. He was on a committee to state the price of sundry articles.

July 8, 1777. Moderator at a special meeting.

March 11, 1778. One of a committee of three to provide for the families of soldiers.

May 7, 1778. One of committee to instruct A. Temple, representative to Concord, to form a government.

October 26, 1778. Moderator at a special meeting.

March 10, 1779. Surveyor of highways.

November 3, 1779. Committee to appraise pews.

December 3, 1779. On minister committee.

March 8, 1780. Surveyor.

June 5, 1780. On minister settlement committee.

September 19, 1780. On committee to hire a minister.

November 13, 1780. One of two delegates to a convention at Walpole.

December 5, 1780. Delegate to a convention to be held at Charlestown, in January, 1781.

February 8, 1781. Delegate to a convention at Cornish.

April 16, 1782. One of a committee to give opinion relative to the Constitution, and also one of a committee to hire a minister.

May 14, 1782 One of a committee to confer with the soldiers, and give each forty pounds in land or money; also on the committee to appraise Glebe lands.

November 11, 1782. On the committee to expound the Constitution.

May 7, 1783. On committee to hire a preacher.

November 8, 1784. On committee to confer with the Rev. Mr. Davis.

March 27, 1786. On committee to hire a minister.

July, 1787. On committee to get a preacher.

For nearly all of his life he was one of the pillars of the Congregational Church, and for many years one of its deacons.

In the early days of the settlement he was often annoyed by the Indians. He built a block house for the protection of his family and the families of his neighbors. Some years ago the site of this block house was determined by the uncovering of the well that was dug at that time.

He married Edith Davis, who was born in 1729, and died February 8, 1805. He died September 13, 1813, aged 85. Both he and his wife, as well as his father, were buried in the "River Burying Ground" in Westmoreland.

The children of Jonathan and Edith (Davis) Cole were:

25. i. Jonathan, b. 1751; d. in Westmoreland, Feb. 8, 1805.
ii. Jedediah, b. Sept. 5, 1765; d. May, 1766.
iii. Abel, b. 1767; d. Oct. 3, 1770.
26. iv. Mary, b. ———; m. Benjamin Gleason; d. ———.
v. Martha, b. ———; m. Noah Whitman. She probably soon after her marriage moved away from Westmoreland, and all trace of the family has been lost.
vi. Susan, b. ———; m. Thomas Wyman. She probably moved from Westmoreland soon after her marriage. All trace of her family has been lost.

14

ABIJAH[5] COLE (*Jonathan,*[4] *John,*[3] *John,*[2] *Thomas*[1]). Very little is known of his brief life, even the date of his death being unknown. He married Sarah Kent, one of the four daughters of Jonathan Kent, of Harvard, Massachusetts. She had no brothers, and of her three sisters Ruth never married. Abigail married a Mr. Crafts, of Roxbury, Massachusetts, and the other married a Mr. Groves. Abijah Cole died in 1768, being probably less than 30 years of age, and as the three youngest of his children are the only ones whose births are recorded there, he may have lived elsewhere in the early years of his married life. Some years after his death his widow married Samuel Garfield, of Harvard or Bolton, by whom she had no children. She spent some of the years of her second widowhood in Gouldsboro, Maine, at the house of her eldest son, who settled there. She died about 1812 in Roxbury, Massachusetts, at the house of her niece, Mrs. Crafts.

It is related by one of her grand-children that at the time of her husband's death Mrs. Cole was overwhelmed with her loss, and refused to be comforted; but finally before the funeral she took her Bible and went out into the orchard alone, and after some time returned calm, resigned, and peaceful.

There is a deed from Jonathan to Abijah Cole, dated at Harvard, May, 1761. Probably this was about the time that Jonathan left for Westmoreland.

The following, in the possession of the Maine branch of the family, is supposed to be a copy of a will:

"I, Abijah Cole, having joined a company or regiment for the capture of Quebec, in view of the uncertainty of human life, do give and bequeath to my father, Jonathan Cole, and to my brothers, Jonathan and John Cole, certain lots of land situated in Harvard, and to my friend Sarah Kent, personal property, consisting of a watch and money."

There is no date, but it was probably about 1755.

The children of Abijah and Sarah (Kent) Cole were:

i. Sarah, b. May 13, 1760; d. unmarried in Westmoreland, N. H., Nov. 3, 1783. She was buried in the River Cemetery, where a stone was afterwards erected to her memory.

27. ii. Abijah, b. Nov., 1761; d. in Prospect Harbor, Me., June 17, 1841, aged 80.

iii. Lois, b. 1764. She m. Solomon Robbins, of Westmoreland, N. H. She had eleven children born in that town, viz.:

Sally, b. March 5, 1782.
Solomon, b. March 10, 1785.
Asa, b. Aug. 28, 1788.
Lois, b. Aug. 19, 1790.
Charles, b. Aug. 22, 1792.
Jonathan, b. March 24, 1795.
Candace, b. June 21, 1800.
Mary, b. June 12, 1805.
Allen, b. Nov. 11, 1806.
Emeline, b. Sept 9, 1807.
Judith, b. July 5, 1810.

Mr. Robbins was for many years ferryman at the place now known as "Britton's Ferry." In 1816 the family moved to Pennsylvania, and all trace of them has been lost. He was elected fish inspector in Westmoreland in March, 1796. He was a private in Capt. Scott's company of Col. Ashley's regiment in the march on Ticonderago in 1777, and again in the Eighth company of Col. Nichols' regiment at the battle of Bennington.

iv. Judith, b. 1767; m. John Hayden, of Cambridge, Mass. At her father's death she went to live with her maternal aunt, Abigail Kent Crafts, who was then a widow. John Hayden was the manager of Mrs. Crafts' business. Judith married him and removed to Cambridgeport, where he went into business as an India merchant. She died in 1810, leaving two son, John Hayden, who died in 1871, and William Hayden. After her death her husband married her cousin, Abigail Crafts.

28. v. Asa, b. Dec. 8, 1768; d. in Westmoreland, N. H., Dec. 6, 1816, aged 48.

15

JOHN[5] COLE (*Jonathan,[4] John,[3] John,[2] Thomas[1]*). The third son of Jonathan and Judith (Bowen) Cole, was born June 29, 1741, and died in Westmoreland, New Hampshire, August 15, 1786. He was one of the prominent men of the town during the Revolutionary times. He was one of the committee to instruct the representative chosen December 12, 1775. He was a sergeant in the Eighth company of Colonel Nichols' regiment, Joseph Hindes captain, in 1776, and was in the battle of Bunker Hill.

His name is to be found on the roll of signers of the test oath of March previous, as is also that of his brother Jonathan.

In November, 1777, a company of sixty-three men was raised for service against Burgoyne, and he was chosen captain.

In August, 1779, he was chosen one of a committee to settle with a committee from the Baptists, the rights in the church building and to move the church to the new site on Park Hill. This change was successfully consummated. In November of the same year he, with others, was selected to furnish the house and appraise the pews.

He was several times surveyor, fence viewer, and committeeman. He lived in the north part of town. After his family became large and the older children had left home, he removed to Windham, Vermont. He died in Westmoreland, while on a visit to his oldest brother, Jonathan, and was buried in the River Cemetery in that town, as was also his wife and one daughter. The oldest sons had not gone with him to Vermont, and they drifted to various parts of the country. The younger children, who were in Windham at the time of his death, remained in and around that region till middle life, and some of them all of their days. The youngest in some way got back to Westmoreland, and lived the remainder of his days there. With him his mother spent her last years.

The wife of Captain John Cole was Lois Davis, born October 12, 1742; died in Westmoreland, September 30, 1830, aged 88.

The children of Captain John and Lois (Davis) Cole were:

29. i. Levi, b. January 10, 1762; d. in Joliet, Ill., Sept. 20, 1850.
30. ii. John, b. Sept. 23, 1763; d. in London, Canada, 1850.
31. iii. Salmon, b. Jan. 13, 1765; d. in Buckingham, Canada, in 1840.
iv. Matawassa, b. May 22, 1766; d. June 14, 1772.
v. Amasa, b. March 12, 1768. The tax records of the town of Chesterfield, N. H., show that he was assessed for a poll tax in 1790, and again the following year, and he married Lois Higgins in Westmoreland, Feb. 5, 1789. Nothing further is known of him, and it is probable that he died in early manhood.
32. vi. Laban, b. Feb. 14, 1770; d. in Troy, N. Y., March 24, 1830.
vii. Hannah, b. April 25, 1772. She married Benjamin Howard, of Jamaica, Vt., and died there in 185–. She had no children.

viii. Derastus, b. Dec. 13, 1772; d. in Coshocton, Steuben county, N. Y., in 1842. His wife, Betsy ———, survived him. They had no children.

ix. Benoni, b. Feb. 8, 1775; d. in New York City, Sept. 25, 1798. He was unmarried.

33. x. Sala, b. Sept. 2, 1776; d. in Tioga, Tioga county, Pa., Feb. 8, 1852, aged 76.

34. xi. Ethan, b. March 5, 1778; d. in Londonderry, Vt., Dec. 14, 1854, aged 76.

35. xii. Simon, b. Feb. 13, 1780; d. in Boston, Mass., June 27, 1856, aged 76.

xiii. Lois, b. Aug. 15, 1781. She married Reuben Robinson, and removed to Canada, where she died Dec. 30, 1803, aged 23.

36. xiv. Heber, b. Aug. 10, 1783; d. in Westmoreland, N. H., Oct. 19, 1857, aged 74.

16

DANIEL[5] COLE (*Samuel,*[4] *Samuel,*[3] *John,*[2] *Thomas*[1]). The first child of Samuel and Bethiah (Hardy) Cole, was born in Boxford, December 10, 1739. He married Elizabeth Day, of Boxford, November 25, 1672, and lived in Boxford, being alive in 1793.

His children were:

37. i. David, b. Jan. 20, 1764. Enlisted in the Revolutionary army, and died of a fever.

38. ii. Jesse, b. Dec. 19, 1765.

39. iii. Moses, b. —— ——, 1767; bapt. Sept. 27.

iv. Elizabeth, b. —— ——, 1770; m. April 1, 1789, Nathaniel, son of Nathaniel Peabody, of Boxford. He was born 1767, and lived in Boxford and then in Dracut. Her children were:

(i.) Hepsibah, b. Aug. 29, 1787; m. Russell Fox.

(ii.) Nathaniel, b. Feb. 26, 1792; m. Mary Gilcrist.

(iii.) Betsy, b. 1799; d. young.

(iv.) Ephraim, b. Aug. 25, 1804; m. Sarah P. Davis.

(v.) Moses, b. Dec. 12, 1806; m. Hannah F. Gray.

40. v. Thomas, b. —— ——; bapt. Nov. 17, 1771.
vi. Sally, b. —— ——; bapt May 22, 1773.
41. vii. Samuel, b. —— ——; bapt. Nov. 17, 1776.
viii. Phebe, b. —— ——; bapt. Feb. 21, 1779.

17

Benjamin[5] Cole (*Samuel,*[4] *Samuel,*[3] *John,*[2] *Thomas*[1]). The second son of Samuel and Bethiah (Hardy) Cole, born in Boxford, November 8, 1741. He was a farmer, and died there February 12, 1774. He married Elizabeth ——, who September 10, 1778, married Samuel Kimball, of Boxford.

His only child was:

42. i. Asa, b. July 22, 1766.

18

Solomon[5] Cole (*Samuel,*[4] *Samuel,*[3] *John,*[2] *Thomas*[1]). The third son of Samuel and Bethiah (Hardy) Cole, was born in Boxford, Massachusetts, April 1, 1743. He married Mehitable Barker, of Andover (pub. Jan. 8, 1766). He settled in Zandaff, New Hampshire, and died there in 1835.

Their children were:

43. i. Timothy, bapt. June 28, 1767.
44. ii. Kimball, b. —— ——.
45. iii. Benjamin, b. —— ——.
46. iv. Isaac, b. ——, 1774.
47. v. John, b. —— ——.
48. vi. Solomon, b. —— ——.
49. vii. Samuel, b. —— ——.
50. viii. Asa, bapt. May 15, 1785.
ix. Catherine, b. —— ——; m. Benjamin Whitcher, of Northfield, N. H., Nov. 30, 1801.
Perhaps other daughters.

19

PHINEAS[5] COLE (*Samuel,*[4] *Samuel,*[3] *John,*[2] *Thomas*[1]). The fourth son of Samuel and Bethiah (Hardy) Cole, was born in Boxford, November 20, 1744. He married Abiah Hazletine, of Bradford, December 20, 1765, and settled in Pelham, New Hampshire. He was an inn-keeper in Boxford and in Pelham, and was living in 1793.

[There is a record in Bradford of the marriage of Phineas Cole, of Bradford, and Catherine Hudson, late of Boston, May 17, 1776.] I think he lived in Bradford for a time, and that he is the one whose name appears as a subscriber of $4.00 to the Social Library of that town.

One of his children was:

Sarah, b. —— ——. She married Capt. Eliphalet Buck, of Haverhill, and moved to Eastport, Me. Her daughter: Lydia Cushing, b. Oct. 17, 1799, in Haverhill, and married in Eastport, Feb. 9, 1820, Peter Thatcher Vose, and died in Robbinstown, Me., Jan. 22, 1865.

20

ELIPHALET[5] COLE (*Samuel,*[4] *Samuel,*[3] *John,*[2] *Thomas*[1]). The fifth son and eighth child of Samuel and Bethiah (Hardy) Cole, born in Boxford, May 23, 1752. He married Ruth Marsh, of Pelham, New Hampshire (pub. July 29, 1775), and was living in 1793.

21

SAMUEL[5] COLE (*Samuel,*[4] *Samuel,*[3] *John,*[2] *Thomas*[1]). The sixth son and ninth child of Samuel and Bethiah (Hardy) Cole, born in Boxford, March 3, 1754, and was living in 1793.

22

SIMEON[5] COLE (*Samuel,*[4] *Samuel,*[3] *John,*[2] *Thomas*[1]). The ninth son and fourteenth child of Samuel and Bethiah (Hardy) Cole, born in Boxford, July, 1762; married Polly Smith, of Rowley, July 5, 1785. He lived in Boxford, and died there December 9, 1843. His wife died there January 5, 1826.

Their children were:

i. Triphena, b. June 20, 1786; m. (1) Gardner Eames, of Boxford, Nov. 12, 1805; (2) Joseph Pike, April 4, 1822. She was living in 1844.

ii. Sally, b. Aug. 24, 1787; m. Samuel W. Clement, an inn-keeper of Boxford, Oct. 24, 1811, and died there Dec. 2, 1877, aged 90.

iii. Caleb Currier, b. March 26, 1789; d. Aug. 8, 1802.

iv. Hannah, b. July 3, 1791; m. John Ladd Davis, of Boxford, May 5, 1808.

v. Judith, b. Oct. 24, 1793; d. Nov. 23, 1797.

51. vi. Samuel, b. Jan. 24, 1797.

52. vii. Manley Hardy, b. Aug. 19, 1800.

24

NATHAN[5] COLE (*John,*[4] *Samuel,*[3] *John,*[2] *Thomas*[1]). The second son and fourth child of John and Eunice (Spofford) Cole, was born in Boxford, Massachusetts, and baptized there February 23, 1755. He removed to Amherst, New Hampshire, with his parents in 1763. He was a soldier of the Revolution, and was at the battle of Bunker Hill, where his only brother, John, was killed.

He probably settled after the war (if he escaped death) in some other place than Amherst, as no trace of his descendants is found in that town.

25

JONATHAN[6] COLE (*Jonathan,*[5] *Jonathan,*[4] *John,*[3] *John,*[2] *Thomas*[1]).

The only son who grew to manhood of Jonathan and Edith (Davis) Cole was born in Westmoreland, New Hampshire, in 1751. He lived on the old homestead with his father, and died before him, February 13, 1807. On June 29, 1775, he married Anna Whitman, who was born in 1753, and died December 7, 1843, aged 90.

The children of Jonathan and Anna (Whitman) Cole were:

53. i. Jonathan, b. April 30, 1776; d. in West Stockholm, St. Lawrence county, N. Y., April 4, 1848, aged 72,

54. ii. Abel, b. Dec. 8, 1777; d. in Westmoreland, N. H., July 11, 1838, aged 61.

iii. Betsy, b. Sept. 14, 1779. She m. Abel Whitman, June 17, 1799, and removed to Wisconsin, and settled in Whitmanville, where she d. July 27, 1859. Her descendants are living there now, and one of her daughters, Mrs. Joshua Fitch, was living in Canandaigua, N. Y., in 1872.

55. iv. Martin, b. Nov. 23, 1781; d. in Mt. Holly, Vt., April 6, 1866, aged 85.

v. Polly, b. Nov. 23, 1783. She married Amos Brown, Jr., of Claremont, N. H., Jan. 23, 1806, and died there Jan. 31, 1840. Her husband was born June 28, 1780, and died Oct. 15, 1834. They spent all their married life in Claremont. They had five children, viz.:

Angela Brown, b. June 12, 1806.

Oscar J. Brown, b. Oct. 22, 1808. Lived in Claremont.

Susan C. Brown, b. Sept. 17, 1811; m. Harvey Hendricks.

Daniel C. Brown, b. April 4, 1814; d. Oct. 28, 1870.

Levi B. Brown, b. Sept. 21, 1822.

vi. Anna, b. Oct. 20, 1778. She married the Rev. Otis Hutchins, son of William and Sally (Whitman) Hutchins. He was born in 1781, and died Oct. 6, 1866. He graduated at Dartmouth College in 1804, and was principal of the old Chesterfield Academy, and afterwards first principal of the Kimball Union Academy at Meridan, N. H. Although he was ordained to the ministry, he never preached much, but after his teaching days were over, retired to his farm in Westmoreland, where he spent the remainder of his days. Anna

Cole was his second wife. They had no children. She died April 2, 1858.

56. vii. Abijah, b. Nov. 1, 1787; d. in Mt. Holly, Vt., March 10, 1865, aged 78.

viii. Susan, b. 1790; d. Sept. 4, 1811.

ix. Sally, b. 1792; d. Oct. 16, 1812.

x. Latty, b. May 12, 1796. She married the Hon. Timothy Hoskins, Aug. 11, 1821. He was a son of Timothy and Susan Hoskins, of Westmoreland, and was a prominent man in his region. He was town clerk in 1850, selectman 1849–52, a member of the House of Representatives of New Hampshire in 1833–34 and 1840, and in 1843–44 a State Senator from Cheshire county. He died Sept. 20, 1857. After his death his widow resided with her adopted daughter, Mrs. Caroline (Wing) Pierce, and died in Pawlet, Vt., Jan. 26, 1881. She had no children.

26

MARY COLE[6] GLEASON (*Jonathan,*[5] *Jonathan,*[4] *John,*[3] *John,*[2] *Thomas*[1]). The oldest daughter of Jonathan and Edith (Davis) Cole, was born in Westmoreland, Cheshire county, New Hampshire. She married Benjamin Gleason, one of the four sons of Isaac and Thankful Gleason, of Petersham, Massachusetts. He came to Westmoreland with his brothers when he was a young man, and lived there all of his life. He survived his wife some years. They are both buried in the old ground in District No. 5, but no stone was ever erected to their memory.

They had nine children, viz.:

i. Mary Gleason, b. Feb. 28, 1776; m. Nathaniel Wilson, of Westmoreland, Dec. 15, 1798. She had four children:

(i.) Eli Wilson, who m. Martha Blake.

(ii.) Mary Wilson, who married Ezekiel Woodard, and had five children: (*a*) Betsy, who m. Lewis Shelley, of Westmoreland. (*b*) Mary, who m. Stephen Gary, of Westmoreland. (*c*) Lucy, who m. Chas. Knight, of Westmoreland. (*d*) Samuel.

(iii.) Lydia Wilson, who m. a Mr. Gilson.

(iv.) Nancy Wilson, who m. Hiram Woodard, of Westmoreland, and d. Oct. 16, 1859, aged 46. Mr. Woodard d. Sept. 27, 1854, aged 50. They had four children: (*a*) Martha, d. unmarried. (*b*) Nancy, who m. Harrison Gary. (*c*) Mary. (*d*) Samuel.

ii. Lucy Gleason, b. Sept. 22, 1777; m. Nathaniel Hazelton, Sept 16, 1801. Their children born in Westmoreland were:

(i.) Clark Hazelton, b. July 24, 1803.

(ii.) John Hazelton, b. May 29, 1805.

(iii.) Clarissa Hazelton, b. July 13, 1807.

iii. Benjamin Gleason, b. Aug. 19, 1783.

iv. Clarissa Gleason, b. Oct. 10, 1785; m. Samuel Boynton, Nov. 27, 1805. Had seven children:

(i.) Greenleaf Boynton, d. unmarried.

(ii.) Clarissa Boynton, m. a Mr. Mussy.

(iii.) Almina Boynton, m. in Canada.

(iv.) Eunice Boynton.

(v.) Samuel Boynton, went South and married.

(vi.) Semira Boynton.

(vii.) Oscar Boynton.

v. Bildad Gleason, b. Dec. 16, 1787; m. in Westmoreland to Cynthia Gilmore, Aug. 1, 1809. His children were:

(i.) Benjamin Gleason, b. May 10, 1810.

(ii.) Osman Gilmore, b. April 25, 1811, and perhaps others after he left town.

vi. Lavina Gleason, b. Dec. 8, 1789; m. Arba Gilmore, Nov. 2, 1809.

vii. Betsy Gleason, b. March 21, 1792; m. Elbridge Chickering, of Westmoreland, July 11, 1815, and d. Sept. 4, 1849 Mr. C. d. Jan. 4, 1851, aged 52. Had six children:

(i.) Caroline Chickering, m. Abiather L. Shaw. No children.

(ii.) Clarissa Chickering, who married Jewett E. Buffum. Had six children: (*a*) Solon. (*b*) Clayton. (*c*) Clement. (*d*) Colburn. (*e*) Alba, who m. Adine L. Cole, and lives in W. (*f*) Alice, who m. Edward Fletcher, and lives in K.

(iii.) Rawson Chickering, who m. Julia Gilkerson.

(iv.) Holland Chickering, who m. Celestia Chamberlain.
(v.) Elbridge Wheelock Chickering, m. Elsa Aldrich. Has four children: (*a*) Dell. (*b*) Vesta; m. Nov. 1886, Lyman Willson, of Gilroy, Cal; d. there Jan., 1887. (*c*) Guy. (*d*) Fred.
(vi.) Shubel Chickering; unmarried.

viii. Joseph Gleason, b. Feb. 27, 1794. He had five children. He married Chloe Bell.
(i.) Mary Gleason; m. a Mr. Brown.
(ii.) ——— ———.
(iii.) Lemuel Gleason.
(iv.) Joseph Gleason.
(v.) Alvin Gleason; d. aged 14.

ix. Eunice Gleason, b. May 30, 1796; m. Alvin Chickering, of Westmoreland, March 27, 1817, and d. Jan. 18, 1836, aged 39. Her children were:
(i.) Lucy Chickering, m. Seaman Wilber.
(ii.) Alvin Chickering, m. Helen Hale.
(iii.) Elbridge Chickering.
(iv.) Eunice Chickering; m. Horace Wilson.
(v.) Benjamin Chickering.
(vi.) Mary Ann Chickering; m. a Mr. Neil.

x. Semora Gleason, b. July 9, 1803; m. Calvin Walker, Jan. 3, 1823.

27

Abijah[6] Cole (*Abijah,*[5] *Jonathan,*[4] *John,*[3] *John,*[2] *Thomas*[1]). The second son of Abijah and Sarah (Kent) Cole. He was born in 1761. The place of his birth is not known, but it was probably in that part of Littleton, Massachusetts, that is now Harvard. His father died when he was about seven years of age, but after a few years his mother married Samuel Garfield, a millwright, who taught the boys, his step-sons, his trade. With his step-father he went down into the State of Maine, building mills, and in Hancock county he purchased property and settled in the village of Prospect Harbor, town of Gouldsboro, where he lived for the remainder of his days. He married Nancy Williams, born September 29, 1762; died March 10, 1851, aged 89. He was a man of prominence in the town, and a public-spirited citizen. He died June 17, 1845, aged 84.

The children of Abijah and Nancy (Williams) Cole were:

57. i. Asa, b. Jan. 24, 1792; d. in Prospect Harbor, Me., April 28, 1861, aged 89.

58. ii. Sarah, b. March 1, 1793; m. Henry Everett; d. Sept. 9, 1871, aged 78.

iii. Abigail, b. March 16, 1794; d. unmarried, June 16, 1826.

59. iv. Nancy, b. Nov. 11, 1795; m. George Moore; d. Sept. 2, 1860.

60. v. Abijah, b. Aug. 14, 1799; d. in Prospect Harbor, March 31, 1876, aged 77.

vi. Judith, b. Nov. 19, 1801. On Dec. 8, 1825, she married David Godfrey, of Lubec, Me. She died Oct. 9, 1863, aged 62. She had no children.

61. vii. Lois, b. Nov. 2, 1803; m. David Moore; d. March 8, 1861, aged 58.

62. viii. Lydia, b. Jan. 30, 1806; m. Joel Moore; d. Oct. 26, 1881, aged 75.

ix. Percilla, b. June 12, 1808. She married Fabens Downing, of East Sullivan, Hancock county, Me., April 20, 1838. She died July 10, 1884, aged 76. Her children were: (1) Theodosia Downing, b. Dec. 9, 1838; m. R. H. Moon, of Hancock, Me., Jan. 11, 1863, and d. Aug. 16, 1869, leaving one son, Frank D. Moon, b. March 24, 1864, now a member of the firm of Moon & McMillan, contractors and builders, Minneapolis and Duluth, Minn.; and (2) Sherman R. Downing, b. June 30, 1847, who m. Lucretia Kenniston, Nov. 26, 1883, and has one child, Ethel, b. Nov. 6, 1884. He resides in East Sullivan, Me.

x. Susan Hayden, b. Oct. 7, 1810. She married Josiah N. Dunbar, of Machias, Me., Oct. 1, 1840. They had two children, (1) Albert Josiah Dunbar, b. Aug. 14, 1846. He enlisted in Co. D, First Maine Heavy Artillery, and was killed at Milford Station, Va., May 24, 1864; and (2) Augustus Dunbar, b. May 20, 1848; m. Mariam C. Smith, Nov. 2, 1872. He lives in Columbia, Me., and has one child, Susie, b.

Aug. 15, 1872. Josiah Dunbar died Sept. 15, 1849. On Nov. 4, 1858, his widow married Morey Nash, of Columbia, Washington county, Me., who died Jan. 20, 1870. They had no children.

xi. Daniel N., b. Nov. 23, 1813; d. at sea, unmarried, Nov. 13, 1842, aged 29.

28

Asa[6] Cole (*Abijah,*[5] *Jonathan,*[4] *John,*[3] *John,*[2] *Thomas*[1]). Born in Harvard, Massachusetts, December 8, 1768; died in Westmoreland, New Hampshire, December 6, 1816. His father died when he was an infant. From his seventh to his fourteenth year he lived with his aunt, Mrs. Chamberlain, in Westmoreland. He then went to live with his step-father, Samuel Garfield, in Harvard, Massachusetts, and learned his trade, that of a millwright. He worked with Mr. Garfield in Massachusetts and Maine till 1793, when he married Anna Goldsmith, of Harvard, who was born January 27, 1772. At the time of his marriage he owned a house in the village of Harvard, and his mother and step-father probably lived with him. Here his eldest son was born. Soon after that he and his step-father moved to Rindge, New Hampshire. They there owned and operated a saw and grist mill for some six or seven years. He then moved to Westmoreland, following his trade as a millwright in that region, working one season on a mill in Coventry, Vermont, and also living some two years in Putney, Vermont. About 1810 he built the Pierce mills, in the south part of Westmoreland, and lived near and managed them for some four years. Here three of the younger children were born. In 1814 the mills were sold, and he went to Boston and worked throughout the summer, returning in the fall and living in a house on the "Brooks place."

In March, 1815, Ephraim Brown, of Westmoreland, who had purchased a large tract of land in Ohio, and was about to emigrate thither, applied to him to join the party. He accepted the proposal and made arrangements to go and take his third son with him, but just one week before the party started he was taken with bleeding at the lungs, and was compelled to give it up. On his recovery from this illness he determined to go eastward, and in June he left for Gouldsboro, Maine, where his brother had settled, hoping to find some place where he could do business to advantage, and also hoping that the change of climate would improve his health. But it was all in vain. He remained away till the autumn of 1816, when he took passage for Boston, arriving home in November, sick, emaciated, and prostrated. Two weeks afterwards he died, and on the following Sabbath was buried in the North Cemetery in Westmoreland. He owned some land in Gouldsboro, Maine, for in 1800 he sold a tract to his mother, and again in 1816 he quit-claimed all his remaining land to his brother. His wife was a superior woman. Left thus alone with a family of eleven children, most of them young, she managed to keep her family together till all were able to care for themselves or to find good homes. She raised her children to be honorable and useful men and women, and they repaid her by lifelong love and reverence. In 1838 she married Amory Pollard, of Bolton, Massachusetts, whom she survived. She died in Montpelier, Vermont, while on a visit to her youngest daughter, September 4, 1852, aged 80, and was buried in Westmoreland, New Hampshire.

The children of Asa and Anna (Goldsmith) Cole were:

63. i. Asa, b. Nov. 19, 1793; d. in West Medway, Mass., April 18, 1872, aged 79.

64. ii. Richard Goldsmith, b. Nov. 7, 1795; d. in Burlington, Vt., Dec. 18, 1864, aged 69.

iii. Sarah, b. in Rindge, N. H., Sept. 24, 1797. She married Asa Farnsworth, of Westmoreland, Nov. 7, 1816, and moved to Londonderry, Vt., where she died Nov. 12, 1832. Her children were: Louisa, who m. a Mr. Batcheldor, of Landgrove, Vt., and moved with him to one of the Western States; Asa; Delham; Daniel, who died at two years of age; Nancy, who died at two years of age; Daniel, who moved to Michigan and died there about 1865; John; Henry.

65. iv. Benjamin Franklin, b. Aug. 11, 1799; d. at Chargres, Panama, March, 1850, aged 51.

66. v. Nancy (Anna) Goldsmith, b. Feb. 6, 1802; m. Rev. Isaac Esty; d. in Amherst, Mass., Dec. 13, 1872, aged 70.

vi. Philena, b. in Putney. Vt., May 25, 1804; d. in Brattleboro, Vt., unmarried, April 3, 1859, aged 55.

67. vii. John, b. Nov. 7, 1806; d. in Westmoreland, N. H., Jan. 8, 1875.

68. viii. Susan Ermina, b. March 10, 1809; m. (1) Elihu Whitcomb, and (2) Orin Pitkin; d. in Montpelier, Vt., 1884.

ix. William, b. in Westmoreland, N. H., March 6, 1811; killed in a steamboat explosion on the Hudson River, at Newburg, April 23, 1830, aged 19.

69. x. Theodore, b. May 11, 1813; d. in Westmoreland, N. H., July 2, 1885, aged 72.

70. xi. Charles Henry, b. Feb. 25, 1816; d. at sea, April 14, 1853, aged 41.

29

LEVI[6] COLE (*John,[5] Jonathan,[4] John,[3] John,[2] Thomas[1]*). Born January 10, 1762; died in Joliet, Illinois, September 20, 1850. He married in Westmoreland, New Hampshire, Lydia Pierce, July 3, 1783, who died, and he then married Chloe Stoddard, June 18, 1787, who was born 1769, and died in Joliet, Illinois, March 13, 1848. He was elected hog reeve in Westmoreland, March 12, 1788. After his marriage he lived for some years in Chesterfield, New Hampshire, and the old assessors' books show the amount of his estate, which seems to have been a fair one for a young man in those days.

About 1795 he moved to the Black River region, in the neighborhood of Watertown, New York, where he lived for many years. When very aged he and his wife went to Joliet, Illinois, to the home of their daughter, Mrs. Doolittle, and there died after a few years.

The children of Levi and Chloe (Stoddard) Cole were:

i. Chloe, b. May 4, 1788. She m. Nathaniel Kittredge, of Dummerston, Vt.; d. in 1868. For a time she lived in Brattleboro, Vt., and then moved west, and at the time of her death was living in Joliet, Ill. She had eight children, two of whom are: C. F. Kittredge, of Rockland, Me., and Mary M., wife of E. B. Holmes, M.D., formerly of Canandaigua, N.Y.

71. ii. Levi, b. Aug. 25, 1790, d. in Sidney, Ia., May 27, 1868.

iii. Arathusa, b. July 9, 1795, d. Apr. 27, 1863. She m. Elijah Doolittle, b. Apr. 11, 1792, d. Mar. 9, 1849. They lived for a time in Ill., but returned to Watertown, N. Y. where he died. Their children were:
Maria E., b. June 26, 1815, m. D. C. Young and lives in Sonoma, Cal.
Phynodia, b. Jan. 13, 1817, d. Sept. 13, 1828.
Lyman D., b. June 12, 1818, d. Apr. 30, 1872, in Watertown, N. Y.
Mary F., b. Sept. 23, 1820, d. July 10, 1854.
Lycurgus, T., b. Apr. 7, 1823.
John W., b. Dec. 10, 1827.
William B., b. Apr. 30, 1837, d. Oct. 27.

iv. Persis, one of the three daughters of Levi and Chloe Stoddard Cole, was b. about 1793, and d. in Sandwich, Ill. She m. John Stiles. When the Mormon faith was preached they embraced that religion and joined the Latter Day Saints, and lived at Kirtland, O., and Navvoo, Ill. They emigrated to Utah with the great body of Mormons, and there remained till about 1864, when they left and settled in Sandwich, Ill., where they died. He was a soldier of 1812. Their only son was:
George P. Stiles, who was a lawyer, settled in Western Ia., and was appointed Chief Justice of the Territory of Utah by President Buchanan. After the expiration of his term of office he removed to Cardington, O. He afterwards held an important position at Washington, and died there. His children were: (1) John M., b. 1850; m. —— ——. Lives in Chicago, Ill. (2) Gertrude, b. 1852; m. —— Scheble; widow, resides at Belton, Tex. (3) Geo. P., Jr., b.

John Cole

JOHN[6] COLE (*John,[5] Jonathan,[4] John,[3] John,[2] Thomas[1]*). The second son of Capt. John and Lydia (Davis) Cole, was born in Westmoreland, New Hampshire, September 23, 1763, and died in London, Canada, in 1850, aged 87. His wife was Hannah ———, born August 21, 1771. He left home before his marriage, and after a time settled near London, Canada. He was a skilled workman at some trade, and was also a farmer part of his life. In his latter years he lived on the outskirts of the town and kept a large tavern. The only knowledge I have of him is from four letters written by him between 1828 and 1840, in which he mentions his family and gives a list of his children in their order.

I quote a portion of his last letter:

DEAR BROTHER—I received your letter on the third day of Aug. dated the fifth day of July and well pleased to hear from you so soon, and well pleased to hear that you are well. Will inform you that I am not very well but so as to take care of my house and do chores. But I am not able to labor at all for I am seventy-six years this day and you cannot expect much of a man at that age. * * You wrote that you wanted us to come to you. I wish that we could, but it is a long way, Heber, and we must be at a great sacrifice to sell at these hard times and must leave all of our children in this distant land and never see them any more and that would be hard. You wrote that it was too hard for me to keep tavern, but it gives me a little cash every day that I should not get in any other way. I have but a small farm but it is all cleared and I value it at a hundred dollars per acre, aside from the buildings and loose property, and what I have got is my own, for I owe nothing and borrow nothing and ask no favors from anybody only my Maker But if I had all of it in my pocket I think that I would go back to my native land, where we could be buried decently among my friends, for here is nothing but Old Country people, and they have a way by themselves, and not Yankee ways. * * * I live about two miles out of London village, that is about three quarters of a mile across it both ways, and thickly settled. Back of the town is the barrack where the soldiers are kept, about 1200 of them. * * * Now you want to know our childrens names,— * * Now Heber I dont know as I shall write to you any more, but if I am able I shall write to you as long as I can write with a pen, and I want you to do the same by me. But if I fail as fast as I have lately I cant last always for I go the way of the world. * * * * You wrote that you were in your fifty sixth year. I am seventy-six this day and the old lady Hannah Cole was 68 on the 21 of Aug. last. So now it is my love to you and your lady.

JOHN COLE,

London, the 23 of Sept., 1839. HANNAH COLE.

To HEBER COLE, Westmoreland, State of New Hampshire.

The children of John and Hannah Cole were:

i. Rogena, b. Nov. 6, 1792. She m. her cousin, Daniel Cole (the oldest son of Salmon). She had nine children. (Three daughters married and two of them having two children each, and three sons men grown in 1839.) In 1839 they moved to the Rock River country, in Wis.

72. ii. Adolphus, b. —— ——. He was m. and lived in and about London. He was crippled with rheumatism, and lived with his father and took care of him in his last days. He had three sons and two daughters.

iii. Sophia, b. —— ——, m. John Smith and moved to Mich. She had nine children and one grand-child in 1839.

73. iv. Benoni M., b. —— ——. Lived in Warwick, Ont. He had eight children in 1839.

v. Parmela, b. —— ——; m. Wm. Allen and moved to Mich. She had no children.

vi. Clarissa, b. —— ——; m. Elezer Smith and moved to Warwick, Ont. She had seven children.

74. vii. Asa, b. —— ——. He m. and moved to Mich., where his wife d. leaving three sons. He m. again before 1839.

viii. Polly, b. —— ——; m. Bemas Pickley and lived in or near London. She had three sons in 1839.

ix. Matilda, b. —— in 1812, and m. Sept. 25, 1827, to Mica Mudge. She went to Mich. and d. about 1830, leaving no children.

75. x. Alvord, b. July 12, 1815. He went to Mich. and was there in 1839. His uncle, Derastus, offered to make

him his heir if he would live with him, but whether the offer was accepted I cannot say.

31

Salmon Cole

SALMON[6] COLE (*John,*[5] *Jonathan,*[4] *John,*[3] *John,*[2] *Thomas*[1].) The third son of John and Lois Cole was born June 13, 1765, died in Buckingham, Canada, in 1849, aged eighty-four. He probably prospected about the then western and northern country and finally settled in Canada. He was in Hawksbury in 1801 and in Chatham for more than ten years previous to 1828, and between 1828 and 1832 he, with his sons, took up land in Buckingham and settled there. In a letter to his brother Heber, dated at Chatham, May 5, 1828, he says:

> "Myself, four sons and two daughters, have drawn two hundred acres of land in Buckingham, fifty miles up the river. Ethan began work there last summer, and has cleared 10 acres for me, 12 for Salmon, 10 for Hiram, 15 for himself, 8 for Bathshebe, and 5 for Allen Davinny, who married Lois."

Mr. Cole was a tall, good looking, good tempered man, and at 70 years of age was straight and active. His wife, Bathsheba Dodge, was a native of Wales, who came to this country with her parents when she was quite young. They settled in the Connecticut Valley, and she was early inured to the hardships and perils of a frontier life. She was a strong tempered, energetic woman of massive frame and great strength. They were married in Westmoreland, New Hampshire, February 7, 1786. She died in Buckingham at the residence of her son Oris, at the age of eighty-four years.

Their children were:

i. Rhoda, b. —— ——, m. ——— Smith, settled near New London.

76. ii. Daniel, b. —— ——

77. iii. Hiram, b. —— ——, d. —— ——

iv. John, b. —— ——. Killed at a barn raising in Buckingham when about twenty years of age. Unmarried.

v. Bathsheba, b. —— ——, m. (1) William Hilliard, of Chatham. He was killed by his oxen running away with him. He left three children, William Hilliard, who went to the home of his uncle Salmon; Thomas Hilliard, who went to the home of his uncle Ethan; and Lois, who was taken by her uncle Oris. She went to Buckingham with her father and brothers and there m. James Hays, by whom she had two children, Saul Hays and Ruth Hays.

78. vi. Salmon, b. Aug. 8, 1795, d. in Buckingham April 15, 1875.

79. vii. Oris, b. Feb. 28, 1801, d. in Buckingham, Sept. 13, 1883.

80. viii. Ethan, b. Nov. 22, 1804, d. in Crescent City, Ia., Jan. 22, 1864.

ix. Lois, b. Aug. 7, 1807, m. Adam Devinny, and d. Mar. 2, 1834. Her husband d. Oct. 22, 1856. They settled in Buckingham in 1824. Their children were:

Salmon Devinny, b. July 20, 1825. He lives in Petuaua. Charles Devinny, b. Sept. 16, 1827. He is a farmer in Buckingham, and has four sons and four daughters. Lucretia Devinny, b. Mar. 21, 1829; Adam Devinny, b. Dec. 6, 1832; Sarah Devinny, b. Feb. 22, 1835; Lois Devinny, b. Feb. 23, 1827. Some of the family spell the name Devine.

x. Ruth, b. in 1809 and d. in Buckingham unmarried.

32

LABAN[6] COLE (*John,*[5] *Jonathan,*[4] *John,*[3] *John,*[2] *Thomas*[1]). The fifth son of John and Lois (Davis) Cole was born in Westmoreland, Cheshire county, New Hampshire, February 4, 1776, and died in Troy, New York, March 24, 1839. He went to Vermont with his father's family, and there married Betsy Mansfield, who died

July 12, 1825. He lived in Brookline, Windham county, Vermont, all of his married life. The year after his wife died his eldest son moved from Brookline to Cataraugus county, New York, and he went to Troy to live with his other son, Reuben. The circumstances of his death are best told in a letter written by Reuben to his uncle Heber.

TROY, NEW YORK, June 23, 1830.

DEAR UNCLE—I write to inform you of the death of my father, murdered by a drunken Irishman named Connolly. On May 11 father was in the store when Connolly came in drunk. They had some words, when Connolly turned and threw father, who was in feeble health, and then went away. He soon returned, and father threatened to knock him down if he did not go away. At this he struck father with a clothes pounder. * * Father died the 24th. Connolly was convicted of manslaughter in the third degree, and sentenced to States Prison for two years. Your nephew, REUBEN COLE.

The children of Laban and Betsy (Mansfield) Cole were:

81. i. Daniel Mansfield, b. Feb. 10, 1794, d. in Ashford, Cattaraugus co., N. Y., Oct. 6, 1880, aged 86.
82. ii. Reuben, b. Sept. 10, 1796, d. in Lansingburg, N. Y., Jan. 28, 1885, aged 89.
iii. Martha, b. Dec. 4, 1801. She m. Warner Marsh, of Andover, Windsor co., Vt., who soon died. She then m. Josiah P. Cook, of Troy, N. Y., and removed with him to Pittsburg, Pa., where she d. Sept. 30, 1857. She left a daughter, Frances Cook, and a son, Charles P. Cook, both of whom lived in Pittsburg.
83. iv. Rebecca, b. Mar. 19, 1804, m. Hollis Gilson.

33

Sala Cole

SALA[6] COLE (*John,*[5] *Jonathan,*[4] *John,*[3] *John,*[2] *Thomas*[1]). The seventh son of John and Lois (Davis) Cole, was born September 2, 1776. Nearly all of his early life was spent in Windham, Windham county, Vermont, and he married Sally Stevens, of

Townsend, an adjoining town, in 1801. She was born July 26, 1781. In September, 1824, he moved to Tioga, Tioga county, Pennsylvania, and two years later he moved on to the place where he spent the rest of his days. His wife died April 26, 1845, and he on February 28, 1852.

The children of Sala and Sally (Stevens) Cole were:

84. i. Heber, b. Sept. 13, 1802.
85. ii. Sally, b. Jan. 15, 1805; m. Thomas Leet; d. Nov. 18, 1876.
iii. Asa, b. Oct. 23, 1806; d. March 2, 1809.
86. iv. Maria, b. April 15, 1809; m. Abram Prutsman; d. Oct. 31, 1878.
87. v. Catherine, b. Feb. 7. 1812; m. Abram Adams; d. April 15, 1845.
88. vi. Adeline, b. March 3, 1815; m. Samuel Cody; d. Dec. 26, 1874.
89. vii. A. Clark, b. Dec. 9, 1819.

34

ETHAN[6] COLE (*John,*[5] *Jonathan,*[4] *John,*[3] *John,*[2] *Thomas*[1]). The ninth son of Captain John and Lois (Davis) Cole, was born March 5, 1778, in Windham, Vermont. He was very young when his father died, and as the family was soon broken up, he experienced the hard life of the small boy who works on a farm for his board. In due time he learned the carpenter's trade, and worked at various places in Vermont and Massachusetts. In 1801, while working in Barre, Massachusetts, he married Lucinda Witherell, of that town. She was born November 25, 1777, and died April 12, 1842. For nine years after their marriage they lived in Barre. In 1810 they moved to Windham, and in 1826 to the adjoining town of Londonderry, where they remained the rest of their lives. Mr. Cole died December 14, 1854, aged seventy-six.

The children of Ethan and Lucinda (Wetherell) Cole were:

90. i. Arnold, b. Aug. 12; 1803; d. in Londonderry, Vt., July 30, 1860.

ii. Arminala, b. Dec. 15, 1804, in Barre, Mass. In 1826 she married Waldo Barton, a farmer and blacksmith of Londonderry. He was born March 15, 1802. In their old age they moved to Chester, Vt., where they died—he March 1, and she June 17, 1879. Their only child was Arminala Barton, b. Aug. 17, 1836. She married J. R. Richardson, a farmer and cattle dealer of Chester. She died January 25, 1885, leaving no children.

iii. Alson, b. in Barre, Mass., June 5, 1807. His boyhood was spent in Windham and Londonderry, Vt. About 1833 he married Tryphenia, daughter of Abraham and Betsy (Whitney) Sanderson, of Sunderland, Mass., b. Nov. 2, 1814, and soon after settled in Springfield, Mass., where he died June 18, 1850. His wife followed him the next year. They had no children.

91. iv. Isabanda, b. June 15, 1809; m. Reuben Harrington, and d. June 16, 1885.

92. v. Alfred R., b. Oct. 19, 1811.

93. vi. Alverado, b. April 20, 1814.

94. vii. Alonzo Ethan, b. March 1, 1817; d. in Londonderry, Dec. 27, 1883.

35

Simon Cole

SIMON[6] COLE (*John,*[5] *Jonathan,*[4] *John,*[3] *John,*[2] *Thomas*[1]). Born February 13, 1780; died in Boston, Massachusetts, June 27, 1856, aged seventy-six. He married Ester Robbins, of Putney, Vermont, who was born July 22, 1780; died December 18, 1840. He lived in various places in Vermont and Massachusetts, but was not, I should judge, very successful in his undertakings. He last lived in Boston with his son David J., and there died.

The children of Simon and Ester (Robbins) Cole were:

i. Louisa, b. March 6, 1811; m. a Mr. Lamb, in July, 1841; d. June 29, 1842.

ii. Sophia, b. Nov. 22, 1813; m. (1) Collins M. Stearns; (2) a Mr. Wetherbee, of Worcester, Mass., where she was living in 1871.

iii. David Jewett, b. July 18, 1815. He went to Boston in early life, and earned his living as a wood-sawyer. He became a well-known character in the north end of Boston, and finally became a hermit and miser. He never married, and after his father's death in 1856, he lived entirely alone. Finally in his old age the authorities were called upon to look after him, by the neighbors, when it was found that he had secreted some $10,000 by his miserly habits. Several articles appeared in the papers about the case at the time. He was placed in the charge of his brother, and is now living in East Boston.

95. iv. Davis Simon, b. Aug. 3, 1817. He moved West, and for a time lived at Nettletonville, Caldwell county, Mo., but he has gone from that region, and none of his family live about there.

v. Kesia, b. Sept. 2, 1819. She never married; she d. —— ——

96. vi. Stephen Robbins, b. June 10, 1821.

vii. Hannah, b. March 2, 1823; m. Fred Robinson, of Harwich, Mass., Oct. 4, 1844.

viii. Betsy, b. March 4, 1823. She lived in Worcester, Mass. She never married; she d. —— ——.

ix. Ester, b. Sept. 22, 1828; d. March 16, 1843, aged 15.

36

HEBER[6] COLE (*John*[5] *Jonathan*,[4] *John*,[3] *John*,[2] *Thomas*[1]). Born August 10, 1783; died October 19, 1857, aged seventy-four. He married (1) Sally Bennett, of Westmoreland, December 11, 1811, who was born May 15, 1787; died January 31, 1827. He lived all his life in Westmoreland, and until 1827 kept a tavern in the north part of the town. He was a man well-to-do in the world, and whose judgment was much respected by his neighbors.

The children of Heber and Sally (Bennett) Cole were:

97. i. Alonso, b. March 15, 1812; d. in Newburyport, Mass.

98. ii. Heber Bennett, b. Sept. 29, 1813; d. in Westmoreland, N. H., Feb. 18, 1885.

iii. Sarah Laurette, b. March 7, 1821; m. Sept. 7, 1847, George W. Daggett, a farmer of Westmoreland, who was born in 1818, and died June 25, 1884. Their children are: (1)George Marshall Daggett, b. Sept., 1848, d. July 11, 1862; (2)Louisa Daggett, b. —— ——; m. Thomas Merrill, a farmer, who moved to Belvedere, Ill., where she died in December, 1881, leaving two daughters; (3)Clara Daggett, b. 1853; m. William Leonard, a farmer of Walpole, N. H., and has one son, Wallace. (4)Walter Daggett, b. —— ——, a blacksmith by trade, but now prospecting in Dakota. (5)Eliza Isabel Daggett, b. July 1, 1857; d. July 22, 1862.

iv. William, b. April 9, 1824; d. in Westmoreland, Dec. 6, 1859. On March 1, 1885, he married Emeline, daughter of Melzer Paine, of Westmoreland. She was born in 1830, and died June 19, 1869. Their children were: Eva, b. March, 1857; d. in Westmoreland, unmarried, Oct. 12, 1875. Luella, b. Aug. 19, 1857; d. March 12, 1858. Emeline, b. Dec. 14, 1858; d. July 5, 1859.

Heber Cole

After the death of his first wife Mr. Cole married May 29, 1828, Prudence Walker, of Westmoreland, who was born January 24, 1800, and died March 16, 1883.

Their children were:

v. Emeline, b. Sept. 1, 1830. She married William M. Whitney, Sept. 12, 1850. He was for many years a conductor on the New York & New England Railroad, and resided in Needham, Mass. She had two sons: (1) William Whitney, b. Sept. 30, 1854, who was a clerk in Boston, and died January 27, 1878. The following tribute to him was published at the time:

Mr. Whitney for several months has been very feeble, and the tenacity and strength of his disease had awakened in his friends the most anxious solicitude. He met the approach of death with calmness, and passed away without a struggle, watched by tender and loving hearts. This death has cast a gloom over our village, because Mr. Whitney was so widely known and esteemed. He was a young man of fine qualities of character, and life opened before him with the promise of usefulness and success. He had gained the entire confidence of the gentleman with whom he had been associated in business, and in a letter to the bereaved family he says: "I never had in my employ any one I thought so much of, or any one in whom I placed so much confidence, as Willie. He was an honest young man."

He also won the respect of all who knew him, and was endeared to his companions. Prompt and faithful in the discharge of every duty, he was ready always cheerfully to do his part in public affairs. For years he was a zealous friend and advocate of temperance, and gave to this cause the power of example, as well as his words. He was very much interested in the Sunday School of the First Parish, and held the office of Treasurer at the time of his death. Even during his lingering illness this was manifested in a way which was both touching and beautiful. As a son and brother he was loving and tender, and lightened the cares of the household by his ready hands and efficient helpfulness.

(2) Frank Cole Whitney, b. Sept. 25, 1856. He was for several years teller in the First National Bank of Santa Fe, N. M., but now with the Lincoln National Bank of Boston.

99. vi. George, b. March 20, 1833; d. in Rochester, N. Y., Feb. 23, 1873.

vii. Martha Ellen, b. Sept. 2, 1838. She married Alonso Burt, of Walpole, N. H., Dec. 1, 1866. They have no children.

viii. Mary Ellen, b. Dec. 6, 1843. She married May 27, 1866, Fred. G. Parker, of Putney, Vt., a contractor and builder. They live on the old Cole homestead in Westmoreland. Their children are: Bertie C.

Parker, b. June 17, 1868. Myrtie B. Parker, b. May 20, 1870. Willie H. Parker, b. May 23, 1876.

38

JESSE[6] COLE (*Daniel,*[5] *Samuel,*[4] *Samuel,*[3] *John,*[2] *Thomas*[1]). The second son of Daniel and Elizabeth (Day) Cole, was born in Boxford, Massachusetts, December 19, 1765.

39

MOSES[6] COLE (*Daniel,*[5] *Samuel,*[4] *Samuel,*[3] *John,*[2] *Thomas*[1]), the third son of Daniel and Elizabeth (Day) Cole, was born in Boxford, Massachusetts, and baptized there September 27, 1767.

40

THOMAS[6] COLE (*Daniel,*[5] *Samuel,*[4] *Samuel,*[3] *John,*[2] *Thomas*[1]), the fourth son and fifth child of Daniel and Elizabeth (Day) Cole, was born in Boxford, Massachusetts, and baptized there November 17, 1771. He married January 11, 1798, Sally Kimball. He died soon after, and on February 9, 1803, his widow married John Downing, of Boxford.

His only child was:

i. Mary L., b. July 10, 1798.

41

SAMUEL[6] COLE (*Daniel*[5], *Samuel*[4], *Samuel,*[3] *John,*[2] *Thomas*[1]), the fifth son and seventh child of Daniel and Elizabeth (Day) Cole, was born in Boxford, Massachusetts, and baptized there November 17, 1776.

42

ASA[6] COLE (*Benjamin,[5] Samuel,[4] Samuel,[3] John,[2] Thomas[1]*). The only child of Benjamin and Elizabeth (———) Cole, born in Boxford, Massachusetts, July 22, 1766. His father died when he was eight years old, and four years later his mother married Samuel Kimball, of Boxford. He married Sally Davis, March 1, 1792, probably in Boxford.

43

TIMOTHY[6] COLE (*Solomon,[5] Samuel,[4] Samuel,[3] John,[2] Thomas[1]*). The first child of Solomon and Mehitable (Barker) Cole, born in Boxford and baptized there 1767. He settled in Richmond, Massachusetts, where he died —— ——

His children were:

104. i. Barker, b. —— ——. Lived in New Jersey.
105. ii. Solomon, b. —— ——. Lived in Lenox, Mass.
106. iii. Isaac Chancy, b. —— ——. He was an evangelist of the M. E. Church.
107. iv. John, b. —— ——. Lived in Richmond, Mass., on the ancestral farm.

And probably others.

44

KIMBALL[6] COLE (*Solomon,[5] Samuel,[4] Samuel,[3] John,[2] Thomas[1]*), the second son of Solomon and Mehitable (Barker) Cole, born 1780, in Boxford, Massachusetts, and died there 1822. He was commonly called Lieutenant Cole. He married Abigail, daughter of William and Rebecca Runnells of Methuen, (published April 2, 1804). She was born in Methuen February, 1780, and died in Boxford, April 7, 1861.

Their children were:

i. Sarah Foster, b. Aug. 23, 1805, m. Ezra Town, Sep 21, 1824, d. Mar. 1834.
ii. Rebecca, b. Apr. 2, 1807, d. Feb. 19, 1834.
108. iii. Ephraim Foster, b. July 6, 1809.
iv. Mehitable Barker, b. June 9, 1811, m. Henry C. Su livan of Boxford, Mar. 27, 1832, d. Mar. 9, 183
v. Abigail, b. Feb. 22, 1813, d. June, 1833.
109. vi. John Kimball, b. Dec. 16, 1814.
110. vii. William Runnells, b. Jan. 15, 1817.

45

BENJAMIN[6] COLE (*Solomon,*[5] *Samuel,*[4] *Samuel,*[3] *John,*[2] *Thomas* the third son of Solomon and Mehitable (Barker) Cole, was bo about 1771. He settled in Richmond, Massachusetts, and I b lieve moved to New York, and there lived and died.

46

ISAAC[6] COLE (*Solomon,*[5] *Samuel,*[4] *Samuel,*[3] *John,*[2] *Thomas*[1]), tl fourth son of Solomon and Mehitable (Barker) Cole, was born Boxford, Massachusetts, January 26, 1774. He moved to Fra conia, New Hampshire, where he lived many years. In 1821 l removed to Franklin, New Hampshire, and built an iron found there. Six years later he removed to Lake Village, New Ham shire, and built another foundery, which he operated until 183 when he sold out to his sons. The business has since grown in the present extensive establishment of the Cole Manufacturi Company. He died in Lake Village July 8, 1854. He marri Hannah Atwood of Atkinson, New Hampshire, in 1792. Sl was born in that town March 27, 1773, and died February 2 1841.

Their children were:

i. Hannah, b. May 23, 1793. She m. John Aldrich of Franconia, and lived there all her life, dying in 1863. Her children were:

(i.) Isaac, b. Jan. 12, 1823. He is a machinist, and resides at Lake Village, N. H. He has been three times married, and has two living children.

(ii.) John, b. June 1, 1827. Is now a merchant and manufacturer in Lake Village. He was major of the 15th N. H. Vols. in the war of the Rebellion. He m. his cousin Mary, dau. of John A. Cole. They have no children.

(iii.) Hannah A., b. Feb. 10, 1827, d. Aug. 20, 1832.

(iv.) Caroline S., b. May 4, 1830. She m. E. E. Webster. He was a member of the N. H. Vol. Cavalry and died in 1878. She has five children and several grandchildren.

(v.) Myra W., b. Oct. 28, 1833, m. A. G. Lane, now a real estate agent of Manchester, N. H. Their only child died in infancy.

(vi.) Martha A., b. Apr. 22, 1833. She is unmarried, and has resided in Europe for several years.

ii. Mehitable, b. Nov. 30, 1794. She m. Joseph Town, of Boxford, Mass., and d. in 1878. Her children were:

(i.) Eleanor, b. in 1814 and d. in 1878. She m. James M. Blake, who d. —— ——. One son, James W. Town, was a member of the 15th N. H. Vols., and d. in the service. There are three other children still living.

(ii.) Abigail, b. in 1816. She m. Jonathan Dow and is living in Lisbon, N. H. She had seven children. One son, Henry Dow, was capt. in a N. H. Reg. and after the war went to Bay City, Mich., and was editor of a paper. He d. several years ago.

(iii.) Mehitable, b. in 1819. She m. E. H. Wheeler, and they live in Lake Village, N.

H. Her children were: (1) Orin F., d. Nov. 22, 1862, in the service as member of 15th Reg. N. H. Vols. (2) Eliza, m. M. A. Dow, and resides in Mass. (3) Emma, m. —— Bump and resides in Vt. (4) Hannah M., resides in Lake Village, unm. (5) Gilman, conductor on B. & L. R. R. (6) George, resides in Mass.

(iv.) Moody, b. in 1821, d. about 1879. He was three times married and left several children but their residence is unknown to me.

(v.) Judith, b. in 1823. She m. Reuben Smith of Lake Village, and after his death E. Maxfield of the same place, where she now resides. She has no children living.

(vi.) Jerusha, b. in 1824. She m. —— Whitcher and moved to Baltimore, Md. She is now a widow, and lives in Baltimore with her only daughter.

(vii.) Joseph W., b. in 1826. He removed to Chicago, Ill., where he lived for many years, and was a prominent citizen. He d. in 1878, leaving a widow and two daughters.

(viii.) Mary, b. in 1828. She m. (1) —— Eastman of Lisbon, N. H., (2) Rev. J. Knowles of Lake Village, and (3) Rev. I. Allen of the same place. She is again a widow. She has one daughter living.

(ix.) Kimball, b. about 1830, d. in 1841.

(x.) John, b. about 1833. He removed to Ill., where he d. in 1875.

(xi.) James, b. in 1835. He never m. He d. in Colorado in 1861.

iii. Isaac, b. Oct. 31, 1796, d. in Franconia in 1880.

iv. Mary, b. May 29, 1799. She m. Perley Putnam of Franconia, N. H., and lived and died there in 1868. Her children were:

(i.) Horace B., b. Feb. 1823. He is still living and has several children.

(ii.) Charles, b. in 1825. He resides in Leominster, Mass., and is married, but has no children living.

(iii.) William, b. in 1825. He lives in Boston, Mass., and has three children.

(iv.) Perley, b. in Franconia in 1830. He resides in Laconia, N. H., where he is extensively engaged in the manufacture of freight and passenger cars. For twelve years he has been postmaster at Laconia. His only child is m. to Mr. Chamberlain, superintendent of the Concord R. R., and resides at Concord, N. H.

(v.) Elizabeth, b. in 1832, d. unm. about 1870.

112. v. John A., b. Apr. 22, 1801, d. in Plymouth, N. H., in 1864.

vi. Elizabeth, b. July 21, 1803. She m. Horace Bugbee of Hartland, Vt. and d. there in 1849. Her children were:

(i.) Marcia, b. in 1822, d. in childhood.

(ii.) Catherine, b. in 1824, d. unm. in 1846.

(iii.) Frances, b. —— ——, m. W. Andrews, and resides in Tacoma, Wash. Ter.

(iv.) Arthur W., b. —— ——. He settled in Kansas, where he now lives. He has several children.

(v.) Horace, b. —— ——. He resides in Lake Village, N. H., and has a son and daughter, both m.

(vi.) James, b. —— ——. Resides in Manchester, N. H. Has no children.

113. vii. Timothy, b. Sept. 22, 1806.

viii. Abigail, b. Apr. 16, 1810, m. Joseph Hill of Springfield, N. H., where she now resides. Her children are:

(i.) Benjamin F., b. —— ——. He resides in Lake Village, N. H., and has two sons and three daughters.

(ii.) Joseph, b. —— ——. Resides in Winchester, Mass., and has several children.

(iii.) Lydia, b. —— ——, m. —— Heath, and lives in Wakefield, Mass. She has no children.

(iv.) Susan, b. —— ——, m. —— Taylor. She lives in Dakota and has several children.

(v.) Emily, b. —— ——. She lives in Springfield, N. H., and has several children.

114. ix. Benjamin James, b. Sept. 28, 1814.

47

JOHN[6] COLE (*Solomon*,[5] *Samuel*,[4] *Samuel*,[3] *John*,[2] *Thomas*[1]). The fifth son of Solomon and Mehitable (Barker) Cole, was born in Rowley, Massachusetts, ——— 1768, and died in Surry, Cheshire county, New Hampshire, October 4, 1807, aged thirty-nine. He married Polly Bemis, who was born in Westminster, Massachusetts, in 1762, and died in Gilsum, New Hampshire, December 30, 1825. He was a shoemaker by trade, but most of the latter years of his life was a teamster from Boston to the towns of Northern New Hampshire and Vermont.

His children were:

115. i. Zackeus, b. March 28, 1791, at Dummerston, Vt.; d. in Westminster, Vt., Oct. 12, 1882.

ii. Betsy, b. Sept. 11, 1792, at Orange, Mass.; d. at Gilsum, N. H., Aug. 9, 1820. She m. Amherst Haywood.

116. iii. John, b. Sept. 13, 1797, at Gardner, Mass.

iv. Polly, b. Aug. 28, 1800, at Gardner, Mass. After her sister Betsy's death, she married the widower, Amherst Haywood, and died at Gilsum, Nov. 21, 1826.

117. v. Asa, b. in Surry, N. H., Oct. 20, 1804.

48

SOLOMON[6] COLE (*Solomon*,[5] *Samuel*,[4] *Samuel*,[3] *John*,[2] *Thomas*[1]). The sixth son of Solomon and Mehitable (Barker) Cole was born ——. He married Sally Howland, and settled in Whitefield, New Hampshire, where he died at the age of eighty.

His children were:

118. i. Samuel, b. —— ——; d. in ———, —— ——.

ii. Havens, —— ——; killed by falling from a building when 18 years of age.

118*a*. iii. Stephen H., b. —— ——; d. in ———, 1877.

iv. Mary, b. —— ——; m. Moses Jewell. She had two children, only one of whom is now living. She d. —— ——.
v. Sally, b. —— ——; m. Peter G. Russell. She had seven children, four of whom are now living. She d. —— ——.
118*b*. vi. Asa, b. —— ——; d. in —— ——.
vii. Kitty, b. —— ——; m. Hubbard Sawyer. She had three children, all of whom are now living. She died —— ——.
118*c*. viii. Solomon, b. —— ——.

49

SAMUEL[6] COLE (*Solomon,*[5] *Samuel,*[4] *Samuel,*[3] *John,*[2] *Thomas*[1]). The seventh son of Solomon and Mehitable (Barker) Cole, b. —— 1781. He became a minister of the Freewill Baptist Church. He settled in Lisbon, New Hampshire, and died there in 1850. He married —— ——.

Their children were:

i. Harriet, b. —— ——.
ii. Louisa S., b. —— ——.
119. iii. Amos J., b. —— ——.
120. iv. Phineas, b. —— ——.
121. v. Mooers, b. Aug. 14, 1815, in Lisbon, N. H.
122. vi. Joseph, b. —— ——.
123. vii. Benjamin, b. —— ——.
124. viii. Samuel, b. —— ——.

On —— —— Rev. Samuel Cole married as his second wife Mary Colby.

Their children were:

ix. Nancy, b. —— ——.
125. x. Isaac, b. —— ——.

50

ASA B.[6] COLE (*Solomon,*[5] *Samuel,*[4] *Samuel,*[3] *John,*[2] *Thomas*[1]). The eighth son of Solomon and Mehitable (Barker) Cole, was born ——— ———; baptized in Boxford, Massachusetts, May 15, 1785. He married Lydia Howland, and settled in Whitefield, New Hampshire, where he died in 1862, aged seventy-seven. His wife died at the age of thirty-nine.

Their children were:

i. Simon, b. ——— ———; d. aged 1 year.
ii. Zelinda J., b. ——— ———; m. A. S. Bartlett. She had eighteen children, eight of whom grew to maturity, and seven are still living.
126. iii. Kimball, b. ——— ———.
iv. Mehitable B., b. ——— ———; m. Joseph French. She had nine children, of whom three have died. She died in 1886.
v. Aurelia C., b. ——— ———; m. William Smith. They have eight or nine children living.
126*a*. vi. George W., b. ——— ———.
vii. Rhoda T., b. ——— ———; m. William Melcher. Mr. M. enlisted in the volunteer service, and died in Andersonville prison. She died about 1881. They left two children.
127. viii. Simon, b. ——— ———.
ix. Mary H. B., b. ——— ———; m. Sabin Noyse. She has two children.

51

SAMUEL[6] COLE (*Simeon,[5] Samuel,[4] Samuel,[3] John,[2] Thomas[1]*). The second son and sixth child of Simeon and Polly (Smith) Cole, born in Boxford, January 24, 1797. He married Clarissa Harlow Pettingill, of Bradford (pub. January 31, 1824). He lived in Salem, New Hampshire. He died in Boxford, Massachusetts, September 7, 1849.

His children were:

i. Mary Ann, b. ——— ———; m. ——— ———.
ii. Prescott, b. ——— ———; d. unmarried.
iii. Leverett S., b. Feb. 9, 1833, in Salem, N. H.; d. unmarried (?) in Groveland, Nov. 29, 1859.

52

MANLY HARDY[6] COLE (*Simeon*,[5] *Samuel*,[4] *Samuel*,[3] *John*,[2] *Thomas*[1]). The seventh and youngest child of Simeon and Polly (Smith) Cole, born in Boxford, Massachusetts, August 19, 1800. He married Hannah Kimball, daughter of Benjamin and Priscilla Robinson, of Boxford, April 1, 1824. She was born in Boxford, July 22, 1802, and died there February 24, 1851. He married (2) Mrs. Betsy (Johnson) Nichols, of West Newbury, November 30, 1853. She was a daughter of Hezekiah and Betsy Johnson, and was born in Stanstead, Canada, in 1805. Mr. Cole was a farmer in Boxford all his life.

His children were:

128. i. David Mighill, b. Sept. 20, 1825.
129. ii. Caleb Manly, b. Jan. 26, 1827.
iii. Joseph Pike, b. Sept. 27, 1829; m. Helen M., daughter of George and Abigail Pearl (pub. Nov. 23, 1853). She was born in Boxford in 1833. He resided in Boxford, and died there Nov. 19, 1877. He had no children.

53

JONATHAN[7] COLE (*Jonathan*,[6] *Jonathan*,[5] *Jonathan*,[4] *John*,[3] *John*,[2] *Thomas*[1]). The oldest son of Jonathan and Anna (Whitman) Cole, was born in Westmoreland, New Hampshire, April 30, 1776, and died in West Stockholm, St. Lawrence county, New York, April 8, 1848, aged seventy-two. He married August 8, 1792, Lydia Daggett, of Westmoreland. In 1803 they moved to Charlotte, Chittenden county, Vermont. He was a shoemaker, and pursued his trade in connection with his farming. In 1815 he joined the Methodist Episcopal Church, of which he remained a consistent member till the day of his death. "He was a man of sound judgment, true to the principles of right, let the opposition be what it might. In politics he was a true Republican." He served in the war of 1812. In 1836 he removed to West Stockholm, St. Lawrence county, New York, where he lived till the time of his death.

The children of Jonathan and Lydia (Daggett) Cole were.

130. i. Tisdale Sabina, b. Dec. 19, 1793; d. in River Falls, Pierce co., Wis., Feb. 2, 1864, aged 71.

ii. Lydia Louisa, b. in Westmoreland, N. H., Sept. 25, 1796; d. unm. in Fayette, Fayette co., Ia., in 1875, aged 79.

131. iii. Betsy Elmira, b. Jan. 1, 1798; m. Anson Wadleigh; d. in Morrison, Whiteside co., Ill., May 26, 1866, aged 68.

iv. Mary Maria, b. Aug. 11, 1800, in Westmoreland, N. H.; d. unm. in Waterbury, Washington co., Vt., Aug. 25, 1864, aged 64.

132. v. Horace Cooley, b. Sept. 29, 1802; d. in Fayette, Ia., Oct. 25, 1864, aged 62.

vi. Serenas Swift, b. Jan. 1, 1805; died May 12, 1809, aged 4.

133. vii. Louisa Durphy, b. Jan. 23, 1807; m. Emery Taylor; d. in Waterbury, Vt., Jan. 26, 1884, aged 77.

134. viii. Osmand Rasselas, b. Sept. 16, 1809.

ix. Charlotte Elmira, b. July 5, 1811, in Charlotte, Vt. She m. Jan. 25, 1842, Milo B. Hawley. They lived in Middlebury, Vt., where she d. in 1874, aged 63. They had no children.

135. x. Clement Carlton, b. Sept. 27, 1813.

136. xi. Celia Caroline, b. Feb. 14, 1816; m. J. D. Sperry; d. in Fayette, Ia., Jan. 15, 1887.

54

Abel[7] Cole (*Jonathan,*[6] *Jonathan,*[5] *Jonathan,*[4] *John,*[3] *John,*[2] *Thomas*[1]). The second son of Jonathan and Anna (Whitman) Cole, was born in Westmoreland, December 8, 1777. Died there July 11, 1838, aged 61. He married Louisa Hutchins, March 24, 1808. She was born April 9, 1786, and died September 16, 1852. Mr. Cole lived all his life on the farm inherited from his ancestors; the same on which the family settled when they first came to the town. His life was devoted to his work as a farmer and also to his trade as a carpenter. In his younger years he was a successful music teacher.

The children of Abel and Louisa (Hutchins) Cole were:

i. Eliza B., b. Apr. 17, 1809; d. unm. in Westmoreland, N. H., Sept. 19, 1855, aged 46.
137. ii. Abel Barton, b. Feb. 21, 1811.
iii. Latty, b. Aug. 4, 1813. She m. June 5, 1855, Palmer Carpenter, a farmer of West Brattleboro, Vt., and went there to reside. They had no children. Mr. Carpenter d. in Mar. 1866, and she Apr. 12, 1870.
138. iv. Anson, b. Apr. 26, 1815, d. in Westmoreland, N. H., June 17, 1881.
139. v. Susan L., b. Nov. 13, 1817; m. James R. Ware.
140. vi. Jonathan, b. June 4, 1820.
vii. Alma, b. Mar. 20, 1822. She m. May 8, 1860, the Rev. Oscar Bissel, a Congregational clergyman. They lived in Dublin and Roxbury, N. H., in which latter place she d. Feb. 25, 1869, leaving no children. Mr. Bissel now lives in Westford, Ct.
141. viii. Larkin G., b. May 9, 1824.
142. ix. George H., b. June 4, 1826.

55

MARTIN[7] COLE (*Jonathan,*[6] *Jonathan,*[5] *Jonathan,*[4] *John,*[3] *John,*[2] *Thomas*[1]). Born in Westmoreland, November 23, 1781; died in Mt. Holly, Vermont, April 6, 1866. He married May 12, 1803, Sally Baker, of Westmoreland, who died in 1863. Soon after his marriage he moved to Mt. Holly, Vermont, where he spent the rest of his days, a quiet citizen, a good neighbor, and a kind and considerate man. He was a deacon in the church for many years.

The only child of Deacon Martin and Sally (Baker) Cole was:

149. i. Larkin Baker, b. April 10, 1804; d. in Louisville, Ky., in January, 1856.

ABIJAH[7] COLE (*Jonathan,*[6] *Jonathan,*[5] *Jonathan,*[4] *John,*[3] *John,*[2] *Thomas*[1]). The fourth son of Jonathan and Anna (Whitman) Cole, was born in Westmoreland, New Hampshire, November 1, 1787, and died in Mt. Holly, Vermont, May 10, 1865, aged seventy-eight. He married Lucy Howe, of Westmoreland, February 11, 1807. She was born April 11, 1791, and died March 2, 1868. Soon after his marriage he moved to Vermont, and settled in Mt. Holly, where the rest of his life was spent. He was a man of a good deal of influence in the town, and several times represented it in the Legislature. He was town clerk for nineteen years, and for many years was a justice of the peace, and in fact was generally known as 'Squire Cole. Of his family, one son, two sons-in law, and eleven grand-children served in the armies of his country.

At the town meeting in March, 1865, the following resolution was unanimously adopted:

"*Resolved*, That the thanks of the town are hereby tendered to Abijah Cole, Esq., for the constant fidelity, the marked ability, and the uniform spirit of urbanity and kindness with which, for the long period of nineteen, years he has discharged the duties of town clerk, and that we express to him our cordial and earnest sympathy in that affliction which renders it necessary for him to decline reëlection to that office."

The children of Abijah and Lucy (Howe) Cole were:

i. Lucy Hutchins, b. May 23, 1808. She married May 17, 1832, Freedom Frost, a blacksmith of Mechanicsville, Vt. They had two children, Sarah Frost, who married John Fuller, of Illinois, and Rodney Frost, who died at the age of 19. Mr. Frost died June 6, 1835, and on May 25, 1838, she married Lyman C. Hammond (who died in December, 1852.) They removed to Illinois, where she died March 5, 1850, in Margaretta, Clark county, leaving four children by her second marriage. Two of them have not been heard from for twenty years, and are supposed to be dead. The others are George Hammond, Martinsville, Clark county, Ill., and Mrs. Emily Parker, Westfield, Clark county, Ill.

144. ii. Curtis Abijah, b. Aug. 23, 1810.
145. iii. Susan Maria, b. June 24, 1812; m. Ezra Newton; d. Aug. 13, 1886.
iv. Sarah Buckley, b. April 21, 1814, in Mt. Holly, Vt. She married Samuel Marshall, of Mechanicsville, Vt., Sept. 21, 1861. He died the following year. She then married Joseph Rodgers, a farmer of Danby, Vt., Aug. 17, 1865. They had no children. He died Aug. 4, 1876. She is living in Mechanicsville.
146. v. Mary Emeline, b. May 18, 1816; m. Isaac Jaquith.
vi. William Henry, b. March 24, 1820; d. Sept. 17, 1823.
147. vii. Emily Betsy, b. Nov. 11, 1822. She married (1) Benj. M. Benson; (2) William Roberts. She died in Weston, Vt., March 8, 1885.
148. viii. William Marshall, b. Nov. 16, 1826.
149. ix. Charles Lewis, b. May 13, 1831.
150. x. Oscar Brown, b. March 26, 1833; d. Nov. 10, 1886.
151. xi. Horace Frederick, b. Jan. 17, 1836.
xii. Julia Anna, b. June 26, 1838. She married May 5, 1861, Joseph W. Durling, and moved to Michigan. He died in Grand Rapids, May 15, 1879, and she married Peter W. Duck, May 3, 1881. She lives in Cardillac, Wexford county, Mich. She has no children.

57

Asa[7] Cole (*Abijah,*[6] *Abijah,*[5] *Jonathan,*[4] *John,*[3] *John,*[2] *Thomas*[1]). The first child of Abijah and Nancy (Williams) Cole, was born in Prospect Harbor, Maine, January 4, 1792; died there April 28, 1861. He married Sarah Godfrey, of Lubec, Maine, who was born November 11, 1795, and died March 1, 1860. Mr. Cole was one of the leading men of the town. He was postmaster for over thirty years, and in 1859 was representative for the town of Gouldsboro.

The children of Asa and Sarah (Godfrey) Cole were:

i. James G., b. Dec. 12, 1819; d. at sea while a young man, unmarried.

ii. Mary Ann, b. Feb. 7, 1820; m. John Bowdoin, of Boston, Mass., and died there in June, 1850. Their only child was James C. Bowdoin, b. June 21, 1850; d. in Boston, April 26, 1871.

152. iii. Edwin, b. Oct. 25, 1822; died in New York City, Sept. 31, 1869.

iv. Peter G. and Harriet L., b. April 11, 1825. The first died at sea, in 1851, unmarried, and the second died in infancy.

v. Harriet L., b. Oct. 25, 1825. She married John Holway, of Machias, Me., Oct. 6, 1863. Her children are:

(i.) Emma L., b. Dec. 17, 1864.
(ii.) Melville C., b. Feb. 15, 1867.
(iii.) Charles B., b. Sept. 22, 1869.
(iv.) Winifred B., b. July 21, 1871.

153. vi. David G., b. Dec. 5, 1829.

154. vii. Buckman, b. March 5, 1832; d. in Cuba, March 29, 1870.

viii. Emily, b. June 2, 1834. On Sept. 26, 1858, she married Henry Smith, who was born June 6, 1830. Their children are:

(i.) Louisa, b. July 20, 1859; d. Sept. 14, 1863.
(ii.) Alisas A., b. Oct. 10, 1861; d. Aug. 7, 1871.
(iii.) Mariam C., b. July 20, 1869; d. Feb. 11, 1870.
(iv.) David B. C., b. Dec 22, 1873.

ix. Frederic, b. March 7, 1838. He was assistant postmaster at Prospect Harbor for several years previous to 1861, and was postmaster from 1861 to his death, March 30, 1877. He never married.

155. x. Melville, b. May 25, 1840. He is unmarried.

58

SARAH COLE[7] EVERETT (*Abijah,*[6] *Abijah,*[5] *Jonathan,*[4] *John,*[3] *John,*[2] *Thomas*[1]). The first daughter and second child of Abijah and Nancy (Williams) Cole was born in Prospect Harbor, Maine, March 1, 1793, and died near that place September 9, 1871, aged seventy-eight. At the age of nineteen (June 6, 1816) she married

Henry Everett, who was lost at sea in 1827, leaving her with six little children. She remained a widow forty-four years, till her death.

Her children were:

i. Timothy B., b. Oct. 30, 1816. He became a sailor, and on. Mar. 9, 1864, he sailed from Portland for Queenstown, and was never again heard of, the vessel of which he was master having probably foundered. He married Sarah L. Hudson, of Portland, Sept 4, 1845.

ii. Clement Everett. He went to Ohio, and married in Cleveland, Ophelia McIlrath, Feb. 18, 1847. She died May 31, 1863. Their children were:

(i.) George H. Everett, b. Nov. 12, 1848; married Achsah J. Ford, Mar. 11, 1868; resides at Weston, Wood county, O., and has four children: (*a*) Willie, b. Dec. 12, 1868, d. May 5, 1868; (*b*) Charles, b. Jan. 1, 1870, d. Sept. 4, 1870; (*c*) Myrtle A., b. Feb. 4, 1871; (*d*) Carrie, b. Oct. 7, 1874, d. Aug. 23, 1875.

(ii.) Lucy A. Everett, b. Dec. 8, 1849; married John J. Higgins, Sept. 19, 1870; resides at Paulding, Paulding county, O.

(iii.) Edward E. Everett, b. July 8, 1852; married Ida W. Alexander, Sept. 2, 1882; resides at Bowling Green, Wood county, O., and has one child: (*a*) Blaine, b. Aug. 6, 1884.

(iv.) Solan A. Everett, b. Sept. 14, 1857.

(v.) S. Ellen Everett, b. Oct. 2, 1859; married Chas. F. Williams, Jan. 7, 1879; resides at Tontogany, Wood county, O.; has children: (*a*) John B., b. Nov. 4, 1879; (*b*) Arthur b. Feb. 1, 1882; (*c*) J. C. Guy, b. Jan. 22, 1885.

(vi.) Cora E. Everett, b. Feb. 8, 1862; married Oscar W. Loash, Dec. 14, 1881; resides at Tontogany, O. Children: (*a*) Harris, b. Feb. 27, 1882; (*b*) Jane, b. June 2, 1884.

iii. Henrietta, b. —— ——; married Amos Boyden, and resided at Boyden Lake, Perry county, Me., where she died in 1870.

iv. Eliza Ann, b. Jan. 24, 1821, and married John Porter, a farmer of Pembroke, Washington county, Me. Her children were:

(i.) Clara A. Porter, b. Feb. 1, 1844; married Apr. 24, 1867, R. P. Fisher, a farmer of West Pembroke, Me.

(ii.) S. Jennie Porter, b. July 31, 1845; married June 8, 1867, L. G. Smith, a farmer of Pembroke.

(iii.) Florence M. Porter, b. Nov. 25, 1847; married Oct. 2, 1869, J. S. Reynolds, a wheelwright of Pembroke.

(iv.) Sandy M. Porter, b. Mar. 1, 1849; is a lumberman in Chicago, Ill.

(v.) William D. Porter, b. Feb. 17, 1852; married Apr. 26, 1881, Adeline M. Birdsey, and is a commercial traveler, residing in Indianapolis, Ind.

(vi.) Stephen C. F. Porter, b. July 17, 1854; m. Apr. 14, 1881, Josie Vale. He is a silverplate worker in Meridan, Ct.

(vii.) Cassius G. Porter, b. Dec. 4, 1857; married Aug. 29, 1880, Eva Dudley. Is a farmer in Pembroke.

(viii.) George R. Porter, b. Mar. 5, 1862; is a shingle manufacturer in Lincoln, Me.

(ix.) Earnest P. Porter, b. Jan. 24, 1866; is a farmer in Pembroke, Me.

v. Charlotte, b. —— ——; married Capt. Abner McAllister, Sept. 18, 1845. She lived in Milltown, Me., and died there very suddenly on Nov. 5, 1881. Their children were:

(i.) Eliza McAllister, b. June 9, 1846; married June 2, 1869, John C. T. Waite, who died Jan. 27, 1871, leaving one child, (*a*) Mary Alice Waite, b. June 12, 1870. She again married William N. Hughes, July, 1878, and died July 17, 1881, leaving a second daughter, (*b*) Lottie M. Hughes, b. Feb. 21, 1880.

(ii.) Maud Mary McAllister, b. July 2, 1854; is unmarried.

(iii.) Lottie Blanche McAllister, b. Aug. 24, 1857; is unmarried.

(iv.) Harrison McAllister, b. Oct. 12, 1859; is unmarried.

(v.) James E. Chaffee McAllister, b. Feb. 18, 1861; is unmarried.

vi. George Henry Everett, b. in 1842. He settled in Eastport, Me., where he died in Feb., 1863.

59

Nancy Cole[7] Moore (*Abijah,*[6] *Abijah,*[5] *Jonathan,*[4] *John,*[3] *John,*[2] *Thomas*[1]). The third daughter and fourth child of Abijah and Nancy (Williams) Cole, was born in Prospect Harbor, Maine, November 11, 1795, and died there September 2, 1860, aged sixty-five. She married George Moore, April 12, 1828. He was born July 24, 1802, and died June 15, 1851.

Their children were:

i. George Augustus Moore. He lived in Gouldsborough, and was never married.

ii. Clifford Moore. Enlisted in the army in 1861, and was never heard of after the company went South.

iii. Harriet Moore. Married Jan. 1, 1862, Nathan F. Holway; resides in Machias, Me. She has children:

  (i.) George M. Holway, b. May 17, 1863; m. Emily Spring in 1884.
  (ii.) Bertie Holway, b. Aug. 21, 1864.
  (iii.) Lendall C. Holway, b. Sept. 28, 1866.
  (iv.) Keller F. Holway, b. Feb. 2, 1869.
  (v.) Edith M. Holway, b. Jan. 28, 1872.
  (vi.) N. Clifford Holway, b. Sept. 14, 1875.

iv. Elizabeth Moore, b. Aug. 26, 1841; m. Capt. Dennis Mahoney, July 27, 1861. Lives in Portland, where Capt. Mahoney died Oct. 24, 1883. Their children were:

  (i.) Girard Mahoney, b. May 17, 1862.
  (ii.) C. H. C. Mahoney, b. July 31, 1864.
  (iii.) Marcus H. Mahoney, b. April 27, 1870.
  (iv.) Eva Belle Mahoney, b. July 20, 1872.
  (v.) Guy C. Mahoney, b. Dec. 29, 1879.

60

Abijah[7] Cole (*Abijah,*[6] *Abijah,*[5] *Jonathan,*[4] *John,*[3] *John,*[2] *Thomas*[1]). The second son of Abijah and Nancy (Williams) Cole, was born in Prospect Harbor, Maine, August 14, 1799, and died there March 31, 1876. He married Rebecca Simonton, who was born April 2, 1803, and died April 10, 1876. He was a quiet and industrious citizen, respected by his neighbors and loved by his family.

The children of Abijah and Rebecca (Simonton) Cole were:

156. i. Mehitable, b. Aug. 24, 1826; m. Capt. Joseph Handy.

157. ii. Adolphus, b. Dec. 30, 1827; d. June 16, 1876.

iii. Judith, b. Feb. 14, 1829; m. ——, ——, Oliver Allen, and moved to Lake county, Ind. (Ill. ?), and died there July 26, 1855. Her children were:

(i.) Ellen S. Allen, b. May, 1848; m. a Mr. Hardin, a farmer in Minnesota.

(ii.) Everett Allen, b. in 1850, and is a farmer in Minnesota.

158. iv. Allen, b. March 11, 1830.

v. Susan, b. Feb. 14, 1832. She married Capt. John Noonah, of Prospect Harbor, June 20, 1852, and died there Feb. 1, 1875. She had no children.

vi. Elizabeth, b. Feb. 26, 1834. She married Feb. 10, 1853, George Weston. He died in New Orleans, while on a voyage there. She is now living in Prospect Harbor. Her children were:

(i.) William Weston, who died at sea when about 20 years of age.

(ii.) Thomas Weston, who died when about 14 years of age.

159. vii. Isabella, b. Oct. 5, 1835; m. Edwin Cleaves.

viii. Francis Lorenzo, b. Jan. 8, 1838; d. unmarried, April 25, 1871.

160. ix. Sarah, b. Sept. 25, 1839; m. Capt. Wm. Handy.

x. Emeline, b. Sept. 24, 1840; m. Ezra Robinson, of Millbridge, Me., Sept. 15, 1862. He was drowned at sea, April 16, 1881. Her children were:

(i.) Everett A. Robinson, b. Oct. 10, 1862; d. July 4, 1871.

(ii.) Lizzie W. Robinson, b. Nov. 12, 1865; d. Feb. 8, 1869. She now lives in Prospect Harbor.

161. xi. James Woodbury, b. Oct. 1, 1843.

162. xii. Charles G., b. Jan. 22, 1845.

61

LOIS COLE[7] MOORE (*Abijah,*[6] *Abijah,*[5] *Jonathan,*[4] *John,*[3] *John,*[2] *Thomas*[1]). The seventh child of Abijah and Nancy (Williams) Cole, was born in Prospect Harbor, Maine, November 2, 1803, and died March 8, 1861. She married David Moore, of Gouldsboro, Maine, January 31, 1828. He died September 7, 1839.

Their children were:

i. Ellen Moore, b. Oct. 30, 1828; m. Dr. Gilbert M. Small, May 23, 1847. Resides in Sumner, Oxford co., Me. Their children are:
   - (i.) Helen M. Small, b. Feb. 29, 1848; m. Capt. Albert Robertson and resides in Harrington, Washington co., Me. She has two children: (1) Enoch B. Robertson, b. in Gouldsborough, Apr. 6, 1872, and (2) Percy M. Robertson, b. in Harrington, Apr., 1878.
   - (ii.) Byron M. Small, b. July 3, 1863.
   - (iii.) Daniel D. Small, b. in Jonesport, Me., Sept. 26, 1864.

ii. Cordelia Moore, b. Oct. 8, 1830; m. Capt. Edwin Cole (whom see).

iii. Emma Moore, b. Dec. 7, 1833; m. Capt. Daniel Deasey, of Prospect Harbor, Aug. 22, 1859. Their children are:
   - (i.) Luere B., b. Feb. 8, 1860, now an attorney-at-law in Bar Harbor, Me.
   - (ii.) Myra B. Deasey, b. June 27, 1872.

iv. Georgiana Moore, b. May 14, 1838; m. Capt. Freeman Joy, of Gouldsborough, Oct. 23, 1858. Their children are:
   - (i.) Ella A. Joy, b. May 3, 1860.
   - (ii.) Emily F. Joy, b. May 26, 1864.
   - (iii.) Alberta D. Joy, b. Oct. 18, 1867.
   - (iv.) Alice M. Joy, b. Jan. 22, 1877.

62

LYDIA COLE[7] MOORE (*Abijah,*[6] *Abijah,*[5] *Jonathan,*[4] *John,*[3] *John,*[2] *Thomas*[1]). The eighth child of Abijah and Nancy (Williams)

Cole was born in Prospect Harbor, Maine, January 30, 1806. She married Joel Moore, of Gouldsborough, January 11, 1827, and died there October 26, 1881. Mr. Moore was born August 3, 1801, died April, 1883. The following is from *Zion's Herald:*

Sister Moore was converted under the labors of Rev. David Richards, and joined the M. E. Church during the pastorate of Rev. Moses Palmer. She was a faithful and devoted member of the church militant for forty-two years, ever constant at the attendance of the church services, and was found on the Sabbath in her place at the house of God. But her worship on earth is ended, for she is now a member of the church triumphant. She gave three of her sons to her country, and when the news of their deaths reached her, she could look up through tears and feel that God doeth all things well. She could say with Job: "The Lord gave, and the Lord hath taken away; blessed be the name of the Lord.

Her home was, and now is, the home of the Methodist itinerant; in it many a weary one has found rest. I visited her in her sickness, and she was sweetly trusting Christ. Speaking about getting well or dying, she said: "God's will be done." She delighted in the Word of God; it was her counsel, and the Holy Spirit was her Comforter. God was her support in the affliction of life, and in death's hour through Him she triumphed. The Monday previous to her death she asked her daughter for the Bible. It was brought, and she took it and read these words from Matt. 7: 7-8: "Ask, and it shall be given you; seek, and ye shall find; knock, and it shall be opened unto you; for every one that asketh receiveth, and he that seeketh findeth, and to him that knocketh it shall be opened."

She had experienced the preciousness of the promises found in the passage when in health, but in her sickness did she seem to realize it as never before.

A husband, who is a member of the church, sons and daughters, mourn her departure. May they all meet that mother in Heaven. W. BALDWIN.

Her children were:

i. Alvah G. Moore, b. Oct. 23, 1831; married Mary C. Runnells, Mar. 12, 1855, and moved to Aroostook county, Me. Their children were:

(i.) Hattie Prescott, b. Mar. 10, 1858; married Alpheus Craig, and lives in Island Falls, Arostook county.

(ii.) Fred L.

(iii.) Genevia.

After about ten years of married life, Mrs. Moore died, and some time after Mr. Moore married Annie Morley. Their children were:

(iv.) Mary E., and

(v.) Annie.

After the death of his second wife he moved to Portland, where he married Olive R. Ray. He lives in Ferry Village, Cumberland co., Me.

ii. Gilbert Moore, b. Oct. 10, 1833. Lived in Gouldsborough. He was a sea captain, and was killed Nov. 3, 1879, by a fall from the masthead of his vessel. He married Victorine H. Fairfield, Nov. 16, 1860. Their children were:

(i.) Charles W., b. Oct. 22, 1861.
(ii.) Cora B., b. Dec. 4, 1863; married Almen Richardson, of Lawrence, Mass.
(iii.) Martha J.
(iv.) Daniel C.
(v.) Nellie.
(vi.) Alston.

iii. Alfred Moore, b. Apr. 5, 1835. Served in Co. L, 1st Me. Heavy Artillery, during the war. On Oct. 26, 1865, he m. Addie C. Sowle, He lives in Emmet, San Benito co., Cal. His children are:

(i.) Abijah C.
(ii.) Arvilla C.
(iii.) Lydia E.
(iv.) Aurelia.
(v.) Ida May.
(vi.) Selinda.
(vii.) Eli.
(viii.) Mabel.
(ix.) Edwin G.

iv. Sophia P. Moore, b. Dec. 23, 1836; m. Geo. S. Staples, Jan. 31, 1863. Lives in Portland, Me. Their children are:

(i.) Alice B. Staples, b. Oct. 12, 1863.
(ii.) John B. Staples, b. Jan. 16, 1865.
(iii.) Emma Staples, b. Dec. 25, 1866.
(iv.) Georgietta Staples.

v. Charles W. Moore, b. July 9, 1839; m. Annie L. Maxwell, Apr. 3, 1864. He was a member of Co. B., 8th Reg. Me. Vol. Inf., and d. in Andersonville, Ga., July 5, 1864.

vi. Abijah Moore, b. Dec. 25, 1840, was a member of Co. A., 13th Me. Vol. Inf., and was killed at the battle of Pleasant Hill, La., Apr. 9, 1864.

vii. Daniel C. Moore, b. Oct. 21, 1842. Member of Co. A., 13th Me. Vol. Inf., d. in the service at Ft. Jackson, La., June 2, 1863.

viii. Adelia Moore, b. April 25, 1845; m. Apr. 26, 1876, Wiley C. Libby. Resides at Greene, Androscoggin co., Me. She has one child:

(i.) Alice Libby.

ix. Bryant E. Moore, b. Nov. 5, 1847; m. Emma S. Walls, Nov. 18, 1869. Resides in Gouldsborough, Me. His children are:

(i.) Bertha M.
(ii.) Cecil J.
(iii.) Lewis K.

x. Edwin Kingsbury Moore, b. June 5, 1850. Was in the U. S. Signal Corps, and d. at Key West, Fla., Oct. 18, 1873.

63

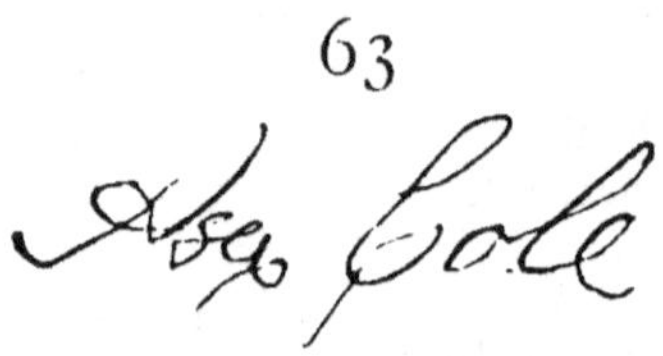

ASA[7] COLE (*Asa,[6] Abijah,[5] Jonathan,[4] John,[3] John,[2] Thomas*[1]). The first child of Asa and Anna (Goldsmith) Cole was born in Harvard, Massachusetts, August 16, 1793, and died in West Medway, Massachusetts, April 18, 1872, aged seventy-eight. On March 10, 1821, he married Marcia Knight, of Rindge, New Hampshire. She was born August 16, 1793, and died March 15, 1839. He was a farmer nearly all of his life. He was a man of immense physical strength and endurance. He represented Medway in the Massachusetts Legislature in 1841. His latter days were spent in feebleness, consequent on a paralysis caused by a physical injury, but he bore the years of suffering with true fortitude.

The children of Asa and Marcia (Knight) Cole were:

163. i. Asa, b. Mar. 11, 1822.
ii. Nancy G., b. Sept. 27, 1824, in Rindge, N. H., and d. unm. in Fall River, Mass., Nov. 22, 1873. She was a teacher in the schools of Fall River and other places nearly all her life.

On November 13, 1836, Mr. Cole married Melitiah Fairbanks, of West Medway, who was born November 24, 1813, and died February 28, 1875, in West Medway.

The children of Asa and Melitiah (Fairbanks) Cole were:

164. iii. Charles H., b. Dec. 2, 1840.
165. iv. George T., b. Mar. 4, 1843.
v. Hattie E., b. Feb. 12, 1843, d. Mar. 16, 1866.
166. vi. Albert M., b. July 6, 1847.

Richard G. Cole.

vii. Ellen M., b. Oct. 13, 1853; married Ezra Pierson, May 24, 1876. Their children are:
- (i.) Bertha Lillian Pierson, b. Dec. 17, 1871.
- (ii.) Hattie Minerva Pierson, b. Sept. 26, 1879.
- (iii.) Ezra Cole Pierson, b. Aug. 4, 1884.

64

RICHARD GOLDSMITH[7] COLE (*Asa,[6] Abijah,[5] Jonathan,[4] John,[3] John,[2] Thomas[1]*). The second child of Asa and Anna (Goldsmith) Cole, was born in Rindge, New Hampshire, November 7, 1795. In 1801 he went to the home of his uncle Hayden, in Cambridge, Massachusetts, where he lived till he arrived at manhood. When fourteen years of age he entered his uncle's store, and was bred a merchant. He followed this business in Cambridge, New York City, and Troy, New York, till 1826, when he became an officer in a bank in Troy. In 1832 he was invited to the position of cashier of a bank in Burlington, Vermont, which place he held till his death, in 1864. As a bank officer and business man, his name was a symbol of inflexible integrity. In 1833 he became a communicant of the Episcopal Church. While in Troy he led the music of St. Paul's Church, and for twenty-five years he held the same position in his church in Burlington. The simple recital of the trusts he held in the church will show the reliance placed upon him and the estimation in which he was held. For thirty years he was vestryman of St. Paul's Church, and for the last seventeen the senior warden. For eighteen years he was trustee of the parish. From 1848 he was delegate to the annual diocesean convention. In 1844 and 1853 he was delegate from Vermont to the general convention of the United States; for twelve years a member of the standing committee; from 1856 a trustee of the Vermont Episcopal Institute, and also a member of the Board of Land Agents. In all these positions his soundness of judgment, the wisdom of his counsels, his firmness of principle, his skill in business, and uniform kindness and courtesy, made him a valuable officer and a most congenial associate. He married Miss Eliza Cutler, of Cambridge, Massachusetts. They had no children. He died December 18, 1864, and his wife survived him less than a year.*

65

Benjamin Franklin[7] Cole (*Asa,*[6] *Abijah,*[5] *Jonathan,*[4] *John,*[3] *John,*[2] *Thomas*[1]). The fourth child of Asa and Anna (Goldsmith) Cole, was born in Rindge, New Hampshire, August 13, 1799. He was seventeen years of age when his father died, and a year or two later he went to West Point, New York, and obtained employment on a North River packet. Most of his life was spent in the freighting business on that river, and a part of the time he was master and owner of a craft running from New York up the river. When he was fifty years of age his health failed and he determined to try a warmer climate. He went out to the Isthmus of Panama, but soon caught the fever, and died at Chargres, in March, 1850. He married Adeline Sherwood in 1821. She was born January 9, 1806, and died in Brooklyn, New York, June 1, 1852.

The children of Benjamin Franklin and Adeline (Sherwood) Cole were:

i. Evelina, b. Sept. 19, 1824, in Highland Falls, N. Y. She m. in Nov., 1852, Warren Rodgers, of Brooklyn, N. Y., who was a boot and shoe manufacturer in N. Y. City. She d. at Cold Spring, L. I., June 1, 1866. Her husband survived her nearly ten years. Their only child living is Oliver V. Rodgers, of Cold Springs, b. Dec. 3, 1854. He is not married.

167. ii. Eliza Ann, b. May 14, 1856; m. Stillman R. Walker; d. in Brooklyn, Dec. 15, 1869.

* For many of the facts here set forth, I am indebted to the funeral discourse, preached by the Rev. D. S. Buell, of Burlington.

168. iii. Almena, b. Oct. 17, 1828; m. (1) Edwin Pelouse, (2) Elias C. Pendelton.

169. iv. Charles, b. Oct. 16, 1830, d. Apr. 16, 1868.

v. John Franklyn, b. Jan. 9, 1833, in Bayonne, N. J. In Feb., 1854, he went to Cal. For the rest of his life he was a miner in Cal. and Nev. He never married. He d. in Virginia City, in 1879.

170. vi. Richard Floyd, b. Dec. 25, 1835; d. Dec. 6, 1872.

vii. Mary, d. while an infant.

171. viii. Jeremiah, b. Jan. 22, 1840.

ix. Julia, d. while an infant.

x. Mary Harriet, b. in Brooklyn, Dec. 13, 1842, and d. there Sept. 6, 1885. She m. Aug. 27, 1865, Chas. Briggs, a native of Charlestown, N. H. They have two daughters:

(i.) Fannie Briggs, b. Apr. 5, 1867.

(ii.) Addie Briggs, b. May, 1869.

Mr. Briggs is a clerk in the Brooklyn Postoffice.

66

NANCY GOLDSMITH[7] COLE ESTY (*Asa,*[6] *Abijah,*[5] *Jonathan,*[4] *John,*[3] *John,*[2] *Thomas*[1]). The fifth child of Asa and Anna (Goldsmith) Cole was born in Westmoreland, New Hampshire, February 6, 1802. She married, February 11, 1829, the Rev. Isaac Esty, of Westmoreland. He was the only son of Isaac Esty (born in Stoughton, Massachusetts, September 11, 1767, died in Westmoreland, May 30, 1830), and Mary Hicks, his wife, (born in Sutton, Massachusetts, February 24, 1774; married in Sutton, June 26, 1794, died in Westmoreland, February 9, 1859). He was born in Sutton, Massachusetts, April 24, 1796, and was prepared for college at Chesterfield and Meridan, New Hampshire, Acadamies, and graduated at Yale College in the class of 1821, and at the Andover Theological Seminary in 1824. He preached at Cape Elizabeth, Maine, 1829-31, at Bridgton, Maine, in 1832; was a farmer in Westmoreland from 1832 to 1840, and in Westminster, Vermont, till 1846; pastor of the Congregational church in Bethleham and Franconia, New Hampshire, till 1851; lived at Westminster till 1855, being pastor in 1853-55, when he removed to Amherst, Massachusetts, where he spent the rest of his days, dying July 31, 1879. During all the years of their married life Mrs. Esty was the strong support and stay of her husband in all his labors. She was a woman of wonderful fertility of resource and strength of purpose, and of the strongest character. She died in Amherst, December 13, 1872.

Their children were:

i. William Cole Esty, b. Apr. 8, 1838, graduated at Kimball Union Academy, Meridan, N. H., in 1856; and at Amherst College in 1860; resident graduate of Harvard College, 1860–61; assistant teacher of Salem High School, 1861–62; tutor of Math. and Astron. at Amherst College, 1862-65; since 1865 he has been Prof. of Math. and Astron. in that College. July 18, 1867, he m. Martha Cushing, of Boston, who d. Jan., 1887. They have children:
  (i.) William, b. July 9, 1868.
  (ii.) Thos. Cushing, b. Dec. 8, 1870.
  (iii.) Edward Tuckerman, b. Aug. 30, 1875.
  (iv.) Robert Program, b. Aug. 5, 1876.

ii. The only other child of Rev. Isaac Esty was Henry Franklin Esty, b. Feb. 1, 1844, d. Feb. 4, 1844.

67

John Cole

John[7] Cole (*Asa,*[6] *Abijah,*[5] *Jonathan,*[4] *John,*[3] *John,*[2] *Thomas*[1]). The seventh son of a family of eleven, was born in Westmoreland, Cheshire county, New Hampshire, on the twenty-seventh day of November, 1806. Here he lived until eight years old, enjoying the home life in the humble cottage by the mill with his brothers and sisters. Then came the sudden death of his father and the struggle of the heroic mother to support her little flock. All who were old enough to work shared the effort, and John early took up the toil of life as "chore boy" upon a neighboring farm. Many hardships were encountered by these children, but their New England pluck and endurance never failed. A few short terms in the winter season was all the schooling John received, but he made excellent use of this. As a boy, he was noted as a skillful wrestler, and was considered good company everywhere. When fifteen years of age he left the New Hampshire hills, on foot, in search of his fortune, and, after a few months spent on a farm in Cambridge, he sailed before the mast on a coasting vessel. Although to the sea-sickness and home-sickness a siege of smallpox was added, he decided during the voyage to become a sailor and the master of a ship.

One voyage followed another, bringing with it rapid promotion. He studied navigation, and soon became expert in all the details of sea life. At the age of twenty-seven he reached the height of his ambition, in having committed to him the command of a fine New Bedford whale ship, and commenced upon a series of very successful voyages.

On the sixth of March, 1838, upon his return from a three-years' voyage as master of the "Hibernia," he married Miss Elizabeth Shaw, of his native place. That the lady of his choice possessed not only rare physical beauty but also a heroic spirit, can be seen in the fact that a former proposal of marriage made by him had been rejected solely upon the ground that he was not a Christian. This humbling defeat doubtless had much influence in leading him to a close study of the Bible, with which he became very conversant. It was upon this voyage that he become what he ever after exhibited in scenes of deep affliction—a sincere Christian. After a few months of wedded life he again sailed upon another voyage. On the sixteenth of December, 1838, his son

John A. was born. After his return from sea, at the most earnest entreaty of his wife and friends, he resolved to give up a sea life, and settled first in Hartford, Connecticut, where his twin daughters, Anna and Ella, were born July 27, 1841, and afterwards in Boston. But the difficulty experienced in obtaining congenial business on land, while flattering inducements were ever drawing him back to his accustomed profession, finally resulted in his accepting the command of the ship Wm. Hamilton, intending that this should be his last voyage. Before leaving he purchased the Carey cottage in Medway, where he left his little family for a three years' absence. Soon after his departure his wife began to fail in health, gradually fading away with consumption until her death, April 13, 1843. One week earlier her little Annie also passed away. Mrs. Cole's sweet Christian spirit, her fortitude and serenity under the trying circumstances of her condition, were wonderful and her death triumphant.

Long afterwards, while cruising in the Northern Pacific, this distressing event was made known to Captain Cole by a letter received from Rev. David Sanford, their pastor. His letter in reply was treasured by this devoted friend until shortly before his own death, when he sent it to the surviving children. This letter is a silent witness, not only to the heart-rending grief of the stricken husband, but also to the depth of his Christian faith and the culture of both mind and heart.

On the ninth of October, 1845, he was married to Miss Mary Wells, of Westmoreland, who was not only his choice but that of his children, to whom she ever proved a most affectionate and devoted mother. He soon after settled in Walpole, New Hampshire, where he resided eight years. Here he had extensive interests, and identified himself with many religious and benevolent enterprises. In the politics of that exciting period he took an intense interest, and was one of the few "Free Soilers" of the town. He was a member of the convention that nominated their

Presidential candidate in 1848, and was an ardent worker for human rights. Many colored fugitives found a helper in him, and his house a home, on their way to Canada. At this time he became a member of a Masonic lodge in Keene. He was also, as a "Son of Temperance," active and successful in efforts to reclaim intemperate men and restrict the liquor traffic in Walpole.

Here his son Frederick Herbert was born—a beautiful, active child, who died suddenly in his arms, before he was five years of age. This death deeply affected the father, and probably occasioned his determination to try the fortunes of the sea again.

Taking his wife with him, he sailed in the ship William Penn, of which he was a part owner, from New York to San Francisco. Upon the return voyage he met the first disaster in his business life in the loss of his ship, which was wrecked on Cape Hatteras, on the thirtieth of September, 1855. The last one to leave the ship, he was separated from his wife and floated alone, with a spar for his only support, for nineteen hours, when he was rescued by a passing vessel. His wife was also rescued from the raft upon which he had placed her as the ship was breaking up. They were united in New York after many days of suspense, both greatly overcome by the hardship of their exposure to sun and waves, but neither of them seriously injured.

March 2, 1856, Arthur Wells was born in Westmoreland, and the same year the family took up their residence once more in the Medway cottage, where they remained until 1872. Here little "Alice" was born and lived her short life—passing away August 21, 1861.

Captain Cole, at this period of his life, was, as ever before, thoroughly alive to all questions relating to the public good. He held his opinions with great pertinacity and maintained them earnestly, lacking certainly the first qualifications of a *politician*, and never the recipient of political honors. His influence was, however, constantly felt and respected. The poor always found a friend in him, and every good cause an advocate. While the war was in progress he several times visited the armies at "the front," and made the acquaintance of many public men. His business habits were very good, his investments were wisely made, and his property carefully managed. He was very liberal in his support of church institutions and charities, and also in many other directions.

His last years were spent at the Shaw homestead, in Westmoreland, amid the scenes of his childhood, and the New Hampshire hills, whose beauty was always very attractive to him. Here he labored earnestly to bring about a harmony of feeling and effect among the churches of the town, which had been greatly divided by a feud of long standing. In this he was happily successful, and the last days of his life were made bright by this union of long divided friends in the old parish church. On the twenty-ninth of December, 1874, he fell, without a moment's warning, by a stroke of apoplexy, and passed away on the following week—January 6, 1875.

In person he was a man of fine physique, stately bearing, and stern but kindly features. He possessed not only dauntless courage, but a tender heart and almost womanly delicacy of feeling. Children were easily won into his arms, and his presence in the social circle was always an inspiration. His remains lie buried in the old Westmoreland cemetery, overlooking the beautiful Connecticut valley, a most fitting spot for the last resting place of one whose manly heart was so keenly sensitive to the phases of nature.

The children of John and Elizabeth (Shaw) Cole were:

172. i. John Adams, b. Dec. 16, 1838.
ii. Anna Elizabeth (twin), b. July 27, 1841; d. 1843.
173. iii. Ella Amelia, (twin), b. July 27, 1841.

The Children of John and Mary E. (Wells) Cole were:

iv. Fred. Herbert, b. Dec. 29, 1848; d. Aug. 24, 1853.
174. v. Arthur Wells, b. Mar. 2, 1856.
vi. Alice M., b. Dec. 22, 1859; d. Aug. 21, 1861.

John E. Whitcomb.

68

SUSAN ERMINA[7] COLE WHITCOMB-PITKIN (*Asa,*[6] *Abijah,*[5] *Jonathan,*[4] *John,*[3] *John,*[2] *Thomas*[1]). The eighth child of Asa and Anna (Goldsmith) Cole was born in Westmoreland, New Hampshire, March 10, 1809, and died in Montpelier, Vermont, in 1884. On January 21, 1831, she married Elihu Whitcomb, of Concord, Massachusetts. They removed to Rutland, Vermont, where, December 12, 1832, her son John Elihu was born. Her husband died on the third of March following. She afterwards returned to Concord, Massachusetts, where she lived till her marriage, May 22, 1850, to Orin Pitkin, of Montpelier, Vermont, where she lived till the time of her death. On her second marriage she found three motherless daughters awaiting her. She proved a kind and devoted mother to them and a helpful wife to her husband. She possessed in a remarkable degree the esteem and confidence of the community in which she lived. Her only son by her second marriage died at the age of nineteen. This was a crushing blow, but her firm Christian faith and confidence in the wisdom and love of the Father enabled her to bear it.

Her children were:

68*a*. i. John Elihu Whitcomb, b. Dec. 12, 1832.
ii. Charles Pitkin, b. ——, 1852, d. —— 1873.

68*a*

JOHN ELIHU[8] WHITCOMB (*Susan E.,*[7] *Asa,*[6] *Abijah,*[5] *Jonathan,*[4] *John,*[3] *John,*[2] *Thomas*[1]). Born in Rutland, Vermont, December 12, 1832. At about one year of age went to Brighton, Michigan; at about five years of age returned east, lived in Westmoreland and Medway for about a year; from six to nine years of age lived in Concord, Massachusetts; from nine years of age to twelve, or until Spring of 1845, lived with Lambert Shaw in Medway,

Massachusetts; then six months in Providence, Rhode Island, with uncle Asa. October 5, 1845, sailed in ship Marengo from New Bedford, on a whaling voyage, Theodore Cole, Master. Arrived home April 22, 1848. November 11, 1848, sailed in ship Cowper, of New Brunswick, on whaling voyage, Theodore Cole, Master. Arrived home March 22, 1851. July 5, 1851, sailed in bark Manuel Ortis, on a whaling voyage, C. H. Cole, Master. Arrived home May 1st, 1854. July 10, 1854, sailed from New York in merchant ship, William Penn, John Cole, Master, for San Francisco. Arrived in San Francisco, December 22, 1854; there left the ship, followed various pursuits (principally mining on the Feather river, Butte county) until August, 1856, when he shipped as boatswain on the clipper ship, Star of the Union, for New York, Frederick A. Stall, Master. Arrived home in November, 1856. Did not go to sea again till April, 1857, then shipped as second mate of merchant bark C. H. Yarrington, (Oliver Gorham, Master), for Smyrna. Arrived home in September, 1857. Tried his hand at butchering business with Mr. Pitkin, the next ten months, until October, 1858, when he shipped in bark Scotland, of Boston, (John Rowe, Master), as second mate, for a voyage to Valiparaiso and the copper ore ports of Chili, South America. Arrived in Baltimore in November, 1859. Spent the Winter at home. In the Spring of 1860 shipped in the Packet service, running between Boston and Philadelphia. Arrived home the last trip in October, 1860. That ended his seafaring life. Thus you will see that from October, 1845, to October, 1860, is fifteen years that his principal occupation was going to sea; nine years of which was in the whaling service. The day before Thanksgiving, 1860, he made his *debut* as a greenhand in a machine shop in Boston, where he remained until April, 1863, when he came to Waltham and entered the employ of the American Watch Company, where he remained until June 1,. 1872, when he left their employ and started the business of manufacturing watch machinery

in connection with Henry N. Fisher and George F. Ballou, under the firm name of Ballou, Whitcomb & Co., located in Boston. In November, 1873, moved the business to Waltham. April, 1874, Ballou retired, selling his interest to Whitcomb and Fisher. November 1, 1876, Ambrose Webster was admitted to partnership. In the Winter of 1876 they built a shop seventy by thirty feet, two stories high. In 1879 enlarged by adding a building forty by thirty feet, two stories high. In 1882 another addition of fifty by twenty feet, two stories high, giving them a capacity at present time to employ ninety hands. Value of present plant is $60,000. He married June 20, 1867, in Waltham, Massachusetts, Hannah Elizabeth Spear, born in West Newton, September 12, 1845.

Their children were:

i. Percival Goldsmith, b. May 29, 1868.
ii. Cliften Spear, b. Feb. 4, 1876.
iii. John Elihu, jr., b. Sept. 11, 1882.
iv. Theodore Joseph, b. Oct. 23, 1884.

69

THEODORE[7] COLE (*Asa,*[6] *Abijah,*[5] *Jonathan,*[4] *John,*[3] *John,*[2] *Thomas*[1]). The tenth son of Asa and Anna (Goldsmith) Cole was born in Westmoreland, New Hampshire, May 11, 1813. At the age of nine years he went to live in the family of Abijah French, a farmer and lumberman of Westmoreland. He lived with Mr. French till the summer of 1834, working on the farm summers and attending district school winters. In the spring of 1835 he left Westmoreland to embark on the sea of active life. He went to New Bedford, Massachusetts, the place then so celebrated for its great whaling interests, and engaged as a seaman under the well known master, Captain James Maxfield. His first voyage lasted eighteen months, and among the various points of interest they visited, were the Azores, South Africa, Madagascar, Comoro Islands, and the Isle of France. In April, 1837, he sailed under Captain Shubel Haws, ship "Frances Henrietta" (Charles W. Morgan, agent), and made a two years' voyage, going around the world, and touching at Van Dieman's Land, Cape of Good Hope, Pernambuco, etc. In the fall of 1839 he set sail under the same master, in the ship Julian (agents, Hathaway and Luce), and cruised for some time on the Atlantic. They then extended their voyage to the northwest coast of New Holland, Australia. At this point he left the Julian, having filled the ship, and went on board the bark Pacific, Captain Webb. They sailed south and southeast along the coast of New Holland, touching at Hobart Town, then east by New Zealand, then around Cape Horn, touching at St. Catherines, Brazil, arriving home in January, 1842. During all these years of sea faring life Mr. Cole had, by diligent and prompt attention to his duties, won the approval of his employers and prepared the way for promotion, and at the age of thirty years he had circumnavigated the globe twice, and in May, 1843, as master of the ship "Parachute" (Benjamin B. Howard, agent) he began his third voyage around the world, stopping at the Sandwich Islands for recruits, thence north to the northwest coast, returning to the Sandwich Islands for water, thence to the South Pacific, around Cape Horn, returning to New Bedford in July, 1845. Captain Cole was married in August, 1845, to Livilla, the second daughter of Captain Wilson and Lucy Atherton Gleason, of Westmoreland, and in October of the same year he sailed in the ship "Marengo" (agent, Jonathan Bourne), touching at Cape Verd, passing west around Cape Horn and on to the Sandwich Islands, and from there to the coast of Kamtchatka. He was absent two years and eight months. In November, 1848, he sailed in the ship "Cowper" (agent, B. B. Howard), on a long voyage for whales in the Arctic ocean. Mrs. Cole accompanied him. They sailed direct for Cape Verd, down the coast of South America, west around Cape Horn, from thence to the Sandwich Islands, then, leaving his wife to await his return, he steered for Behring Strait, passing in June the western extremity of Oonalaska. He remained one season in the Arctic Ocean, discovering the Plover Islands, July 15, 1849, although he never claimed the title or credit of a discoverer. On his return to the Sandwich Islands his wife rejoined him. They sailed for Hong Kong, China, where they passed a month in preparing for another Arctic voyage. From there they sailed through the Japan Sea and the Matsumai Strait, north along the coast of Kamtchatka, stopping at Petropulaski, then on to the Arctic Ocean, where Captain Cole completed his cargo and started for home. The voyage of two years and a half, though full of interest and with opportunities of seeing many distant lands, and abounding in varied experience, was long to Mrs. Cole, and she heartily rejoiced when the hills and spires of New Bedford came in view, March 22, 1851, and she could once more stand upon land. Captain Cole had now for nearly sixteen years followed the sea continuously, and by his practicality, prudence, and perseverance had acquired a competency, and he decided to give up his maritime profession and enjoy the well-earned fruits of his labors, but being naturally an energetic man, idleness was not to his taste, and he engaged in manufacturing and merchandising in Brattleboro, Vermont, where he remained until 1859, when he removed to Westminster, Vermont, and purchased a farm. There he lived about seven years, identifying himself with the affairs of the town, which he represented in the Legislature in 1862. After leaving Westminster he resided in Keene, New Hampshire, one year, and then made his home in Waverly Village, Belmont, Massachusetts, for nine years, in order to give his children better educational facilities. In 1875 he made a pleasure trip to Colorado, Wyoming, and California, and then returned to Westmoreland, New Hampshire, his native place, where he afterwards resided, and employed his leisure in farming. He was a member of the New Hampshire Legislature in 1881–82, as a representative of the Republican party, to which he belonged after 1856, when he cast his vote for Fremont.

Captain Cole was a sea captain of pronounced ability, and a natural leader of men; and as shipmaster, merchant and farmer, impressed others with a sense of his fitness to lead and direct, and was an important factor in the community where he resided.

He improved the opportunities of his later life for reading and study, so that men of a more liberal education were amazed at his extensive and accurate knowledge of history and general literature. He was an able and good counselor to the younger men who often resorted to him for advice. Since 1876 he was a member of the Congregational church, and contributed liberally to its support. He was a kind husband and father, a loyal citizen and good man. He died in Westmoreland, July 2, 1885.—[*Hurd's Cheshire and Sullivan Counties.*]

The children of Captain Theodore and Livilla (Gleason) Cole are:

175. i. Frank Theodore, b. June 22, 1853.
176. ii. William Henry, b. Aug. 19, 1854.
iii. Lucy Anne, b. Feb. 29, 1856; d. Mar. 7, 1856.
iv. Sarah Gleason, Feb. 15, 1857. d. Apr. 30, 1874.

SARAH GLEASON COLE.

At Waverly, Mass., April 30, Sarah Gleason Cole, aged 17 years, and 2 months. The death of Miss Cole is one of those real mysteries of Providence which are so trying to faith. Possessed apparently of uncommon vitality and vivacity, and just at the point where she seemed entering on the full and free exercise of her varied powers, her health suddenly gave way, like a fortress undermined by an insidious foe, and only a brief but distressing illness prefaced her departure. To a good education she was adding a generous musical culture; and was not only a favorite by reason of her accomplishments, but beloved for her many endearing traits; a dutiful daughter, an affectionate sister, an agreeable companion; in many ways ministering to the happiness and welfare of those around her. Her funeral took place at the Congregational church the Sabbath afternoon following her death, a crowded and saddened attendance testifying to the common sense of loss and the universal sympathy with the bereaved household.—*From Congregationalist.*

v. Richard Goldsmith, b. Mar. 21, 1860; d. Feb. 12, 1863.

70

CHARLES HENRY[7] COLE (*Asa,[6] Abijah,[5] Jonathan,[4] John,[3] John,[2] Thomas[1]*). The youngest child of Asa and Anna (Goldsmith) Cole, was born in Westmoreland, New Hampshire, February 25, 1816, and died at sea, April 4, 1853. He was an infant when his father died and he lived with his mother till he was nine years of age, when he went to live with "good old deacon" Blake, of Rindge, New Hampshire, a man who regarded all boys as vicious and not to be trusted. After a year or so he left there and went to the home of Stephen Jewett, in the same town, under the promise that he should attend school summer and winter. Finding that he could not be spared in the warm weather he spoke of the promise. Mr. Jewett replied: "Youngster, if you are not satisfied you had better go to sea with your brother John." This brother was a whaling captain, sailing from New Bedford, and as Charles had a great horror of the sea, Mr. Jewett was surprised to receive the reply: "I guess I will." He walked from Rindge to New Bedford to see his brother, who thought best to take him. He provided books and looked after Charles' studies while he was at sea, so that with his love for reading and desire to learn he was able to acquire a very fair education, while his ready wit and genial disposition made him a man whose memory is warmly cherished by all who knew him. At twenty-five he was master of a ship, the Adelaide, and after a very successful voyage he returned to Rindge and married, March 17, 1846, Caroline G. Cutler. In 1848 he went to California, and for two years ran the schooner Caroline between San Francisco and the Sandwich Islands, as a passenger and freight packet. In 1850 he took the barque Manuel Ortez for a four years cruise around the world, to trade at the islands and ports, and to catch a cargo of oil. While in the Okhotsk sea he was injured by a whale staving his boat. This injury resulted in his death while on his way home on the ship Syren. He was buried at sea, near Christmas Island, three days out from the Sandwich Islands.

His children were:

i. Richard G., b. Apr. 14, 1847, and d. the same day.
177 ii. Charles Ward, b. Oct. 23, 1848.

In 1855 the widow of Mr. Cole married Dr. Edmund Seyffarth, of Altenberg, Germany, a surgeon of much repute, who settled in Lawrence, Massachusetts, and died in 1874.

71

Levi[7] Cole (*Levi,*[6] *John,*[5] *Jonathan,*[4] *John,*[3] *John,*[2] *Thomas,*[1]). The only son of Levi and Chloe (Stoddard) Cole was born in Chesterfield, New Hampshire, August 25, 1790, and died in Sidney Fremont county, Iowa, May 27, 1868. Before he was of age he "went west" to Watertown, New York, where he married Lygusta Allen, who was born in Herkimer county, near Little Falls, New York, May 25, 1788. She died at Riverton, Fremont county, Iowa, January 2, 1877. He lived in Watertown and kept tavern there during the war of 1812, and was well acquainted with the incidents of war in that region. He served in the militia at the time of the British attack on Sackett's Harbor (Watertown). After the close of the war he moved into Upper Canada, where he was engaged in the manufacture of lumber, on the bay of Quinta, and shipping it to Rochester, New York. About 1829 or 1830 he moved to Chautauqua county, New York, and afterwards to Buffalo; from thence to Cleveland, Ohio, and in 1837 to Monroe, Michigan. Here he lived for many years, engaged in business as a carpenter and builder. His last years were spent in Iowa at the home of his son, Gilbert L. Cole.

The children of Levi and Lygusta (Allen) Cole were:

178. i. Julia Ann, b. in Watertown, N. Y., March 26, 1809; m. Henry Webb, at Nashville, Chautauqua co., N. Y., in 1830.

179. ii. Egbert L., b. ————, d. in Louisville, Ky., in June, 1863.

iii. Maryette, b. in Watertown, N. Y. She m. at Nashville, Chautauqua co., N. Y., Elijah Holmes, about 1832. They removed to Louisville, Ky. Her husband d. there in 186–. She d. in Apr., 1885. She had three children,

(i.) George,
(ii.) Newton,
(iii.) Isabella.

180. iv. Caroline, b. in 1821, m. George Batcheldor.

181. v. James E., b. June, 1822.

vi. Isabella, b. in Coburg, Canada, June 14, 1824. She m. Jacob Hunt, at Monroe, Mich., in 1842. They removed to Toledo, Ohio, where they lived till Mr. Hunt d. She now lives with her children. They are

(i.) Nellie Hunt, m. a Mr. Savidge and lives in Spring Lake, Mich.
(ii.) Minnie Hunt, m. David Patterson, and lives in Michigan City, Mich.
(iii.) Alice Hunt, m. a Mr. Cutler.
(iv.) Horace Hunt, lives in Toledo, O.

182. vii. Gilbert L., b. July 22, 1828.

72

ADOLPHUS[7] COLE (*John,*[6] *John,*[5] *Jonathan,*[4] *John,*[3] *John,*[2] *Thomas*[1]). The oldest son of John and Hannah Cole, was born in ————. He lived in London, Canada, and took care of his parents in their old age. His children were three sons and two daughters.

73

BENONI M.[7] COLE (*John,*[6] *John,*[5] *Jonathan,*[4] *John,*[3] *John,*[2] *Thomas*[1]). The second son and fourth child of John and Hannah Cole was born in ————. He married and settled in Warwick, Ontario, and had eight children.

74

ASA[7] COLE (*John,*[6] *John,*[5] *Jonathan,*[4] *John,*[3] *John,*[2] *Thomas*[1]). The third son and seventh child of John and Hannah Cole, was born in ————. He married and moved to Michigan, where his wife died, leaving the three sons. Before 1840 he married again.

75

ALVORD[7] COLE (*John,*[6] *John,*[5] *Jonathan,*[4] *John,*[3] *John,*[2] *Thomas*[1]). The fourth son and the tenth and youngest child of John and Hannah Cole was born in London, Ontario, July 12, 1815. In 1839 he was in Michigan, but his uncle Derastus, of Coshocton, Steuben county, New York, had offered to make him his heir if he would come and live with him. Whether he did so or not I can not find out.

76

DANIEL[7] COLE (*Salmon,*[6] *John,*[5] *Jonathan,*[4] *John,*[3] *John,*[2] *Thomas*[1]). The oldest son and second child of Salmon and Bathsheba (Dodge) Cole was born in ————, Vermont. He married his cousin, Rogena Cole (oldest daughter of John), and for many years lived in Canada. They had nine children. Two of the boys were men grown and three of the daughters were married before 1839. In that year Daniel Cole moved to the Rock river country in Wisconsin.

77

HIRAM[7] COLE (*Salmon,*[6] *John,*[5] *Jonathan,*[4] *John,*[3] *John,*[2] *Thomas*[1]). The second son of Salmon and Bathsheba (Dodge) Cole was born in ————, Vermont, in ———. He went with the family to Chatham, Quebec, and then to Buckingham. His first wife died young and he married again, and about 1826 he moved to Lake Huron. He died from exposure in working on a wreck during a storm. He left a large family, but I have not been able to get trace of any of them.

78

SALMON[7] COLE (*Salmon,[6] John,[5] Jonathan,[4] John,[3] John,[2] Thomas[1]*). The second son of Salmon and Bathsheba (Dodge) Cole was born in Vermont, August 8, 1793, and about three years later was taken to Canada by his parents. He took the oath of allegiance on the twenty-ninth of August, 1812. He served in the war of 1812, and was discharged from the army in 1819. He was a black and white smith by trade, and settled in Chatham, and afterwards moved to Buckingham, Providence Quebec, where he died April 16, 1875. He was a large, fine looking man, and almost a giant in strength. He married Isabella Heatley in Ogdensburg, New York, February 8, 1819, who died August 16, 1885, aged eighty-nine.

Their children were:

183. i. Thomas, b. Dec. 1, 1820.
ii. Elleanor Anderson, b. Sept. 16, 1822; m. in Dec., 1845, to O. Leroy, of Grenville, Que. She had three children:
(i.) Peter Napoleon Leroy.
(ii.) ———, a daughter who m. (1) —— Robennia, and (2) —— Hemmings, of Grenville.
(iii.) Elleanor Augusta, who m. Edwin Cook, of ~~Papeneauville~~, in May, 1855, and was left a widow the following Feb.
184. iii. James (twin), b. March 4, 1826.
iv. Jane (twin), b. March 4, 1826; m. in 1854, D. Longe, in Ingram co., Mich., where they both live.
185. v. William Heatley, b. May 3, 1828.
vi. Elizabeth, b. Sept. 16, 1830; d. Feb., 1848.
186. vii. Mark Douglas, b, July 16, 1836.

187. viii. Willard, b. April 22, 1838.
ix. Margaret Gray, b. Feb. 14, 1843; m. Columbus Cook, of Grenville, Jan. 22, 1862. Her children are:
(i.) Mark E. Cook, b. March 15, 1863; d. Sept. 8, 1884.
(ii.) Isabella R. Cook, b. May 17, 1865.
(iii.) Amanda Augusta Cook, b. May 10, 1867.
(iv.) Ida Adelaide Cook, b. Sept. 11, 1872.
(v.) Lydia Jane Cook, b. March 23, 1875.
(vi.) Leonard Herbert Cook, b. Oct. 15, 1876.
(vii.) Emerson Cook, b. Jan. 21, 1879.
(viii.) Catherine Caroline Cook, b. July 14, 1883.

79

ORIS[7] COLE (*Salmon,[6] John,[5] Jonathan,[4] John,[3] John,[2] Thomas[1]*). The fifth son of Salmon and Bathsheba (Dodge) Cole was born in Hawksbury, Upper Canada, February 28, 1801, and died in Buckingham, Providence, Quebec, September 13, 1883. He was a very eccentric and strong-willed man. It is related of him that when a small boy he went with the older boys across the Ottawa river in a canoe, and not agreeing with them he put a piece of board under his breast and swam back across the river, which at that point was a mile wide. He was among the first settlers of Buckingham, and for many years was a pilot on the Ottawa and St. Lawrence rivers. He accumulated a large property, but through unfortunate investments lost most of it. On October 12, 1829, he married Mary Gillson, daughter of Eleazer Gillson, who was born January, 1808, and died June 18, 1881.

The children of Oris and Mary (Gillson) Cole were:

188. i. Oris, b. Aug. 17, 1830.
ii. Catherine, b. Aug. 14, 1832. She m. Richard Newton, and now lives in Buckingham, Que.
189. iii. Lemuel, b. June 7, 1834.
190. iv. Daniel and George, b. Aug. 23, 1836. George d. in 1838.
v. Harriet, b. in Buckingham, Canada, Aug. 20, 1838. She m. Wm. McFarland, May 6, 1862, of Lochabar

tp., Ottawa co., where they lived several years. They removed to Wisconsin, and now live in Clintonville. Their children are:

(i.) Emily McFarland, b. March 1, 1863; m. Gustavus E. Ahart, and has one son, William.
(ii.) Daniel McFarland, b. Nov. 13, 1864.
(iii.) Harriet Ellen McFarland, b. Sept. 12, 1866; m. Andrew D. Bennett.
(iv.) Margaret R. McFarland, b. Feb. 13, 1869.
(v.) Frederick William McFarland, b. June 22, 1871.
(vi.) Charles McFarland, b. Aug. 1, 1873.
(vii.) Alice McFarland, b. April 27, 1875.
(viii.) Allen McFarland, b. April 27, 1875.
(ix.) Oris McFarland, b. Sept. 5, 1879.
(x.) George Percival McFarland, b. April 8, 1882.

vi. Mary, b. in Buckingham, Canada, Sept. 27, 1840. She m. Allen McLean, who was b. in Glengarry co., Canada, Sept. 4, 1836 About 1878 they moved to Wisconsin, and now live in Clintonville.

Their children are:

(i.) Oris McLean, b. in Buckingham, Canada, May 30, 1863; d. Nov. 24, 1880.
(ii.) Donald McLean, b. in Cumberland, Canada, March 8, 1865; d. April 25, 1865.
(iii.) John McLean, b. in Cumberland, Canada, May 8, 1866; d. Feb. 23, 1867.
(iv.) Norman McLean, b. in Cumberland, Canada, Feb. 17, 1868.
(v.) Alexenia McLean, b. in Cumberland, Canada, Nov. 14, 1869; d. Dec. 25, 1869.
(vi.) Allen Godfrey McLean, b. in Cumberland, Canada, Sept. 25, 1872.
(vii.) Addie Cole McLean, b. in Cumberland, Canada, Jan. 25, 1874.
(viii.) Beatrice Kate McLean, b. in Buckingham, Canada, May 22, 1877.
(ix.) Emily Edith McLean, b. in Bear Creek, Wis., June 1, 1879.
(x.) Mary Zela McLean, b. in Bear Creek, Wis., March 16, 1882.
(xi.) Pinkie Belle McLean, b. in Bear Creek, Wis., May 25, 1884.

vii. Eleazer, b. in Dec., 1842; died in childhood.

viii. Emily, b. in Buckingham, Canada, Oct. 5, 1844. On Aug. 11, 1865, she m. Archibald McDermid, who was b. in Buckingham, May 30, 1839. Soon after their marriage they removed to Bear Creek, Wis., where they lived till the last year or so, and where their children were born. They now live in Clintonville, Waupaca co., Wis. Their children are:

(i.) Mary McDermid, b. April 9, 1871.

(ii.) Jennie McDermid, b. July 25, 1873.

(iii.) Jessie McDermid, b. Nov. 6, 1882.

(iv.) Archibald McDermid, b. Oct. 26, 1884.

ix. Ellen, b. May 18, 1847. She m. Thos. Moore. She is now a widow, living in Dosert, Pr. Que. Mr. Moore was for a time in the Hudson Bay Co.'s service as head man at Dosert. He resigned and opened a store at D., and was also P. M. and engaged in farming. He d. Sept. 15, 1884, leaving the business involved, but his widow has re-established it and cleared off the debts.

x. Norman, b. Oct., 1849; d. in 1878. He was an invalid for ten years before his death. He never married.

191. xi. Frederick, b. Nov. 15, 1852.

80

ETHAN[7] COLE (*Salmon,[6] John,[5] Jonathan,[4] John,[3] John,[2] Thomas[1]*). The eighth child of Salmon and Bathsheba (Dodge) Cole was born in Canada, November 22, 1804, and died in Crescent City, Iowa, January 22, 1864. He married Lucretia Gillson, March 11, 1829. She was born in Vermont, August 1, 1810, and three years later her parents moved to Canada. She died in Omaha, Nebraska, November 22, 1873. They removed from Canada to New York late in 1848, to Illinois in 1851, and to Iowa in 1859, and there made a good property, but by unfortunate investments lost a large portion of it.

His children were:

i. Zirna, b. June 23, 1830, in Buckingham, Canada. She m. Roger Wolcott, Aug. 14, 1853, in Elgin, Ill. He was b. in Coburg, Canada, May 23, 1827. His occupation was farming. He d. June 8, 1884.

Their children were:

(i.) Asa Wolcott, b. June 17, 1854, in Dundee, Ill.; m. Eliza James, April 13, 1876, at Mo. Valley, Ia., where he is engaged in farming. His children are: (*a*) Bertha, b. Jan. 24, 1877; (*b*) Frances M., b. Sept. 14, 1878; (*c*) Ida Z., b. Dec. 1, 1880; (*d*) Edna, b. Aug. 19, 1883, d. Feb. 16, 1885.

(ii.) Ethan C. Wolcott, b. in Lafayette co., Wis., April 13, 1856; m. Julia L. Johnson, Nov. 16, 1885, in Delaware, O., where she was b. Nov. 13, 1860. He is an attorney-at-law.

(iii.) Eleazer J. Wolcott, b. in Mo. Valley, Ia., May 14, 1862. He is a farmer and is unmarried.

(iv.) Roger J. Wolcott, b. in Mo. Valley, March 24, 1864. He is a farmer and is unmarried.

(v.) Mary E. Wolcott, b. Jan. 14, 1866; d. Oct. 22, 1869.

192. ii. Ethan, jr., b. March 9, 1832.

iii. Eleazer L., b. in Buckingham, Canada, Jan. 25, 1836. He enlisted in the U. S. Vols. in 1862, and d. in the hospital in Helena, Ark., July 26, 1863.

193. iv. Enos, b. Jan. 25, 1836.

v. Eleizar, b. in Buckingham, Canada, Jan. 26, 1838; d. in Campville, Canada, May 21, 1841.

194. vi. Isaac, b. Sept. 11, 1839; d. at Loveland, Ia., June 23, 1880.

vii. Abigail, b. at Campville, Canada, April 28, 1842; m. Joseph McCoid at Honey Creek, Ia., March 30, 1862, and d. July 27, 1869, at Council Bluffs, Ia. Mr. McCoid was b. in Ind. in 1826, and is now a stock dealer. Their only child is Sherman McCoid, b. Feb. 27, 1865.

viii. Lucretia, b. in Campville, May 24, 1844; m. at Council Bluffs, Ia., July 3, 1870, Augustus Mischke, a native of Germany. She d. in Council Bluffs, March 26, 1871.

195. ix. Cyrus, b. Sept. 1, 1846.

196. x. John G., b. Feb. 12, 1848.

xi. Mari V., b. in Batavia, Ill., Feb. 20, 1851; m. at

Loveland, Ia., Dec. 14, 1870, Henry F. Davidson, of that place. He was b. in Mass., March 19, 1847. Their children are:

(i.) Henry H. Davidson, b. Oct. 10, 1871.
(ii.) Cyrus E., b. Aug. 30, 1878.
(iii.) Roger M., b. Nov. 25, 1875; d. Sept. 29, 1876.
(iv.) Sarah M., b. Sept. 24, 1878.

81

DANIEL MANSFIELD[7] COLE (*Laban,*[6] *John,*[5] *Jonathan,*[4] *John,*[3] *John,*[2] *Thomas*[1]). The eldest son of Laban and Betsy (Mansfield) Cole was born in Brookline, Windham county, Vermont, February 10, 1794. He married Polly Bigelow, of Brookline, November 24, 1816. About 1826 he moved to Ashford, Cattaraugus county, New York, and remained there until his death, October 6, 1880. He was a farmer and carpenter. His wife, Polly, died September 22, 1834, and having a large family of small children to care for, he was married again December 26, 1834, to Nancy Bigelow, who died in May, 1838.

The children of Daniel Mansfield and Polly (Bigelow) Cole were:

197. i. Aljarman A., b. Oct. 4. 1817.
198. ii. Edwin F., b. Feb. 3, 1819; d. in Blue Earth co., Minn., in 1861.
199. iii. Seymore, b. Feb. 5, 1821.
200. iv. Alvin T., b. March 5, 1823.
201. v. Vernon, b. April 11, 1825.
vi. Phrenillia, b. in Ashford, Cattaraugas co., N. Y., Sept. 16, 1827. She m. Jesse Bemis, a farmer of East Ashford, where she now resides. She has no children.
202. vii. Chesselton, b. July 28, 1829.

203. viii. Byron, b. April 17, 1831.

ix. Myrion, b. in Ashford, Cattaraugus co., N. Y., June 22, 1833. She m. Sept. 22, 1869, Monson Willis, a farmer, of East Ashford. She has four children:

(i.) Grace Willis, b. Jan. 27, 1867.
(ii.) Herbert Willis, b. Nov. 29, 1869.
(iii.) Middleton Willis, b. March 26, 1874.
(iv.) Robert Willis, b. Oct. 14, 1876.

The only child of Daniel Mansfield and Nancy (Bigelow) Cole was:

204. x. Ozro, b. Oct. 1, 1835.

82

Reuben Cole

REUBEN[7] COLE (*Laban,[6] John,[5] Jonathan,[4] John,[3] John,[2] Thomas[1]*). The second child of Daniel and Betsy (Mansfield) Cole was born in Brookline, Vermont, September 10, 1796, and died in Lansingburg, New York, January 28, 1885. He married in Vermont, Chloe Ann Daggett, October 15, 1818. He moved to Albany, New York, and thence to Troy, where he was in business as a grocer. About 1857 he removed to North Greenbush, New York, and in 1867 to Lansingburg. During all his latter years he was a farmer. His wife, Chloe, died May 16, 1859, and he married Lucy C. Wager, June 19, 1860.

The children of Reuben and Chloe Ann (Daggett) Cole were:

i. Dennison, b. July 19, 1821. He d. in Troy, N. Y., Aug. 11, 1845. He was a teacher and unmarried.

205. ii. Russell, b. June 30, 1823. He died about October, 1883, probably in West Va. Nothing is known of his family, if he had one.

iii. Harriet, b. May 30, 1827; d. March 10, 1839.

iv. Jane Ann, b. April 13, 1839.

v. Frederick, b. Oct. 4, 1843; d. May 25, 1859.

83

Rebecca[7] Cole Gilson (*Laban,*[6] *John,*[5] *Jonathan,*[4] *John,*[3] *John,*[2] *Thomas*[1]). The youngest child of Daniel M. and Betsy (Mansfield) Cole was born March 19, 1804. She married Hollis Gilson, of Troy, New York, September 25, 1826. He was a farmer and carpenter, and lived in Dunkirk, New York, where he died. He was born July 12, 1805, and died March 13, 1851.

Their children were:

i. Holland R., b. April 11, 1826, and d. in Boston, Mass., April 15, 1878. He left a widow and children, viz: Mary, Alice, Holland, Herbert, and Etta.
ii. Martha A., b. Aug. 9, 1829; married William Creasy and lives in West Medway, Mass. She has two sons and a daughter.
iii. Harriet L., b. June 27, 1831.
iv. Willard Cole, b. March 26, 1833; died in West Medway, Mass., Sept. 5, 1861, leaving a widow and one son.
v. Warner H., b. May 20, 1835. He lived for a time after his marriage in West Medway, and then removed to Philadelphia, Pa., where he now resides.
vi. Mary, b. May 5, 1837; d. 1842.

84

Heber[7] Cole (*Sala,*[6] *John,*[5] *Jonathan,*[4] *John,*[3] *John,*[2] *Thomas*[1]). The first child of Sala and Sally (Stevens) Cole was born in Windham county, Vermont, September 13, 1802. In 1824 he moved with his father to Tioga, Pennsylvania, and there, in April, 1836, he married Louisa Stevens. She died November 17, 1863. Mr. Cole was a farmer, and is still living on his farm enjoying a serene old age.

Their children were:

i. Celestia, b. Feb. 9, 1837; d. Aug. 28, 1848.
206. ii. George, b. Dec. 25, 1838.

iii. Oscar E., b. May 10, 1841; d. May 5, 1864.
iv. Emeline, b. July 2, 1843; d. Nov. 1, 1848.
v. Delia, b. Aug. 8, 1849, in Tioga, Tioga co., Pa., and m. Wayland Symonds, Jan. 21, 1869.

85

SALLY[7] COLE LEET (*Sala,*[6] *John,*[5] *Jonathan,*[4] *John,*[3] *John,*[2] *Thomas*[1]). The second child of Sala and Sally (Stevens) Cole was born in Windham county, Vermont, January 15, 1805, and died in Middlebury, Tioga county, Pennsylvania, November 18, 1876. She married, October, 1830, Thomas Leet, who died about 1871. He was a farmer in Middlebury.

Their children were:

i. Mandana Leet, who m. a Mr. McWhorter and lives on the old farm in Middlebury. She has two sons who live with her.
ii. Alfred T. Leet, m. in 1874, Emma Stevens. He is a farmer in Middlebury, and has one son, Thomas, b. in 1876.
iii. Clark A. Leet, is a farmer in Hammond, Tioga co., Pa. He m. his cousin, Sally Adams, and has children:
  (i.) Arthur A., b. in 1861; resides in Corning, N. Y., and is unm.
  (ii.) George W., b. in 1864; d. Aug. 27, 1886.
  (iii.) Frederick H., b. 1872.
  (iv.) Frank L., b. 1874.
iv. Orpha Leet, m. Aug., 1861, A. B. Rundell, a carpenter of Mansfield, Tioga co. Their children are:
  (i.) Edward Rundell, b. June, 1862; in business with his father.
  (ii.) Kate J. Rundell, b. June, 1866.
  (iii.) Burt B. Rundell, b. Jan., 1868.
  (iv.) Helen L. Rundell, b. Sept., 1870; d. March, 1874.
  (v.) Rosel J. Rundell, b. June 11, 1875.
v. Kate Leet, m. Waldo White. She d. 1874. Her children are:
  (i.) Helen, m. Wallace Mitchel, a farmer of Middlebury, Pa.

(ii.) Nettie, unm.

vi. Helen Leet, m. William Mitchel, a farmer of Middlebury. She d. in 1886, leaving two sons:

(i.) W. S., b. 1864; a R. R. employe.

(ii.) William, b. 1876.

86

MIRIA B.[7] COLE PRUTSMAN (*Sala,[6] John,[5] Jonathan,[4] John,[3] John,[2] Thomas[1]*). The third child of Sala and Sally (Stevens) Cole was born in Windham county, Vermont, April 15, 1809, and died in Tioga county, Pennsylvania, October 31, 1878. She married in April, 1826, Abram Prutsman, a farmer. He died, June 1, 1882.

Their children were:

i. Sarah Adeline Prutsman, b. March 17, 1827; m. John B. Everett, a farmer of Jackson, Tioga co., Dec. 30, 1852. Their children are:

(i.) Charles E. Everett, a farmer in Jackson, who m. Annie Sheldon, and has two children: (*a*) Addie and (*b*) Myrtle.

(ii.) Abram P. Everett, a farmer in Lawrenceville, Pa., who m. Carrie Ostrander, and has one child, Mildred.

(iii.) George Everett, a farmer at Horseheads, Chemung co., N. Y., who m. May Longwell, and has one child, Helen.

ii. Andrew Jason Prutsman, b. July 12, 1829. On Nov. 14, 1854, he m. Jane C. Westbrook. He is a farmer in Tioga, Pa. His children are:

(i.) Frank C., a farmer in Tioga, who m. Rosa Shappe, and has children: (*a*) Clyde, (*b*) Lynn, and (*c*) Myra.

(ii.) Flora E., m. Charles Robinson, a commercial traveler, of Addison, Steuben co., N. Y., and has children: (*a*) Nellie and (*b*) Carl.

(iii.) Stella M., m. Charles Adams, M. D., and has one child, Ethel.

(iv.) Hattie, unm.

(v.) Effie, unm.

iii. William Randell Prutsman, b. Oct. 17, 1833. He m., July, 1855, Mary Adams, and is now a farmer in

Buda, Bureau co., Ill. His children are:

(i.) Marshall, a farmer in Buda, who m. Dora Adams, of Nebraska.

(ii.) Ella, who m. James Giffin, a R. R. man, in Mo., and has one child.

(iii.) Ida May, unm.

iv. Rachael M. Prutsman, b. Oct. 17, 1833; m. Horace F. Westbrook, a farmer, of Tioga, Sept. 26, 1850. In 1861 he enlisted in Co. D, 57th Pa. Vols., and d. in the service, July 1, 1862. Their children were:

(i.) Willis H. Westbrook, who is now a book-keeper in Wellsboro, Pa., and was m. to Stella M. Marsh, who d. in 1881, leaving one son, (*a*) Claude H. He m. again in 1884, Rilla Coolidge.

(ii.) Edgar L. Westbrook, a farmer in Middlebury, Pa.; m. Helen H. Johnson, and has two children: (*a*) Mamie and (*b*) Nida.

(iii.) Ada B. Westbrook, m. Atis L. Coolridge, a book-keeper at Morris, Tioga co., Pa., and has one child, (*a*) Ross A.

(v.) George E. Prutsman, b. May 9, 1836; m. Lizzie M. McClure, of Chester co., Pa., Jan. 6, 1870. He is a farmer in Buda, Bureau co., Ill., and has six children: (*a*) Mabel F., (*b*) George, (*c*) Sybil, (*d*) Paul, (*e*) Claude, d. 1880; (*f*) Bruce.

(vi.) Wilber H. and Willis C. Prutsman, b. Nov. 17, 1839, and d. April 8 and May 3, 1841, respectively.

87

CATHERINE[7] COLE ADAMS (*Sala,*[6] *John,*[5] *Jonathan,*[4] *John,*[3] *John,*[2] *Thomas*[1]). The fourth child of Sala and Sally (Stevens) Cole was born in Windham county, Vermont, February 7, 1812, and died in Tioga county, Pennsylvania, April 15, 1845. She married Abram Adams, August, 1835. He died March 4, 1879.

Their children were:

i. Martha K. Adams, who m. Sept., 1874, Mortimer

Kerney, of Hammond, Pa., and has one son, Clarence A., b. 1876. She now lives in Middlebury, Pa.

ii. Sally Adams, who m. her cousin, Clark Leet (whom see.)

iii. Fannie Adams, m. first a Mr. Clark, by whom she had one daughter:

(i.) Nellie, b. 1865.

After Mr. Clark's death she m. John Stevens, of Tioga, Pa. She has one son:

(ii.) John Stevens, jr., b. 1882.

88

Adeline[7] Cole Cody (*Sala,*[6] *John,*[5] *Jonathan,*[4] *John,*[3] *John,*[2] *Thomas*[1]). The fifth child of Sala and Sally (Stevens) Cole was born in Windham county, Vermont, March 3, 1815, and died in Tioga county, Pennsylvania, December 26, 1874. She married in April, 1832, Samuel Cody, who died March 21, 1880.

Their children were:

i. Francis A. Cody. He is m., but has no children.

ii. Gardner S. Cody, m. Angie Goodwin, and has children:

(i.) Grace, b. 1874.

(ii.) Glenn, b. 1882.

(iii.) Robert, b. 1884.

iii. Celestia W. Cody, m. a Mr. Keeler and has one son,

(i.) John Keeler, who m. Ida Burley, and has a son, (*a*) Roy, b. 1879, and (*b*), a daughter, b. 1882.

iv. Porter W. Cody; enlisted Sept., 1864, in Co. D, 207th Reg. Pa. Vols., and was killed before Petersburg, April 2, 1865. He was m. and left two daughters:

(i.) Adeline, unm.

(ii.) Helen, unm.

v. Sala V. Cody, m. Nov. 8, 1882, Jane Clark, of Middlebury, Pa. He has one daughter, Leonette. He is a farmer in Middlebury.

89

A. Clark[7] Cole (*Sala,*[6] *John,*[5] *Jonathan,*[4] *John,*[3] *John,*[2] *Thomas*[1]). The youngest child of Sala and Sally (Stevens) Cole was born in Windham county, Vermont, December 9, 1819. He moved to Pennsylvania in 1824 and has always lived in Tioga county, in that State. His present home is in Hammond. He married Delia Patten, June 5, 1845.

Their children are:

i. Frank H., b. Dec. 1, 1852, d. June 21, 1860.
ii. Edith Kittie, b. Feb. 12, 1855. In 1874 she m. John W. McInroy, of Wellsboro, Tioga county, Pa. They have a daughter:
(i). Narvah, b. Mar., 1882.
iii. Arthur Clark, b. Feb. 4, 1859, d. May 22, 1860.
206. iv. Herbert H., b. May 30, 1861.
v. May, b. Jan. 6, 1864.

90

Arnold[7] Cole (*Ethan,*[6] *John,*[5] *Jonathan,*[4] *John,*[3] *John,*[2] *Thomas*[1]). The oldest son of Ethan and Lucinda (Witherell) Cole was born in Barre, Worcester county, Massachusetts, August 12, 1803. When he was seven years of age the family moved to Windham, Windham county, Vermont, where he grew to manhood. On the twentieth of March, 1827, the year after his father's removal to Londonderry, he married Sally Axtell, of Jamaica, Vermont, a neighboring town. He spent nearly all of his life in the town of Londonderry, and died there July 30, 1860. His wife survived him nearly eighteen years, dying January 26, 1878.

Their children were:

i. Louisa, b. Dec. 19, 1827. On May 15, 1847, she m. Jerome W. Benson. They had two children:
(i.) Lenora, who m. Bradford Williams, of Winhall, Bennington co., Vt.,

(ii.) Angelina, who m. John Barrett, of Rutland, Vt., and lives in Chicago, Ill.

Mr. Benson having died, she m. Oct. 25, 1866, William G. Williams, a farmer of Jamaica, Vt., by whom she had two daughters:

(iii.) Olive.

(iv.) Dora Williams. Both unm.

ii. Lucinda, b. Aug. 25, 1831; m. Jan. 1, 1853, Daniel S. Howe, a farmer of Marlboro, Windham co., Vt. She has three children:

(i.) William Howe, a clerk in New York City.

(ii.) Fred Howe, a farmer in Marlboro.

(iii.) A young daughter.

iii. Liantha, b. May 24, 1834; m. Mar., 1852, James C. Vail, of Winhall. They had three children, two sons, both of whom are dead, and a daughter, who m. Elbridge Blodgett, a farmer of Wardsboro, Windham co., Vt. After Mr. Vail died she m. Lyther G. Perry, of Winhall, July 4, 1860. They have two children:

(iv.) Frank Perry, a farmer, who in July, 1886, m. Hattie Williams, of Jamaica, Vt.

(v.) Sarah, who m. John Dewaine, a chair manufacturer of Landgrove, Bennington co., Vt.

iv. Lorenzo A. Cole, b. Dec. 8, 1837; d. May 22, 1866, unmarried.

v. Sarah M. Cole, b. Aug. 21, 1840; m. Oct., 1864, M. J. Holden, a farmer and musician of Mt. Holly, Windsor co., Vt. They have no children.

vi. Angelina Cole, b. Dec. 22, 1844; d. Sept. 20, 1860.

vii. Silas Cole, b. July 27, 1847; d. May 24, 1867.

91

ISABANDA[7] COLE HARRINGTON (*Ethan,[6] John,[5] Jonathan,[4] John,[3] John,[2] Thomas[1]*). The fourth child of Ethan and Lucinda Witherell was born in Windham, Windham county, Vermont, June 15, 1809. Her husband was Reuben Harrington. He was a son of Daniel Harrington, of Orange, Franklin county, Massachusetts, and was born in that town, January 27, 1795. With his three brothers, Daniel, Lyman and Emery, he emigrated to Londonderry, Vermont, about 1817. He and Daniel became farmers, Lyman a merchant, and Emery a wool carder, in that town. After a few years spent in clearing his farm, near the foot of Glebe Mountain, he went to Massachusetts, and married Abigail Abbott, of Warwick, Worcester county, Massachusetts, and returned to his farm. His wife died in 1828, leaving no children.

In 1830 he married Isabanda Cole. Mr. Harrington was a prominent man of the town. He was justice of the peace and first selectman for many years, and represented the town in the Legislature in 1845-46. In 1848 he sold his farm and bought a large farm in Manchester, Bennington county, Vermont, where he resided till 1865, when wishing to retire from active work he sold and came back to Londonderry, and bought a small place in the South Village, where he lived until his death, October 7, 1881. His wife after his death went to her daughter in Chester, Windsor county, Vermont, where she died June 16, 1885.

They had twelve children, two of whom died in infancy. The others were:

i. Abigail A. Harrington, b. in Londonderry, July 26, 1831. In 1853 she m. Charles T. Holman, who was b. Aug. 20, 1830. They moved to Dement, Ill., and thence to Algona, Kossouth co., Ia., where they now reside. Their children are:
  (i.) Lyman H. Holman, d. in Ill., April 9, 1863.
  (ii.) George A. Holman.
  (iii.) Fred H. Holman.
  (iv.) Rosa M. Holman.

ii. Laurenza L. Harrington, b. Sept. 10, 1832. She m., in Manchester, Vt., Calvin B. Walker, b. Aug. 6, 1830, a farmer of Londonderry, where they now reside. They have no children.*

iii. Laurencie I. Harrington, b. June 12, 1837; m. Nov. 1, 1859, Samuel H. Walker, b. Nov. 1, 1832, a farmer in Manchester, Vt., where she resided and where she d., Sept. 7, 1880, leaving four children:
  (i.) Addie C., b. July 16, 1860; d. Aug. 4, 1881.
  (ii.) Henry S., b. Feb. 28, 1861.

*The editor is under obligation to Mrs. Walker for the collection of the records of the family of her mother.

(iii.) Frank H., b. Feb. 27, 1862.
(iv.) Hattie L., b. July 19, 1864.

iv. Harrison H. Harrington, b. Sept. 3, 1839; m. Freelove Amidon, b. May 11, 1839, of Woodford, Bennington co., Vt. Their only child was Mary, b. in Chester, Vt., Aug. 22, 1866. They now live in Dexter, Dallas co., Ia.

v. Ellen L. Harrington, b. Dec. 30, 1841. She m. George C. Allen, b. Dec. 21, 1840, a farmer and harness maker, of Chester, Vt. He was a member of the 11th Vt. Vols. She d. Jan. 4, 1881, leaving no children.

vi. Elsie F. Harrington, b. March 4, 1844. She m., Dec. 20, 1862, in Wallingford, Rutland co., Vt., Abram Straight, who deserted her, and she resumed her maiden name in accordance with the decree of the court. Her children are:
(i.) Fred H. Harrington, b. Nov. 20, 1863.
(ii.) Lulu I. Harrington, b. Nov. 18, 1865.

vii. Viola J. Harrington, b. Oct. 23, 1846. She m. Alvaro D. Whitman, b. March 19, 1845, a machinist of Rutland, Vt., in 1870. Their children are:
(i.) Adelbert K. Whitman, b. Sept. 23, 1871; d. Oct. 28, 1886.
(ii.) Pearl S., b. July 30, 1873.
(iii.) Lyman C., b. May 6, 1876.
(iv.) Louisa, b. Dec. 1, 1878.
(v.) Addie E., b. March 18, 1881.
(vi.) A daughter b. Dec. 1, 1885.

viii. Lyman A. Harrington, b. Aug. 4, 1850; m. Dec. 20, 1881, in Chester, Vt., Jennie Pomroy, who was b. in. South Hampton, Mass., Nov. 3, 1853. He is a carriage smith in Chester. They have no children.

92

ALFRED R.[7] COLE (*Ethan,*[6] *John,*[5] *Jonathan,*[4] *John,*[3] *John,*[2] *Thomas*[1]). The fifth child of Ethan and Lucinda (Witherell) Cole was born in Windham, Windham county, Vermont, October 19, 1811. In March, 1834, he married Liantha Person, of Windham, who was born September 20, 1809. He moved to Lewis county, New York, and settled on a farm near Counstableville, where he now resides.

The children of Alfred R. and Liantha (Person) Cole were:

i. Lawrenza W., was b. in Counstableville, Lewis co., N. Y., May 8, 1836. On Oct. 6, 1861, she m. Allen Dunton, who was b. Mar. 19, 1840. They live in Malone, Franklin co., N. Y., and have two children:
(i.) Ella N. Dunton, b. Jan. 27, 1869.
(ii.) Eugene Dunton, b. July 1, 1876.

ii. Olive H., was b. in Counstableville, Lewis co., N. Y., July 27, 1841. On Jan. 1, 1866, she m. Nelson W. Delain, who was b. Oct. 5, 1845. They lived at Brandon, N. Y., where she d. Feb. 8, 1882, leaving two children:
(i.) Almira H. Delain, b. Nov. 11, 1866.
(ii.) Frank Delain, b. Feb. 25, 1879.

207. iii. Lorenzo W., b. Nov. 7, 1846; d. in Malone, N. Y., Apr. 4, 1879.

93

ALVARADO[7] COLE (*Ethan,*[6] *John,*[5] *Jonathan,*[4] *John,*[3] *John,*[2] *Thomas*[1]). The sixth child of Ethan and Lucinda (Witherell) Cole was born in Windham, Windham county, Vermont, April 20, 1814. On September 27, 1840, he married Theodosia Reed, of Londonderry, who was born September 22, 1812. He learned the trade of a brick maker and also that of a painter, and worked at both at times during his life. He is now a farmer in Londonderry. The editor is under great obligations to him for assistance in the preparation of the portion of this book which relates to the family of Ethan Cole. Both Mr. Cole and his estimable wife are living in old age, surrounded by children and grand-children, and enjoying the comforts that come after a life well spent. The editor had great pleasure in spending a day with them while engaged in the preparation of this work.

The children of Alvarado and Theodosia (Reed) Cole were:

208. i. Warren, b. Dec. 5, 1841.

ii. Henrietta, b. Nov. 12, 1843; she m. Feb. 7, 1869, Geo. A. Howard, of Londonderry, who was b. July 18, 1844. He is a butcher and has been in business in Chester and Manchester, Vt., and Chelmsford, Mass. He is now located in Londonderry. They have no children.

iii. Julia, b. Nov. 12, 1843, and m. Jan. 20, 1866, John Gibson, of Londonderry, who was b. Dec. 22, 1843, and d. June 16, 1877. Their children are:

(i.) Alley C. Gibson, b. May 9, 1869, a clerk in a store in Londonderry.

(ii.) Etta C. Gibson, b. Apr. 25, 1871.

94

ALFONZO ETHAN[7] COLE (*Ethan,[6] John,[5] Jonathan,[4] John,[3] John,[2] Thomas[1]*). The seventh and youngest child of Ethan and Lucinda (Witherell) Cole was born in Windham, Windham county, Vermont, March 1, 1817. He married, June 30, 1840, Sylvia Cheaney, of Londonderry, who was born in 1820, and died March 31, 1847. Mr. Cole was a brick maker and farmer, and spent all of his life in Londonderry.

The children of Alfonzo Ethan and Sylvia (Cheaney) Cole are:

209. i. Winslow A., b. Dec. 9, 1841; d. in Worcester, Mass., June 21, 1884.

ii. Emeline, b. Aug. 28, 1843; m. Charles Rawson, Aug. 19, 1862. They live in Worcester, Mass., and have one son, Frank Rawson, b. June 3, 1871.

iii. George W., b. Nov. 15, 1845; d. Dec. 28, 1845.

On January 4, 1848, Mr. Cole married Mary Babbett, of Londonderry, who survived him. The children of Alfonzo Ethan and Mary (Babbett) Cole are:

iv. Alson, b. March 15, 1850.

v. Almerette M., b. April 29, 1853; m., Oct. 1, 1870, Melvin Vails, a farmer in Londonderry. Their only child is Everett Vails, b. Dec. 24, 1874.

95

DAVIS SIMON[7] COLE (*Simon,[6] John,[5] Jonathan,[4] John,[3] John,[2] Thomas[1]*). The fourth child and second son of Simon and Ester (Robbins) Cole was born August 3, 1817. He moved west and for a time lived in Nettleton, Caldwell county, Missouri, but he has gone from there, and all traces of him are lost.

96

STEPHEN ROBBINS[7] COLE (*Simon,[6] John,[5] Jonathan,[4] John,[3] John,[2] Thomas[1]*). The sixth child of Simon and Ester (Robbins) Cole was born June 10, 1821, in Brookline, Vermont. He married Hannah Carney. He has lived most of his life in and around Boston, and is a machinist.

His children are:

210. i. William A. D., b. Dec. 27, 1853.
211. ii. Frank E., b. April 17, 1855.
iii. Minnie C. E., b. Feb. 1, 1857; died March 15, 1865.
212. iv. Stephen R., jr., b. Dec. 17, 1859.
v. ———, b. March 4, 1864.
213. vi. Howard E., b. June 8, 1870.

97

ALONZO[7] COLE (*Heber,[6] John,[5] Jonathan,[4] John,[3] John,[2] Thomas[1]*), was born in Westmoreland, New Hampshire, September 29, 1813, and died in Newburyport, Massachusetts, December 15, 1877. He married, in Springfield, Massachusetts, December 29, 1833, Louisa Caldwell, who was born December 1, 1813, and died in Newburyport, November 27, 1879.

Their children were:

i. Henry Alonzo, b. Nov. 9, 1836; d. April 7, 1838.

98

Heber Bennett[7] Cole (*Heber*,[6] *John*,[5] *Jonathan*,[4] *John*,[3] *John*,[2] *Thomas*[1]). The second child of Heber and Sally (Bennett) Cole was born in Westmoreland, New Hampshire, September 29, 1813. In early life he began those habits of industry and economy which distinguished him through his life. When over half his life was passed he married Mary Ann Knight, the widow of Charles Cobb, of Westmoreland, January 13, 1856. For nearly twelve years they lived together, he caring for her property and rearing her two children. She died October 31, 1867, at the age of forty years. He continued in charge of the property until the step-son became of age, when he turned the farm over to him, and for the rest of his life made his home with his sister, Mrs. Daggett. He never had any children. He died February 18, 1885. All of his life was spent in Westmoreland, and he was one of the best known men of the town, and he was honored by his townsmen with several of the minor offices in their gift. His frugality and industry, together with his strict integrity, enabled him to accumulate a large fortune, which he disposed of by testament just before his death.

99

George[7] Cole (*Heber*,[6] *John*,[5] *Jonathan*,[4] *John*,[3] *John*,[2] *Thomas*[1]). The second child of Heber and Prudence (Walker) Cole was born

Heber B. Cole.

in Westmoreland, New Hampshire, March 20, 1833. He married (1) Lydia A. Richardson, of Keene, New Hampshire, December 10, 1853. She was born April 4, 1836. He married (2) Eliza Stratton, by whom he had no children. He was an engineer in Rochester, New York, where he died February 23, 1873.

The only child of George and Lydia (Richardson) Cole was:

214. i. George, b. April 6, 1854.

108

EPHRAIM FOSTER[7] COLE (*Kimball,[6] Solomon,[5] Samuel,[4] Samuel,[3] John,[2] Thomas[1]*). The third child and oldest son of Lieutenant Kimball and Abigail (Runnells) Cole was born in Boxford, Massachusetts, July 6, 1809. He married Eliza Spofford, December 10, 1830. She was born in Chester, New Hampshire, and died April 25, 1832, and he married Sarah Spofford, March 5, 1833. She was born in Danville, New Hampshire. He was a farmer in Boxford, and died there April 23, 1879.

His children were:

i. Eliza Spofford, b. Sept. 10, 1831; d. Dec. 19, 1831.
ii. William Kimball, b. Jan. 6, 1834; d. unmarried in Hillsborough, Ia., Oct. 23, 1856.
220. iii. George Spofford, b. July 2, 1836.
iv. John Foster, b. Jan. 20, 1841. He enlisted in Co. F, 35th Mass. Volunteers, and was wounded, and died in McClellan Hospital, Philadelphia, from the effects of his wound, June 14, 1864. He was unmarried.
v. Charles Warren, b. April 3, 1844; enlisted in Co. F, 35th Massachusetts Volunteers; d. at Newport News, of fever, March 3, 1863.
iv. Sarah Jane, b. Mar. 13, 1846; m. May 14, 1846, Melville T. Wadlin, of Biddeford, Me., who was b. Apr. 23, 1839. They reside in South Lawrence, Mass. His children are:
(i.) Chas. Melville, b. July 10, 1868.

(ii.) Margaret Eugenia, b. Sept. 16, 1869.
(iii.) Geo. Leslie, b. Sept. 14, 1871.
(iv.) Ida Louisa, b. Dec. 22, 1875.
(v.) Jennie Alice, b. May 26, 1880.

221. vii. Arthur E., b. Sept. 30, 1848.
222. viii. Joseph Franklin, b. Sept. 28, 1851.
223. ix. Wallace E., b. Nov. 19, 1855.
224. x. Roscoe Kimball, b. Feb. 28, 1861; m. ——. Has no children. Andover, Mass.

109

JOHN KIMBALL[7] COLE (*Kimball,[6] Solomon,[5] Samuel,[4] Samuel,[3] John,[2] Thomas[1]*), the sixth child of Lieutenant Kimball and Abigail (Runnells) Cole, was born in Boxford Massachusetts, December 16, 1814. He married Mary S. Town, of Boxford. He resides in his native town, is a farmer, and has been a deacon in the First Church since 1852. He was a member of the State Legislature in 1862.

His children were:

225. i. Jefferson Kimball, b. Oct. 25, 1838.
ii. Abbie Rebecca, b. Dec. 14, 1840; m. Roscoe W., son of Abel and Annie M. Gage, Nov. 24, 1863. He was b. in Pelham, N. H., and d. in Boxford in 1868, where his widow and her two children are living.
iii. Mary Ellen, b. Jan. 28, 1844; m. Wm. G., son of Geo. A. and Edna G. Todd, Sept. 22, 1863. They have two children.
226. iv. John Newton, b. Mar. 21, 1857.

110

WILLIAM RUNNELLS[7] COLE (*Kimball,[6] Solomon,[5] Samuel,[4] Samuel,[3] John,[2] Thomas[1]*), the seventh and youngest child of Lieut. Kimball and Abigail (Runnells) Cole, was born in Boxford, Massachusetts, January 15, 1817. He married, June 17, 1855, Mary

H. daughter of John and Prudence Runnells, of Andover. She was born in North Andover in 1825. He was a farmer in Boxford, and died there November 18, 1865. His widow is postmistress at West Boxford.

Their children are:

227. i. William Kimball, b. June 2, 1856.
ii. Abbey L., b. July 27, 1858, d. Dec. 26, 1865.
227*a*. iii. Norman, b. July 3, 1860.
228. iv. Morris Lee, b. Apr. 29, 1863.
v. Mary, b. Sept. 20, 1865, d. Sept. 3, 1867.

111

Isaac[7] Cole (*Isaac,[6] Solomon,[5] Samuel,[4] Samuel,[3] John,[2] Thomas[1]*), the third child and oldest son of Isaac and Hannah (Atwood) Cole, born October 31, 1796. He married Lucy Knapp and settled in Franconia, New Hampshire, where he died in 1880, aged eighty-four.

His children were:

i. Emily, b. in 1818; m. (1) A. Woodman and (2) —— Dwyer. Now lives in N. J. Her children were:
  (i.) Dunbar Woodman, b. in N. H. —— ——. Now lives in Chicago, Ill. Was a soldier in an Ill. Reg. and officer in a Colored Reg.
  (ii.) John Dwyer, b. in 1846, d. in 1866.
  (iii.) Edgar Dwyer, b. in 1848. Served in regular army, 1865–68. Lives in Jersey City and has several children.
ii. Harriet, b. —— ——; m. Daniel E. True, of Leominster, Mass., where they now reside. They have one daughter who is married and has three children.
iii. Isaac P., b. in 1825; d. in Lake Village, N. H., 1865, leaving a wife and one daughter; she is now married and has a family.
iv. Abbie, b. —— ——; m. G. Andrews and lives in Chicago. Has one son.
v. Susie, b. 1842; m. C. W. Chase. He was Capt. in 12th N. H. Vols. Removed to Ia. and has been Judge of the Superior Court. Resides at Clinton, Ia. Four children.

112

John A.[7] Cole (*Isaac,*[6] *Solomon,*[5] *Samuel,*[4] *Samuel,*[3] *John,*[2] *Thomas*[1]). The second son of Isaac and Hannah (Atwood) Cole, was born April 22, 1801. He married Mary Ryan and lived in Plymouth, New Hampshire, where he died in 1864.

His children were:

i. Mary Elizabeth, b. Aug. 5, 1826. She m. J. Aldrich in 1846. Has no children.

ii. Marcia B., b. Aug. 5, 1828; m. C. P. S. Wardwell, who d. in 1879. Their children are:

(i.) Marion, b. —— ——; m. C. Blaisdell, and has three children.

(ii.) Charles, b. —— ——. Has two children.

(iii.) Warren R., b. —— ——. Unmarried.

She subsequently m. L. Marston, of Hoopstown, Ill., where they now reside.

iii. Belinda R., b. April 2, 1831; m. A. D. Stanwood, of Me. They are both dead. They had two sons, only one of whom is living, to-wit: Chas. S., of Chicago.

iv. Mehitable R., b. Jan. 5, 1833; m. John S. Young, of Belmont, N. H. They are both dead, leaving five children:

(i.) Herbert S., resides in Buffalo, N. Y. Has one daughter.

(ii.) Harley A., resides in Buffalo.

(iii.) Mary; m. —— Dockham, of Gilmantown, N. H., and has two children.

(iv.) John B.; lives in Laconia, N. H., and has one child.

(v.) Percy, b. in 1873. Lives in Buffalo.

v. John L., b. Oct. 25, 1834; d. in Cincinnati, O., in 1868. Unmarried.

vi. Stephen, b. Apr. 28, 1838; d. in infancy.

For a second wife Mr. Cole married Abigail Davis.

Their only child was:

229. vii. Stephen B., b. Apr. 30, 1840.

113

TIMOTHY[7] COLE (*Isaac,[6] Solomon,[5] Samuel,[4] Samuel,[3] John,[2] Thomas[1]*). The third son of Isaac and Hannah (Atwood) Cole was born September 22, 1806. He became a clergyman of the Christian denomination. He married Susan Hill, and died in Springfield, New Hampshire, in 1868.

His children were:

i. Susan, b. —— ——; m. R. P. Sanborn. She d. in 1875, leaving two daughters, one of whom m. F. E. Busill, of Laconia, N. H.

ii. Francis, b. —— ——, m. ——— Cheever. Lives in Haverhill, Mass., and has several children.

230. iii. Timothy, b. —— ——. Resides in Mich.

114

HON. BENJAMIN JAMES[7] COLE was born in Franconia, New Hampshire, September 28, 1814. In 1821 his father removed to Franklin, New Hampshire, and in 1827 to Lake Village in the town of Gilford, where the family have since resided. In 1836 he, with his two brothers, John A. and Isaac, succeeded their father in the foundry business which he had established there. Later he purchased their interest, and added to and developed the same until it became one of the largest establishments of the kind in the State. In 1873 it was organized into a joint stock company as the "Cole Manufacturing Company," with a capital stock of $60,000, which has since been increased, he retaining nine-tenths of the stock and continuing to manage the business for ten years, when he relinquished the active part of the same to his son-in-law, Col. H. B. Quinby.

He married June 17, 1838, Mehitable A. Batchelder, of Lake Village. He represented the town of Guilford in the State Legislature in 1849 and 1850; was also elected a member of the Governor's Council in 1866 and 1867; was elected a member of the State Constitutional Convention in 1868, and also a delegate to the National Republican Convention at Baltimore which renominated President Lincoln in 1864; was one of the Presidential electors in the following election.

"He has long been a prominent member of the Free Baptist "Church and a trustee of New Hampton Institution. Mr. Cole is "a man of influence in his town and church and throughout a large "business acquaintance. He has a kind, social and affectionate "nature, and cherishes home and friends. To these he is loyal, "and he enjoys to an unusual degree the marked confidence of the "better portion of society and leading business men. He is generous in the highest degree in contributing to religious and charitable objects, and no case of deserving need ever appealed unsuccessfully to him. He is not only a prominent and leading "business man, an active temperance worker, but, higher yet, a "consistent Christian, whose active zeal has done much for the "church and society of his locality."*

Children of Benjamin James and Mehitable (Batchelder) Cole are:

i. Ellen Atwood Cole, b. —— ——.
ii. Octavia M. Cole, b. —— ——; m. Henry B. Quinby, now superintendent of the Cole Manufacturing Co. Their children:
(i.) Harry Cole, b. —— ——.
(ii.) Candace E., b. —— ——.

115

ZACKEUS[7] COLE (*John,*[6] *Solomon,*[5] *Samuel,*[4] *Samuel,*[3] *John,*[2] *Thomas*[1]). The eldest child of John and Polly (Bemis) Cole was born in Dummerston, Vermont, March 28, 1791, and died in

*From History of Belknap and Merrimack Counties, New Hampshire.

Westminster, Vermont, October 12, 1882. He became a plater and metal worker in Westminster, where he spent most of his life, and was a very industrious and ingenious workman. He was a great reader, particularly of history, and a man of very original turn of mind. He married May 31, 1815, Annis Harlow, widow of Giles Marvin.

Their children were:

i. Cynthia, b. Nov. 29, 1817; m. James Smith, of Fillmore, N. Y., June 25, 1845, where they now reside. They have two children.

ii. Lucia Ann, b. May 31, 1820; m. Charles Williard, of Westminster, Nov. 25, 1847; d. Oct. 25, 1880. She had no children.

231. iii. George, b. Dec. 2, 1822.

232. iv. Charles, b. June 16, 1825; d. Dec. 2, 1879.

v. Frances, b. Aug. 3, 1828; m. Benj. F. Richmond, July 4, 1860, who was b. in Grafton, Vt., in 1826. Their children are:

(i.) John Cole, b. June 5, 1861.
(ii.) Geo. Makepeace, b. Feb. 9, 1863.
(iii.) Willie Frank, b. Apr. 16, 1864.
(iv.) Harry Luke, b. Nov. 25, 1865.

116

JOHN[7] COLE (*John*[6], *Solomon*,[5] *Samuel*,[4] *Samuel*,[3] *John*,[2] *Thomas*[1]). The second son of John and Polly (Bemis) Cole was born in Gardner, Massachusetts, September 13, 1797. He now resides in Keene, New Hampshire, with his brother and nephew.

117

ASA[7] COLE (*John*,[6] *Solomon*,[5] *Samuel*,[4] *Samuel*,[3] *John*,[2] *Thomas*[1]). The youngest child and third son of John and Polly (Bemis) Cole was born in Surry, New Hampshire, October 20, 1804. He was but three years of age when his father died. On September 3,

1829, he married Sarah Pitts, of Uxbridge, Massachusetts, who was born November 5, 1808. He settled in Gilsum, New Hampshire, where he lived till late in life, when he removed to Keene, where he now resides.

His children were:

i. Charles Pitts, b. in Gilsum, Jan. 20, 1832; d. Sept. 4, 1832.

233. ii. Daniel Read, b. in Gilsum, Aug. 20, 1835.

118

SAMUEL[7] COLE (*Solomon,*[6] *Solomon,*[5] *Samuel,*[4] *Samuel,*[3] *John,*[2] *Thomas*[1]). The first child of Solomon and Sally (Howland) Cole, of Whitfield, New Hampshire, born —— ——.

118*a*

STEPHEN H.[7] COLE (*Solomon,*[6] *Solomon,*[5] *Samuel,*[4] *Samuel,*[3] *John,*[2] *Thomas*[1]). The third son of Solomon and Sally (Howland) Cole, of Whitfield, New Hampshire; born —— ——; died ——, 1877.

118*b*

ASA[7] COLE (*Solomon,*[6] *Solomon,*[5] *Samuel,*[4] *Samuel,*[3] *John,*[2] *Thomas*[1]). The sixth child and fourth son of Solomon and Sally (Howland) Cole, of Whitfield, New Hampshire, born —— ——.

118*c*

SOLOMON[7] COLE (*Solomon,*[6] *Solomon,*[5] *Samuel,*[4] *Samuel,*[3] *John,*[2]

Thomas[1]). The eighth child and fifth son of Solomon and Sally (Howland) Cole, of Whitfield, New Hampshire.

119

AMOS J.[7] COLE (*Samuel*,[6] *Solomon*,[5] *Samuel*,[4] *Samuel*,[3] *John*,[2] *Thomas*[1]). The eldest son of the Rev. Samuel Cole, of Lisbon, New Hampshire, was born —— ——.

120

PHINEAS[7] COLE (*Samuel*,[6] *Solomon*,[5] *Samuel*,[4] *Samuel*,[3] *John*,[2] *Thomas*[1]). The second son and fourth child of the Rev. Samuel Cole, of Lisbon, New Hampshire, was born —— ——.

121

MOOERS[7] COLE (*Samuel*,[6] *Solomon*,[5] *Samuel*,[4] *Samuel*,[3] *John*,[2] *Thomas*[1]). The fifth child and third son of the Rev. Samuel Cole, was born in Lisbon, New Hampshire, August 14, 1815. He married Elizabeth, daughter of Cyrus Latham, of Lowell, Massachusetts, March 11, 1851. He studied theology and became a minister of the Free Will Baptist Church in 1838, and has been settled in Salem, Massachusetts; Dover, Nashua, Danville and Belmont, New Hampshire; and Gray, Maine. He says:

"For the last nine years I have devoted my time to visiting schools of all grades. Spend from five to twenty-five minutes in each school. Tell the children: 'Never utter a lie. Obey their parent in the Lord. Never use a profane or vulgar word. Never drink a drop of strong drink or use tobacco in any form.' Have taken a line of schools from Hyde Park, Mass., to Fergus Falls, Minn., about two thousand miles. Drove horse and buggy all the way out and back. Visited between five and six hundred schools during the trip. In last nine years visited about seventeen hundred in twelve States."

His children were:

i. Kate Evelyn, b. May 26, 1853; m. Albert Bradley, of Danville, N. H., June 27, 1874.
234. ii. Wm. Latham, b. Feb. 10, 1857.
iii. Helen May, b. Sept. 28, 1860. Is a teacher in Boston.

122

JOSEPH[7] COLE (*Samuel,*[6] *Solomon,*[5] *Samuel,*[4] *Samuel,*[3] *John,*[2] *Thomas*[1]) The sixth child and fourth son of the Rev. Samuel Cole, of Lisbon, New Hampshire, born —— ——.

123

BENJAMIN[7] COLE (*Samuel,*[6] *Solomon,*[5] *Samuel,*[4] *Samuel,*[3] *John,*[2] *Thomas*[1]). The seventh child and fifth son of the Rev. Samuel Cole, of Lisbon, New Hampshire, born —— ——.

124

SAMUEL[7] COLE (*Samuel,*[6] *Solomon,*[5] *Samuel,*[4] *Samuel,*[3] *John,*[2] *Thomas*[1]). The eighth child and sixth son of the Rev. Samuel Cole, of Lisbon, New Hampshire, born —— ——.

125

ISAAC[7] COLE (*Samuel,*[6] *Solomon,*[5] *Samuel,*[4] *Samuel,*[3] *John,*[2] *Thomas*[1]). The youngest child of the Rev. Samuel Cole, of Lisbon, New Hampshire, by his second wife, Mary Colby; born —— ——. Resides on the old home place in Lisbon.

126

KIMBALL[7] COLE (*Asa B.*,[6] *Solomon*,[5] *Samuel*,[4] *Samuel*,[3] *John*,[2] *Thomas*[1]). The second son of Asa B. and Lydia (Howland) Cole, of Whitfield, New Hampshire; born —— ——.

126*a*

GEORGE W.[7] COLE (*Asa B.*,[6] *Solomon*,[5] *Samuel*,[4] *Samuel*,[3] *John*,[2] *Thomas*[1]). The sixth child of Asa B. and Lydia (Howland) Cole, of Whitfield, New Hampshire, was born —— ——.

127

SIMON[7] COLE (*Asa B.*,[6] *Solomon*,[5] *Samuel*,[4] *Samuel*,[3] *John*,[2] *Thomas*[1]). The eighth child of Asa B. and Lydia (Howland) Cole, of Whitfield, New Hampshire, was born —— ——.

128

DAVID MIGHILL[7] COLE (*Manly H.*,[6] *Simeon*,[5] *Samuel*,[4] *Samuel*,[3] *John*,[2] *Thomas*[1]). The first child of Manly H. and Hannah S. (Robinson) Cole, born in Boxford, Massachusetts, September 20, 1825. He married November 17, 1852, Eunice Chadwick, born 1830, and resides in Boxford.

Their only child is:

235. i. Warren Mighill, b. ——, 185–, in Boxford.

129

CALEB MANLY[7] COLE (*Manly H.*,[6] *Simeon*,[5] *Samuel*,[4] *Samuel*,[3] *John*,[2] *Thomas*[1]). The second son of M. H. and H. S. (Robinson) Cole, was born in Boxford, January 26, 1827. He married Louisa W. R., daughter of Mark and Mary O. Jenness, of Boxford. (Published February 22, 1823). She was born in 1831.

His children are:

i. Hannah Madora Osgood, b. July 5, 1857; m. March 22, 1876, Daniel Withan, son of Alvah C. and Effa (Allen) Withan, of Boxford. He was b. in North Berwick, Me., in 1850. He lives in Boxford.
ii. Helen G., b. March 11, 1859.
236. iii. William H. A., b. May 9, 1865.

130

TISDALE SABINA[8] COLE (*Jonathan,*[7] *Jonathan,*[6] *Jonathan,*[5] *Jonathan,*[4] *John,*[3] *John,*[2] *Thomas*[1]). The first child of Jonathan and Lydia (Daggett) Cole, was born in Westmoreland, New Hampshire, December 19, 1793, and died in River Falls, Pearce county, Wisconsin, February 2, 1864. He was married in Madrid, St. Lawrence county, New York, November 24, 1820, to Laurancy Hallock. He was a carpenter and farmer and some time after his marriage he moved to Wisconsin, where he spent the remainder of his days.

His children were:

237. i. George.
238. ii. Serenus.
iii. Clarissa, d. at 14 years of age.

131

BETSY ELMIRA[8] COLE (*Jonathan,*[7] *Jonathan,*[6] *Jonathan,*[5] *Jonathan,*[4] *John,*[3] *John,*[2] *Thomas*[1]). The third child of Jonathan and Lydia (Daggett) Cole was born in Westmoreland, New Hampshire, January 1, 1798, and died in Morrison, Whiteside county, Illinois, May 26, 1866. She married in Charlotte, Chittenden county, Vermont, September 20, 1820, Anson Wadleigh. They moved to St. Lawrence county, New York, where Mr. Wadleigh died in 1841.

Her children were:

i. Mary L. Wadleigh, b. —— ——. m. William Ward, and has six children.

ii. Willard C. Wadleigh, a farmer in West Stockholm, N. Y.; m. Alma Dowd, and has three children.
iii. Truman D. Wadleigh; d. in childhood.
iv. Ann B. Wadleigh; m. Royal Felton; had four children, and d. in Potsdam, St. Lawrence co., N. Y.
v. Luther Wadleigh, who m. Hannah Seeley; has two children. He is an attorney-at-law in Potsdam, N. Y.

132

HORACE COOLEY[8] COLE (*Jonathan,*[7] *Jonathan,*[6] *Jonathan,*[5] *Jonathan,*[4] *John,*[3] *John,*[2] *Thomas*[1]). The fifth child of Jonathan and Lydia (Daggett) Cole was born in Westmoreland, New Hampshire, September 29, 1802, and died in Fayette, Iowa, October 25, 1864. In 1825, at Madrid, New York, he married Delinda Smith, who was born in Malone, Franklin county, New York, February 15, 1806, and died in Fayette, March 22, 1876. He was a carpenter and also a shoemaker by trade.

The children of Horace Cooley and Delinda (Smith) Cole were:

239. i. Myron S., b. Jan. 18, 1826.
ii. Charlotte, b. in Madrid, N. Y., Sept. 29, 1829. In 1847 she m. Henry Childs, and in 1854 moved from New York to Illinois. In 1858 they moved to Iowa, where they lived until Mr. Child's death in 1869. She now lives with her daughter in Kearney, Neb. Their children were:
(i.) Simon Childs, b. in 1849; is m. and has three children. He is a farmer in Nebraska.
(ii.) Carroll Childs, b. in Ill. in 1856. He is a shoemaker; resides in Iowa, and has one child.
(iii.) Sidney Childs. He is a farmer in Nebraska, and has one child.
(iv.) The youngest child is a daughter, who is m. and lives in Kearney, Neb. Has three children.
iii. Amanda, b. June 4, 1833; d. Jan. 12, 1848.
240. iv. Oscar C., b. June 15, 1840.

133

LOUISA DURPHY[8] COLE (*Jonathan,*[7] *Jonathan,*[6] *Jonathan,*[5] *Jonathan,*[4] *John,*[3] *John,*[2] *Thomas*[1]. The seventh child of Jonathan and

Lydia (Daggett) Cole, was born in Charlotte, Chittenden county, Vermont, January 23, 1807, and died in Waterbury, Washington county, Vermont, January 26, 1884. She married in Starksboro, Addison county, Vt., October 4, 1837, Emery Taylor, of Huntington, Chittenden county. They afterwards moved to Waterbury, where they lived for many years, and where he died April 3, 1879.

Their children were:

i. Caroline Taylor, b. Feb. 8, 1840; d. Nov. 6, 1841.
ii. Bertram Taylor, b. Aug. 25, 1841; enlisted in the army and d. in the service Jan. 22, 1864.
iii. Ezra Carlton Taylor, b. June 11, 1843; m. Martha Mussy, of St. Albans, Vt., and is a passenger conductor on the C. Vt. R. R.
iv. George Emory Taylor, b. July 6, 1847; m. Maud Prentiss, of Milton, Vt., Oct. 1, 1879. He is a passenger conductor on the C. Vt. R. R.
v. Corrilla Taylor, b. Sept. 18, 1849; m. Frank H. Atherton, of Duxbury, Vt., Dec. 23, 1867. Has two sons:
(i.) Bertram Frank Atherton, b. Sept. 18, 1868.
(ii.) Luther Henry Atherton, b. Feb. 13, 1870.
Mr. Atherton is now sheriff of Washington co. and resides in Waterbury.
vi. Emma Louisa Taylor, b. Jan. 5, 1851.

134

Osmond Rasalas[8] Cole (*Jonathan,*[7] *Jonathan,*[6] *Jonathan,*[5] *Jonathan,*[4] *John,*[3] *John,*[2] *Thomas*[1]). The eighth child of Jonathan and Lydia (Daggett) Cole was born in Charlotte, Vermont, September 16, 1809. He married Betsy Boswick, October 20, 1831. In 1834 he removed to St. Lawrence county, New York, where he was a farmer for many years. He now resides in Elgin, Illinois.

The children of Osmand R. and Betsy (Boswick) Cole were:

i. Helen A., b. in Charlotte, Vt., July, 1832. Removed with the family to St. Lawrence co., N. Y., when a child. On April 7, 1853, she m. George Cass, in Stockholm, N. Y. Their children are:

(i.) Clarence Eugene Cass, b. in Elgin, Ill., Oct. 7, 1854; d. May 13, 1859.
(ii.) Maria Eliza Cass, b. in Swansey, N. H., March 15, 1861; d. Dec. 21, 1865.
(iii.) Alice Isabel Cass, b. in Swansey, N. H., Oct. 9, 1862; m. Ed E. Purington, Nov. 11, 1882.
(iv.) Ellen Elmira Cass, b. in Swansey, N. H., June 8, 1864.
(v.) Francis Burton Cass, b. in Erving, Mass., June 22, 1872. They reside in Erving, Mass.

241. ii. Lucius O., b. Jan. 15, 1834.

iii. Marcia Boswick, b. in St. Lawrence co., N. Y., March 20, 1838. On Dec. 31, 1855, she m. Hiram O. Day. They have five children:
(i.) Herbert Forest Day, b. Sept. 27, 1856.
(ii.) Effie Jenette Day, b. Jan. 1, 1859.
(iii.) Bertha Gertrude Day, b. June 3, 1861.
(iv.) Charles Horace Day, b. July 23, 1864.
(v.) Walter Vincent Day, b. April 23, 1867.

iv. Julius Isaiah, b. Feb. 11, 1840; d. Aug. 22, 1840.

242. v. Cyrus Jonathan, b. Sept. 26, 1841.

vi. Elizabeth Mabel, b. Oct. 1, 1843; d. July 9, 1845.

243. vii. Charles Wesley, b. March 8, 1846.

viii. Betsy Elmira, b. in St. Lawrence co., N. Y., Sept. 24, 1848. On Feb. 17, 1867, she m. George Parker. She d. June 12, 1878. Their children are:
(i.) Edward Justus Parker, b. Aug. 2, 1869.
(ii.) Carrie Isabel Parker, b. Jan. 22, 1872.
(iii.) Wilhelmina Parker, b. Aug. 23, 1874; d. Aug. 30, 1874.

135

CLEMENT CARLTON[8] COLE (*Jonathan,[7] Jonathan,[6] Jonathan,[5] Jonathan,[4] John,[3] John,[2] Thomas[1]*). The tenth child of Jonathan and Lydia (Daggett) Cole was born in Charlotte, Vermont, September 27, 1813. He married Fidelia Myers in 1840, born July 29, 1821, and moved to Illinois; thence to Fayette, Fayette county, Iowa, and thence to Sibley, Osceola county, Ia. He is a carpenter and joiner.

The children of Clement C. and Fidelia (Myers) Cole were:

244. i. Martin E., b. Nov. 17, 1840.

ii. Jane A., b. Dec. 21, 1844; m. Rev. J. C. Magee, an

M. E. clergyman, and lives in Albion, Ia. Her children are:

(i.) Lois Eastor, b. April 9, 1871.
(ii.) Carroll Cole, b. Jan. 5, 1873.
(iii.) Gertrude Mabel, b. Jan. 21, 1875.
(iv.) Jessie Eunice, b. Dec. 6, 1876.
(v.) Roy Frampton, b. April 15, 1878.
(vi.) Ralph Junius, b. June 3, 1880.
(vii.) Rollo S., b. Jan. 8, 1883.
(viii.) Percival Emera, b. Jan. 16, 1885.

iii. Jerusha A., b. April 17, 1848; m. D. C. McCausland, a real estate agent in Sibley, Osceola county, Ia. Their children are:

(i.) Mamie, b. ——. (iii.) Kittie, b. ——.
(ii.) Almeda, b. ——. (iv.) Flossie, b. ——.

245. iv. Frank, b. Nov. 30, 1856.

136

Celia Caroline[8] Cole (*Jonathan,[7] Jonathan,[6] Jonathan,[5] Jonathan,[4] John,[3] John,[2] Thomas[1]*). The eleventh and youngest child of Jonathan and Lydia Cole, was born in Charlotte, Vermont, February 14, 1816; moved in 1836 to St. Lawrence county, New York, with her father, having married the previous year (October 12, 1835) D. C. Sperry. They afterwards moved to Fayette, Iowa, where they lived, and where she died January 15, 1887.

Their children were:

i. David C. Sperry, b. in West Stockholm, N. Y., July 7, 1837; m. Alice J. McCausland, Nov. 13, 1866; was a merchant and banker in Fayette, Ia., and died May 22, 1873. He had four children, viz:

(i.) Bertha L., b. Oct. 16, 1867; m. Walter Brooks, Sept. 5, 1886.
(ii.) Walter Mack, b. Aug. 25, 1868; d. the same year.
(iii.) Willis A., b. March 5, 1870
(iv.) David C., b. July 31, 1873, and d. in 1874.

ii. Byron A. Sperry, b. in 1841, and d. in 1844.

iii. Olin H. Sperry, b. in 1843, and d. in 1844.

iv. Charles W. Sperry, b. in West Stockholm, N. Y., Nov. 27, 1847; m. Belle Franklin, Sept. 16, 1869. He was a merchant and banker of Fayette, Ia., and

C. W. Sperry.

is now a dealer and shipper of live stock at the same place. His children are:

(i.) Fred. B., b. Jan. 18, 1870.
(ii.) Louisa Lavin, b. Aug. 13, 1874.
(iii.) Maud F., b. April 9, 1878.

137

ABEL BARTON[8] COLE (*Abel,[7] Jonathan,[6] Jonathan,[5] Jonathan,[4] John,[3] John,[2] Thomas[1]*). The second child and oldest son of Abel and Louisa (Hutchins) Cole, was born in Westmoreland, New Hampshire, February 21, 1811. He was married (1) November 17, 1842, to Elizabeth Leach, of Westmoreland, who was born January 15, 1811, and died January 29, 1847. On May 27, 1848, Mr. Cole married (2) Maria Miller, of Putney, Vermont, who was born July 20, 1822. He inherited from his father the old farm on which the family first settled in Westmoreland, and has always occupied it. He has been a quiet and industrious farmer, never seeking or holding office; a man respected by his neighbors, attentive to his own affairs, and prosperous in the world.

The children of Abel Barton and Elizabeth (Leach) Cole were:

i. Louisa M., b. Sept. 29, 1843; m. Sept. 11, 1873, Andrew Pollard. They have one daughter, Sadie E., b. June 26, 1874. They live in Worcester, Mass.
ii. Martha E., b. Aug. 24, 1846; m. March 9, 1875, Edward E. Newton, a farmer of Royalston, Mass. They have one daughter, b. Sept. 15, 1877.

The children of Abel B. and Maria (Miller) Cole are:

iii. Francis M., b. Aug. 20, 1852; d. Aug. 22, 1852.
246. iv. Fred. F., b. Oct. 14, 1854.
247. v. Frank W., b. Sept. 9, 1864; d. in Bellows Falls, Vt., Feb. 7, 1887.

138

ANSON[8] COLE (*Abel,[7] Jonathan,[6] Jonathan,[5] Jonathan,[4] John,[3] John,[2] Thomas[1]*). The fourth child of Abel and Louisa (Hutchins) Cole, was born in Westmoreland, New Hampshire, April 26, 1815, and died there June 17, 1881. During nearly all of his manhood he was a merchant of Westmoreland South Village. He represented the town in the Legislature in 1860–61, and was town clerk in 1846, '47, '48, '49, '51, '52, '64. He married Harriet, a daughter of Increase Warren, Esq., of Westmoreland, October 16, 1838.

The children of Anson and Harriet (Warren) Cole were:

i. Luthera, b. March 12, 1840; d. unm. July 25. 1861.
ii. Stella, b. in Westmoreland, N. H., May 19, 1846. She married C. D. Miles, of Iowa, Dec. 26, 1866. She now lives in Denver, Col. Her children are:
(i.) John S. Miles, b. Nov. 15, 1867.
(ii.) Charles Henry Miles, b. Dec. 23, 1870.
(iii.) William Demming Miles, b. Aug. 15, 1874.
(iv.) Sarah A. Miles, b. Sept. 17, 1875.
248. iii. Dan Warren, b. May 10, 1851.
iv. Adine, b. Nov. 6, 1855. On April 15, 1885, she m. Alba Buffum, youngest son of Jewett E. Buffum, Esq., of Westmoreland. They reside in W.
249. v. Fred. Anson, b. March 17, 1858.

139

SUSAN L.[8] COLE WARE (*Abel,[7] Jonathan,[6] Jonathan,[5] Jonathan,[4] John,[3] John,[2] Thomas[1]*). The fifth child of Abel and Louisa (Hutchins) Cole, was born in Westmoreland, New Hampshire, November 13, 1817. She married March 15, 1838, James Royal Ware, a son of Levi and Peggy Ware. He was born April 11, 1811, and died on his farm in Westmoreland, November 25, 1857.

Their children were:

i. Eliza Cole Ware, b. Dec. 23, 1838; m. J. Frank Kathan, a contractor and builder of Westmoreland. They have two children:
(i.) Lilla Kathan; married to Charles Leach.
(ii.) Myrtie Kathan.
ii. Ann Elizabeth Ware, b. Jan. 14, 1841; d. May 5, 1857.
iii. Charles Leroy Ware, b. Dec. 3, 1843; unmarried; clerk in Keene, N. H.
iv. Oscar James Ware, b. May 27, 1846; m. Lizzie L. Franklin, March 23, 1880. Had three children,

only one of whom is now living. Is a farmer at the homestead in Westmoreland.

v. Wallace King Ware, b. July 22, 1848; m. Feb. 8, 1881, Grace Darling, of Chesterfield, N. H., where he now resides.

vi. Ellen Amelia Ware, b. Aug. 29, 1850; m. C. H. Bachelder, of Whitmanville, Mass.; now resides in East Douglas, Mass., and has several children.

vii. Frank H. Ware, b. Feb. 21, 1853; m. Nellie Cresey Foster, of Chesterfield. Is a druggist in Boston.

viii. Clara Louisa Ware, b. Sept. 16, 1855; d. July 21, 1873.

140

JONATHAN[8] COLE (*Abel,[7] Jonathan,[6] Jonathan,[5] Jonathan,[4] John,[3] John,[2] Thomas[1]*). Born in Westmoreland, New Hampshire, June 4, 1820. Married Hannah Howe, of Westmoreland, March 24, 1842. They have no children. Mr. Cole has for many years been one of the leading teachers of vocal music in Portland, Maine.

141

LARKIN G.[8] COLE (*Abel,[7] Jonathan,[6] Jonathan,[5] Jonathan,[4] John,[3] John,[2] Thomas[1]*). Born in Westmoreland, New Hampshire, May 9, 1824. Married Ellen E. Kathan, of Westmoreland, April 10, 1858. Has been a hotel keeper in Chester, Vermont, and other places. Now lives in West Brattleboro. Has no children.

142

GEORGE H.[8] COLE (*Abel,[7] Jonathan,[6] Jonathan,[5] Jonathan,[4] John,[3] John,[2] Thomas[1]*). Born June 4, 1826. Has been for many years a hotel keeper, residing in Chester, Vermont, and Leominster, Massachusetts, and is now proprietor of the American House, in Fitchburg, Massachusetts. He married, June 1, 1853, Elizabeth E. Stratton, of Walpole, New Hampshire.

The children of George H. and Elizabeth (Stratton) Cole are:

i. Lizzie E., b. Mar. 8, 1854; d. Sept. 2, 1855.
ii. Ella I., b. Feb. 4, 1856; m. Edward Howe, a professor of music in Worcester, Mass.
250. iii. William A., b. Nov. 6, 1857. Associated with his father in business.
251. iv. Walter S., b. Sept. 26, 1859.
v. Hattie A., b. Dec, 28, 1861.
vi. Mabel A., b. June 20, 1867.

143

LARKIN BAKER[8] COLES (*Martin,[7] Jonathan,[6] Jonathan,[5] Jonathan,[4] John,[3] John,[2] Thomas[1]*). The only child of Martin and Sally (Baker) Cole was born in Westmoreland, 1803. He early adopted the final s to his name. He was not much at home after his fourteenth year, all his early manhood being spent at school and in teaching. He studied medicine at Middlebury and at Castleton, Vermont, graduating at the latter place. He settled in Fitzwilliam, New Hampshire, and was afterwards located in Groton and Lowell, Massachusetts. Soon after his graduation he married Sarah Marshall Dyar, the daughter of a retired Boston merchant, then living in Leominster, Massachusetts, as a gentleman farmer. Miss Dyar was a very accomplished woman, and at the time of her marriage was the principal of a ladies' seminary. About 1837 Mr. Cole determined to study for the Baptist ministry, and after graduating at the Newton Theological Seminary, he was settled over the Baptist Church in Windsor, Vermont. He afterwards preached in Hopkinton, New Hampshire, and other towns in that region, and then went to South Reading (now Wakefield),

Massachusetts. His health was poor, and he gave up preaching and moved into Boston and devoted himself to lecturing and general literary work. He bought a place in Cambridgeport, Massachusetts, where he spent the last years of his life. In 1851 he published through Ticknor, Reed & Fields, of Boston, a book called the "Philosophy of Health." He had previously published a book against the use of tobacco. He was earnestly engaged in the Anti-Slavery movement of his time. About 1852 he began traveling in the interests of his book and also in the temperance work. While on one of these trips, he was stricken with pneumonia, in Louisville, Kentucky, and died at the Galt House in that city in January, 1856, and was buried in the Cave Hill Cemetery there. His wife reached his side less than an hour before his death.

Of the children of Larkin Baker and Sarah (Dyar) Coles, three died in early childhood. The others were:

i. Charlotte, b. —— ——. She m. Silas F. Smith, of Syracuse, N. Y. He was a salt manufacturer for several years, and during the late war he was Internal Revenue Collector, and is now in the fire insurance business in Syracuse. For many years he was the owner and editor of the *Syracuse Daily Journal*. Their children:

(i.) Stanley G. Smith, b. in June, 1853, and m. June, 1882, Effie Didina, of Syracuse.

(ii.) Isabel Augusta Smith, b. in Apr., 1855; m. in December, 1882, Rev. Geo. A. Gates, pastor of the Congregational Church in Upper Montclair, N. J.

ii. Georgiana, b. —— ——. She m. the Rev. Wm. A. Simmons, an M. E. clergyman of Georgia. They spend their winters in Florida, where they have a home, and their summers in travel. They have no children.

iii. Frances Sarah, b. —— ——. She resides in Syracuse, and is unmarried.*

---

*The editor is indebted to her for facts in regard to her father and his family.

144

Curtis Abijah[8] Cole (*Abijah,[7] Jonathan,[6] Jonathan,[5] Jonathan,[4] John,[3] John,[2] Thomas[1]*). The second child of Abijah and Lucy (Howe) Cole, was born in Westmoreland, New Hampshire, August 23, 1810. On March 16, 1842, he married (1) Olive Murphy, who was born January 29, 1823, and died July 24, 1849. On May 9, 1850, Mr. Cole married (2) Harriet E. Miller, who was born August 30, 1824.

The children of Curtis Abijah and Olive (Murphy) Cole were:

252. i. Charles Augustus, b. May 24, 1843.
ii. Henry Theodore, b. May 26, 1844; d. Oct. 31, 1844.
iii. George Winfield, b. March 7, 1846. He enlisted in Co. B, 2d Reg., Michigan Sharp-shooters, and served through the war. He died in Hot Springs, Middle Park, Col., April 5, 1884. He never married.
253. iv. Eugene, b. Sept. 10, 1847.
v. Lydia, b. July 22, 1849; d. July 22, 1849.

The children of Curtis A. and Harriet (Miller) Cole were:

vi. Charlotte E., b. Feb. 1, 1851; m. Oct. 20, 1867, William Rector, and lives in Mason, Ingham county, Mich.
254. vii. Carlisle R., b. Feb. 7, 1853.
viii. Lucy S., b. March 18, 1856; d. Nov. 9, 1869.
ix. Julia A., b. Feb. 26, 1861; m. George W. Lampson, Sept. 6, 1882. She lives in Riverdale, Gratiot co., Mich.
255. x. William H., b. Oct. 11, 1863.
xi. Clarence, b. Dec. 17, 1866; d. March 6, 1868.

145

Susan Maria[8] Cole Newton (*Abijah,[7] Jonathan,[6] Jonathan,[5] Jonathan,[4] John,[3] John,[2] Thomas[1]*). The third child of Abijah and Lucy (Howe) Cole, was born in Westmoreland, New Hampshire, June 24, 1812. She married Ezra Newton, April 29, 1830, who died December 3, 1883. She died in Oakdale, Worcester county, Massachusetts, August, 1886.

Her children are:

i. William L. Newton, resides in Cleveland, O.
ii. George B. Newton, died in Baltimore, Md.
iii. Polly D. Newton, m. Edward Oaks, and d. soon after.
iv. Delia Newton, m. Jerry Shepherd, of Oakdale, Mass.
v. Susan T. Newton, m. Mr. York, of Oakdale.
vi. Windsor Newton, a soldier, lives in Cincinnati, O.
vii. Lucius Newton, a soldier; killed on the railroad at Oakdale.
viii. William Newton, a soldier.

146

MARY EMELINE[8] COLE JAQUITH (*Abijah,[7] Jonathan,[6] Jonathan,[5] Jonathan,[4] John,[3] John,[2] Thomas[1]*). The fifth child of Abijah and Lucy (Howe) Cole, was born in Chesterfield, New Hampshire, May 18, 1816. She married Isaac Jaquith, of Mount Holly, May 10, 1838. He was born in Mount Holly, and died there December 11, 1884. On their marriage they settled on the farm where he died.

Their children were:

i. William H. Jaquith, b. in Mt. Holly, April 1, 1839. He was in Wisconsin when the war broke out, and enlisted in Co. G, 21st Wisconsin Vols. After the war he returned to Vermont, and engaged in the manufacture of lumber and chair stock in Weston for a number of years. In 1880 he was burned out for the third time, when he gave up business and removed to a farm in Landgrove, Bennington county. The following year he built a steam mill there and is engaged in his old business. He married Jan. 4, 1870, Mary P. Rideout, and has two children:
   (i.) Millard, b. June 30, 1872.
   (ii.) Ervin, b. Sept. 29, 1878.
ii. Mary Ellen, b. in Mt. Holly, July 3, 1841. She m. Aug. 1, 1866, William Johnson, a farmer of Mt. Holly, and settled in East Putney, Vt.

iii. Rollin Buckley, b. in Mt. Holly, March 19, 1844. He is engaged in lumber and chair manufacturing in Weston, Vt., on quite an extensive scale. He m. Aug. 15, 1869, Susan E. Shedd, of Mt. Holly. His children are:
- (i.) Grace Belle, b. July 14, 1872.
- (ii.) Harlan Clinton, b. March 20, 1874.
- (iii.) Maud Louise, b. Nov. 2, 1878.
- (iv.) Ray Burnette, b. July —, 1881.
- (v.) Arthur Floyd, b. May —, 1884.
- (vi.) A babe, b. Nov. 21, 1886.

iv. Julia Anna, b. Dec. 15, 1849, in Mt. Holly. She m. Dec. 15, 1868, David S. Persons, a farmer of Weston, Vt. . They now live in East Putney, Windham county, Vt., and have children:
- (i.) Minnie Eva, b. Sept. 20, 1869.
- (ii.) Julia Belle, b. March 13, 1875.

v. Frank Smith, b. in Mt. Holly, Jan. 18, 1852. He was for six years an attendant at the insane asylum at Middletown, Conn., and two years an overseer at the Connecticut State prison. He is now an attendant in the hospital at Cromwell, Ct. He is unmarried.

147

EMILY BETSY[8] COLE BENSON-ROBERTS (*Abijah,[7] Jonathan,[6] Jonathan,[5] Jonathan,[4] John,[3] John,[2] Thomas[1]*). The seventh child of Abijah and Lucy (Howe) Cole was born in Mt. Holly, Vermont, November 1, 1822. She married April 25, 1839, Benjamin McClure Benson, of Mt. Holly.

Their children were:

i. Henry McClure Benson, lives in Weston, Vt.

ii. Orison Benson, who was a member of a Vt. Reg. and d. in the service.

iii. Rodney Benson, who was a member of a Vt. Reg. and d. in the service.

iv. Lewis Eugene Benson; lives in Orwell, Vt.

v. Olive E. Benson; m. Alvin Atherton, of Ludlow, Vt.

vi. Clara I. Benson; m. Anthony Shuttuck, of Mechanicsville, Vt.

vii. Charles Benson; lives in Wilmington, Vt.

After Mr. Benson's death in August, 1858, she married William Roberts, of Weston, Vermont, October 16, 1864. She died there in March, 1885.

148

WILLIAM MARSHALL[8] COLE (*Abijah,[7] Jonathan,[6] Jonathan,[5] Jonathan,[4] John,[3] John,[2] Thomas[1]*). The eighth child of Abijah and Lucy (Howe) Cole was born in Mt. Holly, Vermont, November 16, 1826. He married October 20, 1853, Cornelia L. Chandler, who was born in Chester, Vermont, October 30, 1829. Mr. Cole lived for many years in Chester and North Springfield, Vermont. He is now a case maker in the Esty Organ Factory in Brattleboro, Vermont.

The children of William M. and Cornelia (Chandler) Cole are:

i. Nellie E., b. in Chester, Vt., Aug. 19, 1856; m. Mar. 24, 1880, Wm. E. Chittenden, who was b. in Wethersfield, Vt., Apr. 12, 1859.

ii. Minnie, b. in Chester, Vt., Apr. 25, 1859; d. in Brattleboro, Vt., Mar. 31, 1884.

iii. Lillie F., b. in Chester, Vt., Sept. 22, 1861.

149

CHARLES LEWIS[8] COLE (*Abijah,[7] Jonathan,[6] Jonathan,[5] Jonathan,[4] John,[3] John,[2] Thomas[1]*). The eighth child of Abijah and Lucy (Howe) Cole, was born in Mt. Holly, Vermont, May 31, 1831. He married (1) Helen E. Crowley, September 11, 1857. She died May 12, 1864, leaving no children. On December 31, 1865, he married (2) Fannie M. Phelen, who was born August 6, 1846. He lives in Mechanicsville, Vermont.

The children of Charles L. and Fannie (Phelen) Cole are:

256. i. William A., b. March —, 1867.
257. ii. George P., b. April 22, 1872.
258. iii. Curtis L., b. Nov. 10, 1876.

150

Oscar Brown[8] Cole (*Abijah,[7] Jonathan,[6] Jonathan,[5] Jonathan,[4] John,[3] John,[2] Thomas[1]*). The ninth child of Abijah and Lucy (Howe) Cole, was born in Mt. Holly, Vermont, March 25, 1833. He married July 5, 1866, Jennie M. Freeman, who was born in Rutland, Vermont, April 17, 1839. Mr. Cole was a case-maker in the Esty organ factory, in Brattleboro, Vermont. He died November 10, 1886.

The children of Oscar B. and Jennie (Freeman) Cole are:

i. Annie R., b. in Weston, Vt., April 17, 1869.
ii. Adah B., b. in Mt. Holly, Vt., June 8, 1874.

151

Horace Frederick Cole (*Abijah,[7] Jonathan,[6] Jonathan,[5] Jonathan,[4] John,[3] John,[2] Thomas[1]*). The tenth child of Abijah and Lucy (Howe) Cole, was born in Mt. Holly, Vermont, January 17, 1836. In 1861 he went to Wisconsin, and in the following year he enlisted in the Twenty-first Regiment, Wisconsin Volunteers, and served through the war. After he was mustered out he returned to Vermont, where he married, January 3, 1873, Abbie I. Hazelton, of Weston, Vermont, who was born February 12, 1848. They now live in Felchville.

D G Cole

The children of Horace and Abbie (Hazelton) Cole are:

259. i. Fred. H., b. Dec. 29, 1874.
260. ii. Bertie E., b. Sept. 6, 1876.
iii. Florence, b. Dec. 25, 1882.
261. iv. Harry J., b. May 13, 1885.

152

EDWIN A.[8] COLE (*Asa*,[7] *Abijah*,[6] *Abijah*,[5] *Jonathan*,[4] *John*,[3] *John*,[2] *Thomas*[1]). Born in Prospect Harbor, Maine, October 5, 1822; died in New York City, September 3, 1869. He was a seaman, and rose to be master of a ship. He sailed several voyages in that capacity from the port of New York. He was accidentally killed by a block falling from aloft while lying at anchor in New York harbor. He married Delia Moore, October 28, 1851. She was born in Gouldsborough, Maine, October 8, 1830.

The children of Edwin A. and Delia (Moore) Cole are:

i. Mary L., b. Aug. 2, 1854; m. Welch Moore, Nov., 1876.
262. ii. Adelbert H., b. April 28, 1857.
iii. Louella H., b. March 30, 1859.
iv. Fannie H., b. March 24, 1861; m. John M. Higgins in 1879; d. March 24, 1881.
v. Ellen S., b. July 8, 1864.
vi. Sara A., b. Feb. 3, 1866.
263. vii. Frank W., b. July 9, 1868.

153

DAVID G.[8] COLE (*Asa*,[7] *Abijah*,[6] *Abijah*,[5] *Jonathan*,[4] *John*,[3] *John*,[2] *Thomas*[1]). Born in Prospect Harbor, Maine, December 5, 1829. Married June 17, 1853, Sarah Allen, who was born November 28, 1834. Mr. Cole was for many years a ship-master in the sugar trade, sailing from New York. He has now retired, and lives in Prospect Harbor, where he is one of the leading citizens. He has long been noted for his kindness to those in trouble and distress.

The children of David G. and Sarah (Allen) Cole are:

i. Alice M., b. Nov. 28, 1854.
264. ii. John R., b. June 21, 1861.
265. iii. Louis P., Feb. 8, 1863.

154

BUCKMAN[8] COLE (*Asa,[7] Abijah,[6] Abjiah,[5] Jonathan,[4] John,[3] John,[2] Thomas[1]*). Born in Prospect Harbor, Maine, March 5, 1832. Died in Havana, Cuba, March 9, 1870. He was a ship-master, sailing from New York, and died in Cuba while on a voyage thither, of yellow fever. He married August 12, 1856, Marion Allen, of Prospect Harbor, who was born April 15, 1832.

The children of Buckman and Marion (Allen) Cole are:

266. i. Everard G., b. May 23, 1858.
267. ii. Henry M., b. May 2, 1860. Lives at Sebago Lake, Maine.
268. iii. Nathan, b. Mar. 8, 1862; m. Jan. 10, 1885, Edith B. Coombs. He lives in Prospect Harbor.
iv. Elizabeth, b. July 20, 1866.

155

MELVILLE[5] COLE (*Asa,[4] Abijah,[3] Abijah,[2] Jonathan[1]*). The youngest child of Asa and Sarah (Godfrey) Cole was born in Prospect Harbor, Maine, May 25, 1840. He has been a seaman and fisherman, and also engaged in business. He is unmarried.

156

MEHITABLE[8] COLE HANDY? (*Abijah,[7] Abijah,[6] Abijah,[5] Jonathan,[4] John,[3] John,[2] Thomas[1]*). The first child of Abijah and Rebecca

(Simonton) Cole, was born in Prospect Harbor, Maine, August 24, 1826. She married, November 8, 1846, Captain Joseph Handy, of Prospect Harbor. In later years Captain Handy has been a merchant in Prospect Harbor, having retired from the sea.

Their children are:

i. Marcus H. Handy, b. June 29, 1847; he m. Linda C. Handy, Oct. 22, 1870. He d. in Centrifugos, Cuba, while master of the ship Mariana. His children are:
(i.) Fred. A., b. March 21, 1872.
(i.) Dan N., b. June 11, 1874.
(iii.) Hattie M., b. July 11, 1876.

ii. Emma Handy, b. Aug. 25, 1853; m. Dec. 7, 1873, Stephen Clark, who was lost at sea while mate of the ship Teekalet, Sept., 1878. On Dec. 13, 1884, she m. Luere B. Deasy, Esq., an attorney-at-law in Bar Harbor, Me.

157

ADOLPHUS[8] COLE (*Abijah,[7] Abijah,[6] Abijah,[5] Jonathan,[4] John,[3] John,[2] Thomas[1]*). The second child of Abijah and Rebecca (Simonton) Cole, was born in Prospect Harbor, Maine, December 30, 1827, and died there June 16, 1876. He was a farmer and fisherman. He married Rachel Noonan, December 10, 1859. Mr. Cole enlisted in 1861, and served through the war as a member of Company C, Second Regiment Maine Volunteers.

The children of Adolphus and Rachael (Noonan) Cole are:

i. Judith Allen, b. Sept. 2, 1860; d. in infancy.
ii. Lois Noonan, b. April 5, 1865.
269. iii. Clarence Frost, b. Jan. 30, 1868.
270. iv. Emerson Tibbetts, b. Sept. 15, 1871.
271. v. Edgar Nichols, b. Feb. 15, 1873.
272. vi. Stephen Clark, b. Jan. 29, 1876.

158

ALLEN[8] COLE (*Abijah,*[7] *Abijah,*[6] *Abijah,*[5] *Jonathan,*[4] *John,*[3] *John,*[2] *Thomas*[1]). The fourth child of Abijah and Rebecca (Simonton) Cole, was born in Prospect Harbor, Maine, March 11, 1830. In his youth he was a seaman. He enlisted in 1861 as sergeant in Company C, Eleventh Regiment, Maine Volunteers, and lost an arm in the service. He was appointed light keeper at Mark Island, and held the place till 1877, when he was appointed postmaster at Prospect Harbor. He married, April 4, 1865, Ellen Wilkerson, of West Gouldsboro, Maine.

The children of Allen and Ellen (Wilkerson) Cole were:

i. Charlotte, b. Oct. 28, 1866; m. George L. Shaw, of Gouldsboro, Me., March 21, 1885.
ii. Jennie, b. Aug. 7, 1868; m. Frank L. Noonan, April 12, 1885.
iii. Rebecca, b. Oct. 19, 1875.
iv. Winnefred, b. March 27, 1882.
273. v. Allen M., b. March 27, 1884.

159

ISABEL P.[8] COLE CLEAVES (*Abijah,*[7] *Abijah,*[6] *Abijah,*[5] *Jonathan,*[4] *John,*[3] *John,*[2] *Thomas*[1]). The seventh child of Abijah and Rebecca (Simonton) Cole was born in Prospect Harbor, Maine, October 4, 1835. She married E. W. Cleaves, of Steuben, Maine, December 18, 1858.

Their children are:

i. Elvira K. Cleaves, b. Dec. 29, 1859.
ii. George Prescott Cleaves, b. Sept. 9, 1868.
iii. Elizabeth W. Cleaves, b. Apr. 3, 1873.
iv. Bell C. Cleaves, b. Feb. 11, 1878.

Mr. Cleaves is a blacksmith, and lives in Prospect Harbor, Maine.

M. A. Handy

160

SARAH[8] COLE HANDY (*Abijah,*[7] *Abijah,*[6] *Abijah,*[5] *Jonathan,*[4] *John,*[3] *John,*[2] *Thomas*[1]). The ninth child of Abijah and Rebecca (Simonton) Cole was born in Prospect Harbor, Maine, September 25, 1839. She married Captain William Handy, April 4, 1858. He died September 11, 1876.

Their children are:

i. Anna Handy, b. May 30, 1859.
ii. Orpha Handy, b. July 27, 1861; m. Stillman Coffin, of Gouldsboro, July 3, 1881.
iii. Arthur Handy, b. July 17, 1862.
iv. Estelle Handy, b. Sept. 11, 1865; m. B. F. Robbins, of East Sullivan, Me., 1883.
v. Edgar Handy, b. Sept. 7, 1868.
vi. Lois Handy, b. Oct. 11, 1873.

161

JAMES WOODBURY[8] COLE (*Abijah,*[7] *Abijah,*[6] *Abijah,*[5] *Jonathan,*[4] *John,*[3] *John,*[2] *Thomas*[1]). The eleventh child of Abijah and Rebecca (Simonton) Cole was born in Prospect Harbor, Maine, October 1, 1843. He married December 2, 1869, Hannah Crowley. Mr. Cole enlisted in Company C, Eleventh Regiment Maine Volunteers, and was wounded at the battle of Fair Oaks. He resides at Prospect Harbor.

The children of James Woodbury and Hannah (Crowley) Cole are:

274. i. George W., b. Oct. 3, 1871.
ii. Clara N., b. May 2, 1875.
iii. William W., b. June 29, 1877; d. Oct. 9, 1878.
275. iv. Ellery W., b. Dec. 12, 1879.
276. v. Edwin C., b. Apr. 29, 1881.
277. vi. Wilber V., b. Dec. 8, 1884.

162

CHARLES G.[8] COLE (*Abijah,[7] Abijah,[6] Abijah,[5] Jonathan,[4] John,[3] John,[2] Thomas[1]*). The youngest child of Abijah and Rebecca (Simonton) Cole was born in Prospect Harbor, Maine, January 22, 1845. He married September 19, 1870, Olive Martin Teale. For a number of years they resided in Pawtucket, Rhode Island, but now live in Gouldsboro, Maine.

Their only child is:

278. i. Casper, b. May 3, 1871.

163

ASA[8] COLE (*Asa,[7] Asa,[6] Abijah,[5] Jonathan,[4] John,[3] John,[2] Thomas[1]*). Born March 11, 1826. He was for several years a teacher in the public schools of Brooklyn, New York, and while there he married Sarah Merwin, of Delhi, New York. They soon after moved to West Medway, Massachusetts, where they have since lived.

The children of Asa and Sarah (Merwin) Cole were:

279. i. Henry Merwin, b. June 11, 1849.
ii. Arthur William, b. Aug. 27, 1853; d. Sept. 1, 1853.
iii. Marcia, b. July 11, 1855.
iv. Fred. S., b. April 17, 1859; d. March 27, 1854.
v. Edward S., b. March 4, 1860; d. March 4, 1860.

164

CHARLES H.[8] COLE (*Asa,[7] Asa,[5] Abijah,[5] Jonathan,[4] John,[3] John,[2] Thomas[1]*). Born in West Medway, Massachusetts, December 2, 1840. He is a shoe worker in the shoe factories of West Medway. He married Mary F. Chadwick, November 30, 1882.

Their children are:

280. i. Harold Otis, b. Jan. 20, 1884.
ii. A daughter, b. Nov. 23, 1885.

165

GEORGE T.[8] COLE (*Asa,*[7] *Asa,*[6] *Abijah,*[5] *Jonathan,*[4] *John,*[3] *John, Thomas*[1]). Was born in West Medway, Massachusetts, March 4, 1843. He married, March 31, 1864, Sibbie Wesson, of Holliston, Massachusetts. They live in West Shrewsbury, Massachusetts.

Their children are:

281. i. George Franklin, b. Feb. 27, 1868.
282. ii. Theodore Otis, b. Feb. 12, 1872.

166

ALBERT M.[8] COLE (*Asa,*[7] *Asa,*[6] *Abijah,*[5] *Jonathan,*[4] *John,*[3] *John,*[2] *Thomas*[1]). Was born in West Medway, Massachusetts, July 6, 1847. He married Ada J. Fish, of Medway, September 24, 1869. He is a shoe worker in the factories at Howard, Rhode Island.

Their children are:

283. i. Clinton D., b. May 4, 1869.
ii. Alice M., b. July 3, 1871.
284. iii. Myron Asa, b. July 13, 1876.

167

ELIZA ANN[8] COLE WALKER (*Benj. F.,*[7] *Asa,*[6] *Abijah,*[5] *Jonathan,*[4] *John,*[3] *John,*[2] *Thomas*[1]). The second child of B. F. and Adeline (Sherwood) Cole, was born in Highland Falls, New York, May 14, 1826, and died in Brooklyn, December 16, 1869. She married Stillman R. Walker, a native of Charlestown, New Hampshire, August, 1845. Mr. Walker was in business at 201 William street, as a manufacturer of and dealer in printers' supplies. He died in Brooklyn, June 30, 1866.

His children were:

i. Stillman R. Walker, b. July 13, 1849; m. Annie B. Boyce, Sept. 28, 1876. She d. in Sept., 1879, leaving a son, S. R. jr., b. March 30, 1878. Mr. Walker is now the head of the firm, carrying on the old business that his father founded.
ii. Edwin Floyd Walker, b. Oct. 16, 1856; unmarried. Lives in Brooklyn.
iii. Mary Eliza Walker, b. 1858; d. in Brooklyn, 1877.

168

ALMENA[8] COLE PELOUZE–PENDLETON (*B. F.*,[7] *Asa*,[6] *Abijah*,[5] *Jonathan*,[4] *John*,[3] *John*,[2] *Thomas*[1]). The third child of B. F. and Adeline (Sherwood) Cole, was born in West Point, New York, October 17, 1828. She married Edwin Pelouze, November 4, 1844. He enlisted in the army as captain, Company D, 155th Regiment New York Volunteers, and was killed in battle at Reams Station, Virginia, August 25, 1864.

Their children were:

i. Edward Pelouze, b. July 14, 1846. He enlisted in the 13th Reg. N. Y. Vols., three months men; re-enlisted and served through the war. He went in as a drummer boy and came out as a dispatch bearer for Gen. Meade. He married Annia B. Sayers, at Camden, N. J., Dec. 23, 1868. Their children are:
   (i.) Edward Albert, b. Oct. 13, 1872.
   (ii.) Geo. Ripley, b. Jan. 5, 1874.
   (iii.) Percy Starr, b. July 30, 1876.
   (iv.) Richard Floyd, b. May 8, 1879.

   He is now superintendent of the Baltimore Type Foundry, Baltimore, Md.
ii. Almena Pelouze, b. Jan. 10, 1850, in Brooklyn; m. Wm. B. Ripley, a R. R. contractor of Brooklyn, Aug. 18, 1866. She has no children.
iii. Richard Floyd Pelouze, b. in Camden, N. J., Sept. 21, 1857; m. in Louisville, Ky., Leila Pearson, Mar. 13, 1883. He is a commercial traveler, living in Louisville.

iv. Fannie Maud Pelouze, b. April 29, 1860; m. Wm. Pendelton, of Brooklyn, June 19, 1883. Has one son:
   (i.) Howard Pendelton, b. Nov. 12, 1884.

After the death of Captain Pelouze his widow married Elias C. Pendleton, of Brooklyn, September 17, 1874. There she now resides.

169

CHARLES[8] COLE (*Benj. F.,*[7] *Asa,*[6] *Abijah,*[5] *Jonathan,*[4] *John,*[3] *John,*[2] *Thomas*[1]). The fourth child of B. F. and Adeline (Sherwood) Cole, was born in Bayonne, New Jersey, October 16, 1830, and died in Brooklyn, April 16, 1868. He married Margaret Murfin in Brooklyn, November (?) 1, 1853.

His children were:

i. Adele E., b. Oct. 13, 1860.
ii. Clara W., b. Oct. 17, 1862; m. Joseph W. Betz, a merchant tailor in Brooklyn, June 12, 1883, and has children:
   (i.) Claude L. Betz, b. April 8, 1884.
   (ii.) Chas. F. Betz, b. Dec. 6, 1885.
iii. Mary M., b. April 22, 1867.

170

RICHARD FLOYD[8] COLE (*Benjamin F.,*[7] *Asa,*[6] *Abijah,*[5] *Jonathan,*[4] *John,*[3] *John,*[2] *Thomas*[1]). The sixth child of B. F. and Adeline (Sherwood) Cole was born in New Windsor, New York, December 25, 1835, and died in Brooklyn, December 6, 1872. He succeeded his brother-in-law, Mr. Walker, in business in printers' furnishings, in William street, and in a few years accumulated a large fortune. He married Catherine Foley, April 4, 1861.

Their children are:

i. Addie E., b. Jan. 8, 1862.
ii. Katie H., b. Feb. 9, 1865.
285. iii. Richard Franklyn, b. Feb. 18, 1872.

171

Jeremiah[8] Cole (*B. F.*,[7] *Asa*,[6] *Abijah*,[5] *Jonathan*,[4] *John*,[3] *John*,[2] *Thomas*[1]). The eighth child of B. F. and Adeline (Sherwood) Cole was born in Brooklyn, January 22, 1840. He married Mary Ferdinand in Brooklyn, July, 1866.

They have one child:

i. Lizzie, b. Mar., 1867.

Mr. Cole enlisted as a private in Company B, Fourteenth Regiment New York Volunteers, and served through the war.

172

John Adams[8] Cole (*John*,[7] *Asa*,[6] *Abijah*,[5] *Jonathan*,[4] *John*, *John*,[2] *Thomas*[1]). The only son of Captain John and Elizabeth (Shaw) Cole, was born in Westmoreland, New Hampshire, December 16, 1838. After an academic course at the Kimbal Union Academy at Meridan, New Hampshire, he entered the engineering office of Thomas Doane, of Boston, Massachusetts where he remained three years; was afterwards engaged as civi engineer on the State survey of the Sudbury, Meadows Mysti Water-works. In August, 1862, he volunteered as a delegate o the United States Christian Commission, and went to the Army o the Potomac, then on the Peninsular. After the battle of Antietam returned to New England and spent three months in addressing public meetings in the larger cities and organizing societies for the commission work. In January, 1863, he was appointed general field agent for the commission for the armies east of the Alleghenies and until the end of the war was engaged in the field. Ove $3,000,000 were expended for supplies, etc., in his department After the surrender at Appomattox, at which he was present, h went in the service of the commission to Louisiana and Texas

For one year he was in New York City as the secretary of the American Christian Commission, and then located in Washington and opened an office as a civil engineer. He was for several years secretary and financial agent of the Howard University, and president of the Lincoln Mission. In 1872 he removed to Chicago, Illinois, and is at present engaged in engineering, and among other public works, has constructed a water tunnel under Lake Michigan one mile in length, for the Hyde Park water-works. He has been city engineer of Hyde Park for many years.

He married December 15, 1870, in Washington, D. C., Julia Maud Alvord, who was born in Boston, Massachusetts, August 8, 1847. She was the daughter of John Watson Alvord (born in East Hampton, Connecticut, April 18, 1807), and Myrtilla Mead Peck (born in Greenwich, Connecticut, October 11, 1819), who were married June 3, 1845.

The children of John A. and Julia (Alvord) Cole are:

286. i. Edward Smith, b. Dec. 19, 1871.
ii. Julia Elizabeth, b. Jan. 31, 1875.

173

ELLA AMELIA[8] COLE-BARROWS (*John,*[7] *Asa,*[6] *Abijah,*[5] *Jonathan,*[4] *John,*[3] *John,*[2] *Thomas*[1]). Daughter of Captain John and Elizabeth (Shaw) Cole, born in Hartford, Connecticut, July 7, 1841. She was educated at Kimball Union Academy, where she graduated in 1858. After graduation she was employed as a teacher in academies at Meridan, New Hampshire, Pittsfield, Massachusetts, and in Ogdenburg, New York. During the war she took an active interest in relief work, and in 1864 went into the service of the Diet Kitchen Department of the United States Christian Commission, having, with one other, charge of the preparation of food in the Cavalry Corps Hospital at City Point, and also at post hospital in Alexandria, Virginia. The duties of these positions were very arduous and important, giving great relief to hundreds of the sick and wounded from the last campaigns of the war. In 1866 she was associated with Rev. E. P. Smith in the freedmen's work of the American Missionary Association at Cincinnati, and afterwards in New York. In 1868–9 she was the representative of that society in Washington, and was very efficient in the organization of the Lincoln Industrial Mission, and in the care of the needy colored people of that city. She was married at her father's house in Medway, Massachusetts, January 23, 1872, to Thomas Barrows, Esq., a wholesale merchant of Chicago, Illinois. For the next two years her residence was in Chicago and its suburbs.

Mr. Barrows was an active member of the Tabernacle Church (Congregational), and superintendent of its Sunday School — one of the largest in the city. Two years later, owing to failing health, they moved to Oakland, California, and still later to Nordhoff, San Beunaventura county, where they still reside in the beautiful Ojai valley.

Their only child:

i. David Prescott, b. June 27, 1873, in Ravenswood, Ill.

174

Arthur Wells[8] Cole (*John,*[7] *Asa,*[6] *Abijah,*[5] *Jonathan,*[4] *John,*[3] *John,*[2] *Thomas*[1]). The only living son of Captain John and Mary E. (Wells) Cole, born in Westmoreland, New Hampshire, March 2, 1856. Most of his early life was spent in Medway, Massachusetts. At the age of fourteen he entered the classical course of Phillips Academy, Andover, Massachusetts, and graduated in 1873. He graduated at Yale College in 1877, and spent the next year in travel in the South and at the Harvard Law school.

The year of 1878–79 was spent in travel in California and Ore-

Frank T. Cole.

gon. In 1880 he settled in Chicago, and engaged in the study of engineering and architecture. He is now a member of a firm in Ashland block, Chicago.

He is unmarried.

175

FRANK THEODORE[8] COLE (*Theodore*,[7] *Asa*,[6] *Abijah*,[5] *Jonathan*,[4] *John*,[3] *John*,[2] *Thomas*[1]). The oldest child of Captain Theodore and Livilla (Gleason) Cole, was born in Brattleboro, Windham county, Vermont, June 22, 1853. When six years of age his parents removed to Westminster, in the same county, and there his childhood was passed. The family left Westminster in 1866, and that year was spent by him in school in Keene, New Hampshire. The home having been established in Waverly Village, Belmont, Massachusetts, he attended the High School of that town. In 1870 he entered the classical course at Phillips Academy, Andover, Massachusetts. After remaining two years he went to Williston Seminary, East Hampton, Massachusetts, where he graduated in June, 1873. He entered the Williams College the same fall, and received his degree of A. B. on his graduation in 1877. That fall he entered the Columbia Law School, New York City, teaching in private schools when not in attendance on the lectures. He graduated in 1879, receiving the degree of LL. B., and was admitted to the New York bar in Kings county. In December of that year he went to Ohio, locating in Columbus, where he was admitted to the bar in February, 1880, and immediately began practice in partnership with his old school and college class-mate and friend, Bryan Collins, under the firm name of Collins & Cole, and has since continued in the practice of his profession. He has been active and prominent in the charitable and public enterprises of the city, especially in connection with the Y. M. C. A., the Law and Order League, the

Sunday School Missions, etc. He is a member of the First Congregational Church, and an efficient worker in church and society.

He is unmarried.

176

William Henry[8] Cole (*Theodore,*[7] *Asa,*[6] *Abijah,*[5] *Jonathan,*[4] *John,*[3] *John,*[2] *Thomas*[1]). Born in Brattleboro, Vermont, August 19, 1854. For two years was a clerk in a Boston wholesale house. In 1874 he went to Wyoming Territory, and remained there until 1877, when, after an eight months' stay in New Hampshire, he went to California. For eight years was a wheat farmer on the San Joaquin river. In the spring of 1886 he returned to New England and settled in Westminster, Vermont. He married Addie M. Greene, daughter of Rev. James B. Greene, of San Joaquin county, California, June 3, 1883.

They have children:

i. Edith, b. June 9, 1884.
ii. Mabel Ruth, b. Feb. 5, 1887.

177

Charles Ward[8] Cole (*Charles H.,*[7] *Asa,*[6] *Abijah,*[5] *Jonathan,*[4] *John,*[3] *John,*[2] *Thomas*[1]). Son of Capt. Charles H. and Caroline (Cutler) Cole, born in Rindge, New Hampshire, October 23, 1848. On January 15, 1871, he married A. M. Hoag. He was in the freight department of the B. H. & E. R. R. at New Haven for some years, and now resides in Birmingham, Connecticut.

Their children are:

i. Florence A., b. 1871.
ii. Caroline Goldsmith, b. 1873; d. 1875.
iii. Lena Susan, b. 1875.

178

JULIA ANN[8] COLE WEBB (*Levi,[7] Levi,[6] John,[5] Jonathan,[4] John,[3] John,[2] Thomas[1]*). The first child of Levi and Lygusta (Allen) Cole was born in Watertown, New York, March 26, 1809. In 1830 she married Henry Webb, of Nashville, Chautauqua county, New York. He was born September 16, 1811. He moved to Michigan, and settled in Monroe, where they have since lived.

Their children are:

i. Egbert Webb, b. Jan. 6, 1834. He m. Hattie E. Nowlen, Jan. 20, 1834. He is a carpenter. His children are:
   (i.) Merrill E., b. Dec. 3, 1862.
   (ii.) Clarence E., b. Apr. 3, 1866.
   (iii.) Frank E., b. Apr. 17, 1870.
   (iv.) Eva M., b. July 29, 1872.
   (v.) Bessie, b. Oct. 10, 1877.

ii. Adeline L., b. Apr. 11, 1835; m. July 5, 1860, Ashley Calkins. Their children are:
   (i.) Burton Calkins, b. Feb. 5, 1861.
   (ii.) Edgar R., b. May 18, 1863.
   (iii.) Henshall V., b. Aug. 24, 1866.
   (iv.) Nora, b. Sept. 21, 1873.

iii. Wm. H., b. Oct. 29, 1836; m. Rosina Ross, Aug. 17, 1862. His children are:
   (i.) Charles B., b. Aug 22, 1863.
   (ii.) Etta May, b. Jan. 17, 1867.
   (iii.) Jennie, b. Sept. 16, 1869.

iv. Rollin S., b. Apr. 6, 1839; m. Sept. 20, 1865, Emma E. Nowlen. His children are:
   (i.) Ida F., b. Nov. 12, 1867.
   (ii.) Olive B., b. Nov. 17, 1872.
   (iii.) Levant E., b. Sept. 6, 1876.
   (iv.) Rollin H., b. Oct. 18, 1881.

v. James E., b. June 2, 1841; m. Mrs. Sarah Sherlock, Oct. 22, 1868. His children are:
   (i.) Jessie, b. Dec. 8, 1870.
   (ii.) Josie, b. Sept. 4, 1874.
   (iii.) Winnie, b. June 3, 1880.

vi. Calvin, b. Jan. 29, 1843; m. Rhoda Bodell, Dec. 29, 1880. Children:
   (i.) Myrtle A., b. Jan. 5, 1883.
   (ii.) Lillie F., b. Aug. 13, 1885.

vii. Alice L., b. June 27, 1847; unm.
viii. J. Ella, b. Dec. 13, 1848; unm.
ix. Fannie E., b. Oct. 1, 1851; m. Thomas P. Bodell, Oct. 11, 1870. Children:
(i.) Benj. F., b. Mar. 4, 1872.
(ii.) Wm. W., b. Feb. 23, 1874.
(iii.) Barton W., b. Nov. 28, 1875.
(iv.) Minnie B., Sept. 24, 1877.
(v.) Bertha E., b. Aug. 19, 1879.
(vi.) Alice A., b. Nov. 4, 1882.
(vii.) Infant, b. Sept. 10, 1886.

179

EGBERT L.[8] COLE (*Levi,*[7] *Levi,*[6] *John,*[5] *Jonathan,*[4] *John,*[3] *John,*[2] *Thomas*[1]). The second child and oldest son of Lygusta (Allen) Cole, was born in Watertown, New York. He married Lucy Davis, of Louisville, Kentucky, in June, 1846. He was a contractor and builder in Louisville, and accumulated considerable property there, but the decline of business at the beginning of the war somewhat impaired his fortune. He died in June, 1863.

His children were:

287. i. Merrill, b. in Louisville. Served in the Confederate army, and after the war enlisted in the U. S. army. At the close of his five years' term of service, about 1870, he settled in Brown county, Texas, where he is supposed to be at the present time.
288. ii. Levi, b. in Louisville. He m. Ella Garnet, of Hart county, Ky., and settled there.
iii. Ida, b. in Louisville, and m. George Payne, a printer of Louisville. They moved to Eureka, Cal., where he is editor of a paper. They have one child, a daughter.

180

CAROLINE[8] COLE BATCHELDOR (*Levi,*[7] *Levi,*[6] *John,*[5] *Jonathan,*[4] *John,*[3] *John,*[2] *Thomas*[1]). The fourth child of Levi and Lygusta (Allen) Cole was born in Coburg, Canada, in 1821. She married

George Batcheldor at Cleveland, Ohio, November 26, 1836, and two years later moved to Louisville, Kentucky, where they remained for two years, when they removed to Bloomfield, Nelson county, Kentucky, where she has since lived. Mr. Batcheldor was an architect and builder, and his work is to be seen in all parts of Nelson and the adjoining counties. The beauty and convenience of the churches and mansions designed by him, is especially noticeable to this day. He was an enthusiastic and devoted member of the Masonic order. He died May 29, 1879.

His children were:

i. Addie Batcheldor, b. in Monroe, Mich., July 18, 1836. She m. Geo. Moore, of Bloomfield. Their children are:
  (i.) Geo. Augustus Moore, a carpenter and builder of Bloomfield. He is m. and has three children.
  (ii.) Carrie Moore; m. Elliott Lewis, of Jefferson co., Ky.
  (iii.) Minnie Moore; m. Wm. Spyby, of Louisville.

ii. Maria Batcheldor, b. in Louisville, Feb., 1840; m. Edward Lewis, of Bloomfield. They have no children.

iii. Madeline Batcheldor, b. in Bloomfield, Jan. 6, 1843; m. Joseph Broadbent, of Bloomfield. They have no children.

iv. George Batcheldor, b. Sept. 3, 1845; moved to Iowa, and m. Jane Buttercase. He is a carpenter and builder in Riverton, Ia., and has five children:
  (i.) Addie.
  (ii.) James.
  (iii.) Robert.
  (iv.) Callie.
  (v.) Joseph B.

  In Nov., 1886, he was elected Clerk of the Courts of his county.

v. Fannie Batcheldor, b. Oct. 30, 1847. She m. Joseph Lindsay, of Bloomfield. He is now a merchant in Wyandotte, Kan. Has six children:
  (i.) Sarah.
  (ii.) Russell.
  (iii.) Charles.
  (iv.) Eugene.
  (v.) Milton.
  (vi.) Elsie.

vi. James Batcheldor, b. Dec. 9, 1849. He m. Lizzie Clark, of Spencer co., Ky. Is an architect and builder in Bloomfield. Has four children:

(i.) Lina. (iii.) Addie.
(ii.) Susie. (iv.) An infant daughter.

vii. Charles Batcheldor, b. Sept. 6, 1851. Is a carpenter and builder in Bloomfield. He m. May Houghton, of Spencer co., Ky., and has two daughters:

(i.) Callie. (ii.) Maggie.

viii. Mary Batcheldor, b. Sept. 15, 1858; m. Isaac Williams. He owns and manages a large flouring mill in Bloomfield. They have no children.

ix. Callie Batcheldor, b. 1860, d. Aug. 11, 1880. The following memorial was published:

EDITOR RECORD:—An unusual sadness has existed in this community for the past few days, caused by the decease of Miss Callie Batcheldor. It pleased God to take her from us on the 11th inst.

She was a young lady of twenty summers, possessing rare personal beauty, of a remarkably modest, retiring and sweet Christian disposition and temper. She was one of the few girls who kept herself absolutely aloof from demoralizing parties and hops. There were two places dearer to her than all others, viz: home and her church.

Two books were her every-day companions, her hymn book and her Bible. Recently, hardly anything has been more interesting to the writer, than to trace her hand through these two volumes. The pencil, geranium leaves and sprigs of bleeding-heart, mark the finest hymns of our collection and the sweetest promises of inspiration. Her cards, mottoes, drawings and compositions show plainly that the current of her thoughts were pure and heavenly.

As a member of the Sunday School and church she was unexceptionally true and faithful.

Her dying testimony was the sweetest of her life. In answer to the inquiries of her pastor, she said: "I can trust the Saviour." "Give my friends my love and good will, and tell them I am happy." She also requested her pastor to use the burial service of the church at her funeral, not to preach a sermon, but to talk comfortingly to her friends, and to sing "Jesus Lover of My Soul" and "Come Ye Disconsolate."

The following lines were written by her during her last sickness: "When I have gone from earth, when my place is vacant, when my pilgrimage is over, with thy faithful heart keep my memory green."

The last night of her stay on earth, we watched at her bedside, witnessing her struggles and triumphs. Without, the face of the sky presented the appearance of alternate clouds and stars; within the chamber of death were scenes of unutterable pain and the "peace that passes understanding." Death lost his terrors, and was viewed as the messenger of sweet release.

The weary night passed, and as the sun came up through the gates of the East, ushering in the rosy morning of a new day, Callie Batcheldor, in the morning of a beautiful womanhood, passed through the portals of death into the bright morning of a blissful immortality.

At the tolling of the bell the great populace assembled in the church, and, with a greater unanimity than I have ever witnessed, thoughtfully and tearfully paid the last tribute of respect to one whom none could think of but in kindness, and then accompanied her to the quiet graveyard. Never were mortal remains handled by human hands more tenderly. Not a clod was heard to fall on her coffin. Loving hands decorated her grave with floral wreaths and crosses, and there loving friends lingered and consecrated her grave with many tears,

"But when the sun in all his state,
Illumed the eastern skies,
She passed through glory's morning gate,
And walked in Paradise."

D. W. R.

IN MEMORY OF CALLIE BATCHELDOR.

Callie has crossed the stream of death,
The cold and chilly tide,
And she has landed safe,
For Jesus was her guide.

They will lay her in the grave,
To sleep her final sleep,
And angels o'er her dust
Will their loving vigils keep.

There'll be a vacant seat at home,
By the evening fireside;
A lovely form will be missed
That was a family pride.

Kind brothers will breathe her name
And tears unbidden flow;
Loving sisters will mourn for her
In accents sad and low.

No more her winning smile
A mother's eye will meet;
No more her gladsome voice
Sisters and brothers will greet.

Oh, you are lonely now,
Your hearts with grief are riven,
But it will soothe each wound to know
You have a tie in heaven.

Weep not, mother, sisters and brothers,
A harp and crown are her's;
She is an angel now,
And shall forever be.

181

JAMES E.[8] COLE (*Levi,*[7] *Levi,*[6] *John,*[5] *Jonathan,*[4] *John*[3], *John,*[2] *Thomas*[1]). The fifth child of Levi and Lygusta (Allen) Cole was born in Coburg, Canada, June, 1822. He m. Janette Hunt, of Maumee City, Ohio, in 1846. He now lives in Helena, Montana Territory.

His children are:

i. Kate, b. —— ——. m. John Ming, of Helena.
ii. Ida; unm.
iii. Vernia; unm.

182

GILBERT L.[8] COLE (*Levi,*[7] *Levi,*[6] *John,*[5] *Jonathan,*[4] *John,*[3] *John,*[2] *Thomas*[1]). The seventh child and third son of Levi and Lygusta (Allen) Cole, was born in Coburg, Canada, July 22, 1828. When he was quite young his father left Coburg, and after residence of several years in New York and Ohio, settled, in 1837, in Monroe, Michigan. The story of his life shall be told by himself:

"BEATRICE, NEBRASKA.

* * * * * * *

"I was early set to work in father's carpenter shop, and had but little schooling when a boy. In April, 1846, I left home; stopped awhile in Louisville, Kentucky, and the same summer went to St. Louis by river, and thence to Galena, Illinois. I stopped off for a day at Navoo, and saw Uncle and Aunt Stiles for the last time. The city was in an uproar, and under martial law, so I left the same day and went up the river to Kickapoo Pinery, Wisconsin. During the year that I spent there the Territory became a State. The next year I went home via Mackinac.

"In 1848 I went to Cincinnati to finish my trade. I worked on the Burnet House, attended the Mechanics' Institute, and took lessons in drawing and modeling. I worked at my trade in Nelson, Anderson, Woodford, Marion, and Bullitt counties, Kentucky, till the fall of 1851, when I returned home to Monroe, Michigan.

"On the 10th of March, 1852, I started, in company with twenty-three men and one woman, on the overland route to California. We crossed the Mississippi at Warsaw, Illinois, and reached St. Joseph on May 1. On the 5th we crossed the

Gilbert L. Cole

Missouri about twenty-five miles above St. Joseph, and on the next morning (Sunday) first saw the beautiful 'plains' of the great Territory of Nebraska.

"We had now left all civilization behind us. I crossed the Big Blue River, which I can now look out of my window and see, about twelve miles below here. On the 9th of May, followed up the Little Blue, and struck the Platte River at Kearney. On the 27th one of our party died. We forded the south fork of the Platte at its mouth, and followed up the north fork on its south side.

"On June 24 we reached South Pass, burned our wagons, and begun 'packing.' On the Big Sandy we halted. The right hand road led to 'Sublett's Cut-off,' the left to Salt Lake City. The majority voted to go to the right, so I did not see the city nor Aunt Stiles.

"We spent July 4 at 'Soda Springs' with the Shoshone Indians. The company had now all broken up, and going down the Humboldt Valley my little party of three had nothing to eat for twenty-one days but dead stock and willow bark. Our sufferings were terrible, as we found no water fit to drink.

"We got to Carson Valley July 28, crossed the summit of the Sierra Nevadas on August 7, and got into 'Hangtown,' now Placerville, California, August 10, after a journey of five months, less six days.

"After a time I returned via Panama, and arrived in New York City January 10, 1854. After a visit to Vermont I returned to Monroe.

"December 4, 1854, I married at Monroe, Michigan, Frederika Wantzschmitt, who was born in Baumberg, Bavaria, Germany, November 17, 1835, and in 1857 moved to Prairie Du Chien, Wisconsin, and in 1859 (April) to Sidney, Iowa.

"On August 15, 1862, I enlisted in Company E, Twenty-ninth Iowa Volunteer Infantry, and served on the Lower Mississippi and in Arkansas; was wounded and sent to Jefferson Barracks, St. Louis. My wife and boys came to see me there, and remained there during the war. On my recovery I was promoted to a lieutenancy in the colored troops, and served in the Eighteenth Regiment in the fall of 1864, against Price in Missouri, and was then sent to Camp Nelson, Kentucky, where I was attached to Company A, One Hundred and Twenty-fourth United States Cavalry Infantry.

"In November, 1865, I was ordered to bring my command to Louisville, and was mustered out. I had earned by competitive examination a first lieutenant's commission in the regular army, and it was offered me by the same hand that held my discharge, but my health being poor, and my parents old and needing my care, I declined it.

"I returned to Sidney, Iowa, and stayed there till father and mother died. I moved to Beatrice, Nebraska, in the fall of 1878, and have moved along in the even tenor of my way ever since."

Mr. Cole is an architect and superintendent.

The children of Gilbert L. and Frederika Cole are:

289. i. Carson V., b. at Adrian, Mich., May 10, 1856.
290. ii. Frank W., b. in Sidney, Ia., July 21, 1859.
291. iii. George M., b. in Sidney, Ia., Sept. 10, 1861.
292. iv. William S., b. at Jefferson Barracks, Mo., April 28, 1864.

293. v. Edward K., b. at Sidney, Ia., Sept. 22, 1866.
vi. Callie B., b. at Sidney, Ia., Oct. 29, 1869.
vii. Mollie E., b. at Riverton, Ia., March 14, 1872; d. there Oct. 8, 1873.
viii. Nellie W., b. at Riverton, Ia., March 30, 1874.
ix. Alice C., b. at Riverton, Ia., Jan. 14, 1876.
x. Josie, b. at Riverton, Ia., March 31, 1878.

183

THOMAS[8] COLE (*Salmon,[7] Salmon,[6] John,[5] Jonathan,[4] John,[3] John,[2] Thomas[1]*). The first son of Salmon and Isabella (Heatley) Cole, was born December 1, 1820; married (1) Mariake Powers, of Lachute, Quebec, in November, 1854. In the following May emigrated to Iowa, where he took up land and commenced life as a farmer. His wife died in 1860, and in 1865 he married (2) Mrs. Verdy (formerly a Miss Douglass). In 1875 he removed to Central Dakota, where he still lives.

His children by his first wife were:

i. ———— (a daughter).
ii. ———— (a daughter).

The children by the second wife were:

iii. ———— (a daughter).
iv. ———— (a daughter).
v. ———— (a daughter).
294. vi. ———— (a son).

184

JAMES[8] COLE (*Salmon,[7] Salmon,[6] John,[5] Jonathan,[4] John,[3] John,[2] Thomas[1]*). The second son of Salmon and Isabella (Heatley) Cole, was born on March 14, 1826. He married in December, 1850, Elizabeth Longe, and emigrated to Ingham county, Michigan, the following year. He was a blacksmith by trade. He died in the year 1882, and left a family who are still living in Ingham county.

185

WILLIAM HEATLEY[8] COLE (*Salmon,*[7] *Salmon,*[6] *John,*[5] *Jonathan,*[4] *John,*[3] *John,*[2] *Thomas*[1]). The third son and fifth child of Salmon and Isabella (Heatley) Cole, was born May 3, 1828. He married, April, 1855, Isabella Thompson, and emigrated to Grand Haven, Michigan, where he died in October, 1863.

186

MARK DOUGLASS[8] COLE (*Salmon,*[7] *Salmon,*[6] *John,*[5] *Jonathan,*[4] *John,*[3] *John,*[2] *Thomas*[1]). The fourth son and seventh child of Salmon and Isabella (Heatley) Cole, was born July 16, 1836. He married, June 5, 1859, Elizabeth Thompson, and emigrated to Michigan in May, 1860.

187

WILLARD[8] COLE (*Salmon,*[7] *Salmon,*[6] *John,*[5] *Jonathan,*[4] *John,*[3] *John,*[2] *Thomas*[1]). The fifth son and eighth child of Salmon and Isabella (Heatley) Cole, was born April 22, 1838. He married, June 5, 1859, Jane Bothwell, of Chatham, Argentine county, Quebec, and now lives at Hawksbury, Prescott county, Ontario, engaged in farming.

His children are:

304. i. Salmon, b. Feb. 4, 1861.
ii. Elizabeth D., b. Feb. 5, 1863.

305. iii. James, b. March 31, 1865.
iv. Emma, b. Sept. 10, 1867.
306. v. Fred. Earnest, b. Feb. 18, 1870.
307. vi. Lemuel Melville, b. Nov. 2, 1874.
308. vii. Willard William, b. July 8, 1878.
viii. Rebecca Maud Mary, b. Jan. 15, 1881.

188

ORIS[8] COLE (*Oris,*[7] *Salmon,*[6] *John,*[5] *Jonathan,*[4] *John,*[3] *John,*[2] *Thomas*[1]). The first son of Oris and Mary (Gillson) Cole, was born August 17, 1830, in Buckingham, Canada. When twenty-one years of age he started out for himself in the only way open then for a young man in Canada, and began as a lumberman. By diligence and care he has accumulated a competence, and is spending his latter days in comfort in Cloyne, Canada, with his family around him. He married, in 1856, Phena Pollard, an English girl.

Their children are:

309. i. Fred., b. in 1858; lives in Cloye, and is lately married.
ii. Emily, b. —— ——; m. Daniel Spicer; has one child, and lives in Cloyne.
iii. Mary, —— ——; m. Peter Storey; lives in Enterprise, Ont., and has two children.
310. iv. Edwin, born in 1863; is in British Columbia, unmarried.
v. Hattie, born in 1865; living at home.
vi. Katie (twin), b. 1871; living at home.
vii. Nellie (twin), b. 1871; living at home.

189

LEMUEL[8] COLE (*Oris,*[7] *Salmon,*[6] *John, Jonathan,*[4] *John,*[3] *John,*[2] *Thomas*[1]). The third child of Oris and Mary (Gillson) Cole, born in Buckingham, Canada, June 7, 1834. He is a lumberman, and resides in Cloyne, Canada. He has six sons and seven daughters. He married Elizabeth Parcher.

[Nos. 310–316 for sons.]

190

DANIEL[8] COLE (*Oris,[7] Salmon,[6] John,[5] Jonathan,[4] John,[3] John,[2] Thomas[1]*). Twin son with George, of Oris and Mary (Gillson) Cole, born in Buckingham, Canada, August 23, 1836. He lived at home in his boyhood, and as a young man worked at lumbering. Being a very strong opponent of slavery, he went to the United States, on February 5, 1862, and enlisted in the Fourteenth United States Infantry, and served three years, participating in the campaigns of the Army of the Potomac from the second Bull Run to the close of the war, his regiment being a part of the Fifth Corps. He was appointed first sergeant June 18, 1865. On August 20 he was wounded in the right arm and nearly captured during the engagement of the Fifth Corps on the Weldon railroad. After the war he returned to Canada with broken health, and married (1) Annie S. Larwell in May, 1865. In 1869 moved to Wisconsin, but the climate was too severe, and in 1871 to Iowa. In November, 1877, his wife died, leaving two children.

i. Minnie L., b. ——, 1869.
317. ii. Percival, b. ——, 1871.

In September, 1878, he married (2) Abbie De La Vergne, who was born in Pennsylvania January 14, 1861. In March, 1885, he moved to Herman, Lincoln county, Kansas, where he is a prosperous farmer and has a quarter section of land.

iii. Lucy A.. ——, 1879.
318. iv. Oris D., b. ——, 1881.
v. Jennie M., b. April 14, 1883; d. March 18, 1885.
vi. Annie B., b. April 22, 1886.

191

FREDERICK[8] COLE (*Oris,[7] Salmon,[6] John,[5] Jonathan,[4] John,[3] John,[2] Thomas[1]*). Born November 15, 1852; farmer in Buckingham, Quebec; married, June 18, 1879, Rebecca Lonsdale, who was born August 25, 1863.

Children:

i. Rebecca Jane, b. Oct. 12, 1880; d. Oct. 15, 1881.
ii. Rhoda Minerva, b. Oct. 8, 1883.
319. iii. Frederick, b. April 5, 1886.

192

ETHAN[8] COLE (*Ethan,[7] Salmon,[6] John,[5] Jonathan,[4] John,[3] John, Thomas[1]*). The second child and oldest son of Ethan and Lucretia (Gillson) Cole, was born in Buckingham, Canada, March 9, 1832 He removed with his parents to New York in 1848; to Illinois in 1851, and to Iowa in July, 1859. He enlisted in the United States Volunteers in April, 1862, and served three years. He married (1) at Logan, Iowa, in February, 1869, Catherine C. Reel She was born in Reelsville, Indiana, in 1847, and died in Logan Iowa, January 14, 1870. He then married (2) Sarah A. (Frazier Reel, widow of H. B. Reel, October 24, 1871, at Missouri Valley, Iowa. She was born in Reelsville, Indiana, January 30, 1838 Mr. Cole's present occupation is farming.

His children are:

i. Della, b. at Missouri Valley, Ia., July 30, 1872.
320. ii. Leonard T., b. at Missouri Valley, Ia., Jan. 7, 1875
321. iii. Cyrus L., b. at Missouri Valley, Ia., June 24, 1880
iv. Mary L., b. at Missouri Valley, Ia., Feb. 16, 1884.

193

ENOS[8] COLE (*Ethan,[7] Salmon,[6] John,[5] Jonathan,[4] John,[3] John, Thomas[1]*). The fourth child and third son of Ethan and Lucretia (Gillson) Cole, born in Buckingham, Canada, January 25, 1836 and moved with his parents to Iowa. He married at Council Bluffs, Iowa, August 23, 1868, Mary E. Lake, who was born in Iowa, September 5, 1842. He is now a lumber dealer.

His children are:

i. Lulu M., b. Oct. 16. 1870, in Loveland, Ia.
322. ii. Clifford C., b. Sept. 3, 1872, in Modale, Ia.
iii. Myrtle A., b. Oct. 16, 1876, in Mo. Valley, Ia.
iv. Mabel C., b. July 3, 1877, in Minden, Ia.

194

ETHAN[8] COLE (*Ethan,*[7] *Salmon,*[6] *John,*[5] *Jonathan,*[4] *John,*[3], *John,*[2] *Thomas*[1]). The sixth child and fifth son of Ethan and Lucretia (Gillson) Cole, born in Buckingham, September 11, 1839, and moved with the family in their journeyings to Iowa. He married at Magnolia, Iowa, in April, 1871, Alice Maine, who was born in Canada in 1849, and died June 23, 1880, at Loveland, Iowa. Mr. Cole was a farmer, and died in Loveland, May 2, 1886.

Their children were:

i. Effie G., b. in Modale, Ia., Feb. 25, 1872.
ii. Nellie, b. in Loveland, Ia., Sept. 19, 1875.
iii. Sarah (twin), b. in Loveland, Ia., Nov. 20, 1876.
iv. Clara (twin), b. in Loveland, Ia., Nov. 20, 1876.

195

CYRUS[8] COLE (*Ethan,*[7] *Salmon,*[6] *John,*[5] *Jonathan,*[4] *John,*[3] *John,*[2] *Thomas*[1]). The ninth child of Ethan and Lucretia (Gillson) Cole was born in Campville, Canada, September 1, 1846. He moved with the family to Iowa, and in 1862 enlisted in the Second Nebraska Volunteer Cavalry, and served nine months. He then went as a substitute in the Third Iowa Battery in 1864, and served one year. In 1870 he went to California, where he married in Sacramento, November 19, 1875, Hannah M. Sullivan, who was born in Galway county, Ireland, June 20, 1855. While in California he was engaged in railroading. He returned to Iowa in

1880 and engaged in farming for three years and then removed to Spokane county, Washington Territory, and took up a farm.

His children are:

323. i. Arthur E., b. in Carson City, Nev., Nov. 1, 1876.
324. ii. Roy, b. in Ia., Apr. 24, 1882.

196

JOHN G.[8] COLE (*Ethan,[7] Salmon,[6] John,[5] Jonathan,[4] John,[3] John,[2] Thomas[1]*). The tenth child of Ethan and Lucretia (Gillson) Cole was born in Wolcott Village, New York, February 12, 1848. He married in Iowa, June 26, 1869, Lucinda Mattox, who was born in Indiana in 1851. He followed the operation of saw-milling and piloting on the Missouri river, and died in Florence, Nebraska, November 2, 1882.

Their children are:

325. i. George W., b. June 27, 1870, at Mo. Valley, Ia.
ii. Minnie A., b. Sept. 2, 1872, at Mo. Valley, Ia.
326. iii. Ethan A., b. Aug. 21, 1876, at Mo. Valley, Ia.
327. iv. John G., b. Mar. 21, 1879, at Mo. Valley, Ia.

197

ALJAMAN ALONZO[8] COLE (*Daniel,[7] Laban,[6] John,[5] Jonathan,[4] John,[3] John,[2] Thomas[1]*). Born in Brookline, Windham county, Vermont, October 4, 1817. He was the son of Daniel Mansfield and Polly (Bigelow) Cole, his wife. When he was nine years of age the family left Vermont, but we give the rest of his history as related by himself:

"In the month of November, 1826, father emigrated to the town of Ashford, Cattaraugus county, New York, and settled on one hundred acres of land in what was then known as the Holland purchase. I lived at home with father until I was nineteen years of age, when I went to the city of Troy, New York, and lived with my Uncle Reuben and Aunt Chloe Cole. I went to school with my cousins, Dennison and Russell Cole, commencing in November, and returning to my father's the following August. I stayed at home until I was twenty-two, and then went to Bolivar, Alleghany county, New York, and studied medicine with Dr. E. C. Pool. From there I went to Springville, Erie county, and studied for two years with Dr. B. A. Batly. I then studied in Buffalo with Dr. Horace Mellin Conger for about a year and six months, when I obtained from the censors of Erie county my diploma to practice medicine.

"I then emigrated and settled in Richmond, McHenry county, Illinois, on August 12, 1844. I practiced my profession there for three years, when I moved to Utica, Winnebago county, Wisconsin, where I obtained forty acres of land, which I worked as I could, besides attending to my practice in the neighborhood. After about three years I sold out and removed to what was known as the Indian lands, now known as the town of Marion, Waushara county, Wisconsin.

"I settled on one hundred acres of land there about the middle of May, 1850, built me a log house, and went to work clearing, fencing, and breaking my new home.

"When the town was organized I was deputized as town clerk, and was elected to that office eight years in succession. I have been superintendent of schools and supervisor several times. I did not give my attention to the practice of my profession, as I wished to make farming my main business, but I had to go out some among the sick in my immediate neighborhood, but did it without thought of remuneration.

"After some years I was compelled to sell my farm, when I bought a stock of drugs and opened business in Waukaw, where I am now located. I was married to Allyna Ann Sanders, June 22, 1845.

"My wife Allyna died January 26, 1881. On November 18, 1883, I married Ester Evelina Mills, of Waukaw.

"Thus I have had various experiences in the journey of life. When I take a retrospective view of my past life, and see how I have been led and influenced by an over-ruling Power beyond my own, I see and feel that God is good, and deserves my every effort to love and obey His mandates while life shall last.

"ALJAMAN A. COLE."

Their children were:

i. Celia Ovanda, b. April 11, 1846, in Richmond, Ill.; m. Judson Convers, and lives in Omro, Winnebago county, Wis. She has two sons and one daughter.

ii. Oliska Melvina, b. in Utica, Wis., Sept. 20, 1849; m. James Watson. He died in 1884. She is now living in Berlin, Wis., with her three sons.

328. iii. Fayette Alonso, b. in Marion, Wis., May 12, 1856.

329. iv. Albert Eugene, b. in Marion, Wis., Jan. 23, 1861.

v. Edith Viola, b. in Marion, July 19, 1865; m. Frederic H. Fletcher, and lives in Waukaw, Wis.

330. vi. Frank Lewellyn, b. in Marion, Sept. 30, 1869, and is now living with his brother at Elcho.

198

Edwin F.[8] Cole (*Daniel M.,[7] Laban,[6] John,[5] Jonathan,[4] John,[3] John,[2] Thomas[1]*). The second son of Daniel Mansfield and Polly (Bigelow) Cole, born in Brookline, Windham county, Vermont, February 3, 1819. Emigrated with the family to Cattaraugus county, New York, in 1826. In 1845 emigrated to McHenry county, Illinois, and worked by the month for various parties till the fall of 1846, when he went to Rosendale, Fon du Lac county, Wisconsin, where he obtained eighty acres of land and built a house on the same. He soon after married Rachel Parsons.

Their children were:

297. i. Perry M., b. —— ——.
331. ii. Alvin T., b. —— ——; died some years ago.
iii. Mary A., b. —— ——.
iv. Clara E., b. —— ——; m. Mr. Drake, Quincy, Ill.

About 1861 he left his family and went to Blue Earth county, Minnesota, where he obtained eighty acres about three miles from Manketo. After making some improvements, he enlisted in the Fifth Minnesota, and was stationed at Fort Ridgely. While there he was killed in a battle with the Indians.

His widow and her children moved from Rosendale to Silver Lake, McLeod county, Minnesota, where she married a Mr. Straw, and where they all now reside.

199

Seymore[8] Cole (*Daniel M.,[7] Laban,[6] John,[5] Jonathan,[4] John,[3] John,[2] Thomas[1].*) The third son of Daniel M. and Polly (Bigelow) Cole was born in Brookline, Windham county, Vermont, February 15, 1821. The family removed to Cattaraugus county, New York, when he was seven years old, and his boyhood was spent in work on the farm with a little schooling in the winter. When about eighteen years of age he left home and for three years worked at blacksmithing till he learned the trade. In 1842 he went to Buffalo and began work as a journeyman. Soon after the press of dull times threw him out of his place, and there being a shipping office in Buffalo for the United States Navy, he, with two other workmen, shipped as blacksmiths for a term of three years. May 9, 1842, they were sent to the receiving ship at Charlestown Navy Yard, Massachusetts, and on August 3 were transferred to the seventy-four-gun ship Columbus, and sailed August 29. The ship visited the Mediterranean, wintering at Genoa, and then went to the east coast of South America, and after a stay on that coast sailed for home, arriving in New York May 29, 1844. The crew were discharged, and he went home via Troy and Albany.

In September he went west with his brother, Dr. A. A. Cole. He worked at his trade in Elgin, Illinois, till the spring of 1845, when he went to Solon, McHenry county, and started in business on his own account. Here he lived several years and prospered. On July 18, 1847, he married Matilda Slocum, only daughter of Amaijah Slocum. She was born in Wooster, Otsego county, New York, August 1, 1818, and went to Illinois with her family in 1844. Soon after his marriage he sold his shop and tools and bought a farm near Solon. Here he lived, working on his farm in the summer and at his trade in the winter, and here his children were born and reared. In October, 1880, he sold his farm, and with his wife and three unmarried daughters removed to Hayti, Hamlin county, Dakota. His son and son-in-law also sold their farms and removed with him. There he has a fine farm and good buildings, and his family around him. He is a member of the Baptist Church. He holds the office of postmaster at Hayti.

The children of Seymore and Matilda (Slocum) Cole are:

i. Clara R., b. Aug. 13, 1848; she m. Sept. 8, 1885, Herman E. Keesler, a capitalist of Watertown, Dak. She is a practicing physician in the same town.

ii. Martha L., b. Mar. 15, 1851; m. Asher Davey, Dec. 7, 1876. He was b. in Brighton, England, and came with his parents to this land when six years old. He is now a farmer in Hayti. She has children:
(i.) Winifred Arthur, b. Dec. 25, 1877.
(ii.) Glenn J. T., b. Dec. 1, 1882.
(iii.) Roy Elmer, b. July 7, 1886.

332. iii. Aljaman E., b. Sept. 11, 1853.

iv. Mary E., b. Jan 9, 1856. She is a school teacher in Hamlin co.

v. Myra M., b. May 30, 1858; m. Mar. 8, 1882, Clarence W. Fosdick, a native of Mich. They have one daughter:
(i.) Millie Ethel, b. Mar. 20, 1885.

200

ALVIN T.[8] COLE (*Daniel M.*,[7] *Laban*,[6] *John*,[5] *Jonathan*,[4] *John*,[3] *John*,[2] *Thomas*[1]). Born in Brookline, Windham county, Vermont, March 5, 1823. In 1826 his father removed to Ashford, Cattaraugus county, New York. He married Jane Bailey, of Springville, New York. In 1862 he raised a company of volunteers in Alleghany county, New York, and joined the One Hundred and Thirty-sixth Regiment, New York Volunteers; served in Virginia till compelled by ill health to resign. He is a lawyer and a Baptist minister. Lives in Waverly, Brenner county, Iowa.

201

VERNON[8] COLE? (*Daniel M.*,[7] *Laban*,[6] *John*,[5] *Jonathan*,[4] *John*,[3] *John*,[2] *Thomas*[1]). The fifth son of Daniel Mansfield and Polly (Bigelow) Cole, was born in Brookline, Windham county, Vermont, April 11, 1825. While he was an infant the family moved to Cattaraugus county, New York. As a young man he learned the carpenter's trade. He married at Springville, New York, June 15, 1851, Sarah Kellogg, a native of Hanover, Grafton county, New Hampshire, and on the 17th of the same month started for Wisconsin via the Great Lakes. At Oshkosh, Wisconsin, they took conveyance and went to Marion township, Waushara county, where they had a claim of 143 acres of land. They built a house and began farming, and here their first child was born. In October, 1856, they sold the farm and moved to Berlin, Green Lake county, where Mr. Cole worked at his trade. In 1860 they moved to Dell Prairie, Adams county, and in 1862 to Portage City. In 1866 they went onto a farm in Warren, Waushara county, where they remained fourteen years. In 1880 they moved to Oconto county, and after living at several places in that county settled, in December, 1885, on a farm of 160 acres in Maple Valley.

Their children are:

334. i. Jabez Daniel, b. in Marion township, Waushara county, Wis., May 21, 1852. He lives in Maple Valley, Wis.; is a widower with one daughter.

335. ii. Clarence De Poister, b. in Marion township, Dec. 22, 1853.

iii. Mary Parizade, b. in Berlin, Green Lake county, Oct. 23, 1857; m. John Hoffman, and lives in Gilett, Oconto county.

iv. Perviz Fielder, b. in Berlin, Nov. 11, 1859; d. in Portage City, in 1862.

v. Violetta Imogene, b. in Dell Prairie, Adams county, Nov. 15, 1861; m. James A. Hinds, a farmer and lumberman.

vi. Carrie Cecelia, b. in Portage City, Feb. 18, 1864; m. John F. Frye, a lumberman of Iron City, Mich.

336. vii. Vernon Earnest, b. in Portage City, Sept. 6, 1865.

202

CHESELTON COLE (*Daniel M.*,[5] *Laban*,[6] *John*,[5] *Jonathan*,[4] *John*,[3] *John*,[2] *Thomas*[1]). The seventh child and sixth son of Daniel

Mansfield Cole and Polly, his wife, was born in Ashford, Cattaraugus county, New York, July 28, 1829. He married Ann Newcomb, of Springville, Erie county, New York. He enlisted as a private in the One Hundred and Eleventh New York Volunteers, and served through the war, being wounded twice. He is now living in Edgerton, Kent county, Michigan, and is a farmer and carpenter.

203

BYRON[8] COLE (*Daniel M.,*[7] *Laban,*[6] *John,*[5] *Jonathan,*[4] *John,*[3] *John,*[2] *Thomas*[1]).

204

OZRO[8] COLE (*Daniel M.,*[7] *Laban,*[6] *John,*[5] *Jonathan,*[4] *John,*[3] *John,*[2] *Thomas*[1]). The tenth and last child of Daniel M., and his only child by his second wife, Nancy (Bigelow) Cole, was born in Ashford, New York, October 1, 1835. He married Martha A. Wheat, of Ashford.

Their children are:

338. i. Herbert, b. Sept. 4, 1860.
ii. Lilian Emma, b. June 26, 1863; m. C. D. Dennison, of East Ashford.
339. iii. Earl J., b. Feb. 25, 1875.

Mr. Cole is a farmer in Ashford. His postoffice address is Springville.

205

RUSSELL[8] COLE (*Reuben,*[7] *Laban,*[6] *John,*[5] *Jonathan,*[4] *John,*[3] *John,*[2] *Thomas*[1]). The second son of Reuben and Chloe Ann (Daggett) Cole, born June 30, 1832. He died about October, 1883, in West Virginia.

206

GEORGE E.[8] COLE (*Heber,*[7] *Sala,*[6] *John,*[5] *Jonathan,*[4] *John,*[3] *John,*[2] *Thomas*[1]). The second child of Heber and Louisa (Stevens) Cole was born in Tioga county, Pennsylvania, December 25, 1838. He married Louisa White, June 4, 1864.

Their children are:

340. i. Oscar E., b. June 9, 1865.
ii. Celestia, b. Apr. 6, 1870; d. in the summer of 1884.
iii. Kate, b. May 20, 1873; d. in the summer of 1884.

Mr. Cole is a farmer in Tioga, Pennsylvania.

---

206 *a*

HERBERT H.[8] COLE (*A. Clark,*[7] *Sala,*[6] *John,*[5] *Jonathan,*[4] *John,*[3] *John,*[2] *Thomas*[1]). The fourth child of A. Clark and Delia (Patten) Cole was born in Tioga, Pennsylvania, May 30, 1861. He is a civil engineer in Landu, Fremont county, Wyoming Territory.

207

LORENZO W.[8] COLE (*Alfred R.,*[7] *Ethan,*[6] *John,*[5] *Jonathan,*[4] *John,*[3] *John,*[2] *Thomas*[1]). The third child and only son of Alfred R. and Liantha (Person) Cole was born in Counstableville, New York, November 7, 1846. In June, 1867, he married Emma L. Barlow. She was born August 15, 1851. He was a carpenter by trade. He died April 4, 1879.

Their children were:

341. i. Edward W., b. Oct. 5, 1872.
ii. Mabel M., b. Mar. 10, 1876.

208

WARREN[8] COLE (*Alvarado,[7] Ethan,[6] John,[5] Jonathan,[4] John,[3] John,[2] Thomas[1]*). The first child and only son of Alvarado and Theodotia (Reed) Cole was born in Londonderry, Vermont. December 5, 1841. Being in New Jersey in 1863 he enlisted in the Twenty-sixth Regiment New Jersey Volunteers, and served two years until the end of the war. He learned the barbers' trade. In 1881 he married Rosa Harris, of Boston, Massachusetts, where he lived some time. He is now located in Nashua, New Hampshire. He has no children.

209

WINSLOW[8] A. COLE (*Alfonzo,[8] Ethan,[6] John,[5] Jonathan,[4] John,[3] John,[2] Thomas[1]*). The first child of Alfonzo Ethan and Sylvia (Cheany) Cole was born in Londonderry, December 9, 1841. He married December 6, 1862, Marietta Rawson, of Jamaica, Vermont. He moved to Worcester, Massachusetts, where he died June 21, 1884.

The children of Winslow A. and Marietta (Rawson) Cole were:

i. Mina M., b. Mar. 23, 1865.
ii. Netta M., b. Sept. 24, 1867.
342. iii. George W., b. July 20, 1873.
343. iv. Earnest R., b. Sept. 13, 1876.
v. Edith S., b. Jan. 6, 1879; d. Sept. 16, 1879.

210

WILLIAM A. D.[8] COLE (*Stephen R.,[7] Simon,[6] John,[5] Jonathan,[4] John,[3] John,[2] Thomas[1]*). Born in Neponset, Massachusetts, February 27, 1854.

211

Frank E.[8] Cole (*Stephen R.,*[7] *Simon,*[6] *John,*[5] *Jonathan,*[4] *John,*[3] *John,*[2] *Thomas*[1]). Born in Worcester, Massachusetts, April 17, 1855.

212

Stephen R.[8] Cole, Jr. (*Stephen R.,*[7] *Simon,*[6] *John,*[5] *Jonathan,*[4] *John,*[3] *John,*[4] *Thomas,*[1]). Born in Charlestown, Massachusetts, December 17, 1859.

213

Howard E.[8] Cole (*Stephen R.,*[7] *Simon,*[6] *John,*[5] *Jonathan,*[4] *John,*[3] *John,*[2] *Thomas*[1]). Born in Charlestown, Massachusetts, June 8, 1870.

214

George[8] Cole (*George,*[7] *Heber,*[6] *John,*[5] *Jonathan,*[4] *John,*[3] *John,*[2] *Thomas*[1]). Born in Keene, New Hampshire, April 6, 1854. On May 2, 1876, he married Clara E. Crosby, of Surry, New Hampshire. They have no children. Mr. Cole is a butcher in Keene.

220

George Spofford[8] Cole (*Ephraim F.,*[7] *Kimball,*[6] *Solomon,*[5] *Samuel,*[4] *Samuel,*[3] *John,*[2] *Thomas*[1]). Second son of Ephraim F. and Sarah (Spofford) Cole was born in Boxford, Massachusetts, July 2, 1836. He married N. Emeline, daughter of Nelson and

Salinda Bodwell, of Boxford, November 29, 1860. She was born in Rochester, New York, in 1835. Mr. Cole is a carpenter and builder in Andover, Massachusetts, and is deputy sheriff of the county.

His children are:

i. R. Fannie, b. May 3, 1862.
360. ii. John M., b. Nov. 4, 1863.
361. iii. George W., b. Jan. 11, 1867.
iv. Emma L., b. Jan. 23, 1869.
v. Maud M., b. June 12, 1875.

221

Arthur E.[8] Cole (*Ephraim F.,[7] Kimball,[6] Solomon,[5] Samuel,[4] Samuel,[3] John,[2] Thomas[1]*). The seventh child of Ephraim F. and Sarah (Spofford) Cole was born in Boxford, Massachusetts, September 30, 1848. He married October 5, 1882, Sarah A. Wood. He resides in Lawrence, Massachusetts, and has four children.

362. i. Charles Kimball, b. Oct. 23, 1873.
363. ii. Wm. Herbert, b. June 25, 1876.
iii. Bertha May, b. Oct. 4, 1878.
363*a* iv. Walter Irving, b. June 14, 1884.

222

Joseph Franklin[8] Cole (*Ephraim F.,[7] Kimball,[6] Solomon,[5] Samuel,[4] Samuel,[3] John,[2] Thomas[1]*). The eighth child of Ephraim F. and Eliza (Spofford) Cole was born in Boxford, Massachusetts, September 28, 1851. He married September 30, 1874, Carrie E. Bodwell, of Andover, Massachusetts, who was born March 31, 1855. They reside in Andover.

Their children are:

364. i. Frank Lewis, b. Sept. 3, 1875.
ii. Blanche Mildred, b. Nov. 29, 1881.
365. iii. Roy Harold, b. Nov. 26, 1885.

223

WALLACE E.[8] COLE (*Ephraim F.*,[7] *Kimball*,[6] *Solomon*,[5] *Samuel*,[4] *Samuel*,[3] *John*,[2] *Thomas*[1]). The ninth child of Ephraim and Eliza (Spofford) Cole was born in Boxford, Massachusetts, November 19, 1855. He married December 24, 1878, Ida D. Colby, of Salem, New Hampshire, where he now resides and is engaged in the provision business.

Their children are:

i. Mabel, b. Jan. 26, 1880.
ii. Minnie F., b. Apr. 25, 1882.
iii. Gertrude C., b. Sept. 16, 1884.

224

ROSCOE KIMBALL[8] COLE (*Ephraim F.*,[7] *Kimball*,[6] *Solomon*,[5] *Samuel*,[4] *Samuel*,[3] *John*,[2] *Thomas*[1]). The tenth child of Ephraim F. and Eliza (Spofford) Cole was born in Boxford, Massachusetts, February 28, 1861. He married ——— ———, and resides in Andover, Massachusetts. He has no children.

225

JEFFERSON KIMBALL[8] COLE (*John K.*,[7] *Kimball*,[6] *Solomon*,[5] *Samuel*,[4] *Samuel*,[3] *John*,[2] *Thomas*[1]). The oldest child of John K. and Mary S. (Town) Cole was born in Boxford, Massachusetts, October 25, 1838. He was educated in the common schools and at the Topsfield, Massachusetts, Academy. He taught in the district schools of Massachusetts for four years, and was then for two years an officer and teacher in the State Reform School for Boys at Westboro, Massachusetts. He served for two years in the army in the Eighteenth and Thirty-second Regiments, Massachusetts Volunteers. After the war he was for eleven years principal of a grammar school in Lawrence, Massachusetts, and then accepted the principalship of the A. M. A. schools, first at New Orleans, and later at Savannah, continuing in that work for three years. He is now teacher in the High School of Peabody, Massachusetts. He married November 27, 1862, Annie G., daughter of Jonathan and Catherine (Marsten) Poor, of Andover.

Their children are.

i. Mabel Eugenia, b. in Andover, Mass., Mar. 14, 1864; d. in Savannah, Ga., Mar. 6, 1880.
ii. John Sawyer, b. in Lawrence, Mass., Nov. 28, 1866; d. in Savannah, Mar. 1, 1880.
iii. Gertrude Poor, b. in New Orleans, La., Oct. 26, 1877.

226

JOHN NEWTON[8] COLE (*John K.,[7] Kimball,[6] Solomon,[5] Samual,[4] Samuel,[3] John,[2] Thomas[1]*). The fourth child and second son of John K. and Mary S. (Town) Cole was born in Boxford, Massachusetts, March 21, 1857. He is commonly known as J. Newton Cole. He married Minnie Clifford Kimball, of Melrose, Massachusetts, June 21, 1882. He resides in Andover, Massachusetts.

His only child is:

366. i. Harold Clifford, b. Feb. 15, 1886.

227

WILLIAM KIMBALL[8] COLE (*Wm. Runnells,[7] Kimball,[6] Solomon,[5] Samuel,[4] Samuel,[3] John,[2] Thomas.[1]*). The oldest child of William R. and Mary H. (Runnells) Cole was born in Boxford, June 2,

1856. He married 188–, Eliza A. Richardson, of Boxford, where he resides, and is one of the Selectmen of the town.

His only child is:

367. i. Henry Lee, b. Oct. 22, 1882.

227 *a*

NORMAN[8] COLE (*Wm. R.,*[7] *Kimball,*[6] *Solomon,*[5] *Samuel,*[4] *Samuel,*[3] *John,*[2] *Thomas*[1]). The second son and third child of William R. and Mary H. (Runnells) Cole was born in Boxford, Massachusetts, July 3, 1860. He married April 18, 1882, Jennie Isabelle, daughter of Abraham and Eliza (During) Kershaw, of North Andover, who was born in 1859.

228

MORRIS LEE[8] COLE (*Wm. R.,*[7] *Kimball,*[6] *Solomon,*[5] *Samuel,*[4] *Samuel,*[3] *John,*[2] *Thomas*[1]). The third son of William R. and Mary H. (Runnells) Cole was born in Boxford, Massachusetts, April 29, 1863.

229

STEPHEN B.[8] COLE (*John A.,*[7] *Isaac,*[6] *Solomon,*[5] *Samuel,*[4] *Samuel,*[3] *John,*[2] *Thomas*[1]). The only son of John A. Cole by his second wife, Abigail Davis, born in Plymouth, New Hampshire, April 30, 1840.

230

TIMOTHY[8] COLE (*Timothy,*[7] *Isaac,*[6] *Solomon,*[5] *Samuel,*[4] *Samuel,*[3] *John,*[2] *Thomas*[1]). The only son of Rev. Timothy and Susan (Hill) Cole, born —— ——. Resides in Michigan.

231

George[8] Cole (*Zackeus*,[7] *John*,[6] *Solomon*,[5] *Samuel*,[4] *Samuel*,[3] *John*,[2] *Thomas*[1]). The eldest son and third child of Zackeus and Annis (Harlow) Cole was born in Westminster, Vermont, December 2, 1822. He removed to Salem, Massachusetts, where he married Caroline Bartlett, January 15, 1846. He resides in Salem, and has no children.

232

Charles[8] Cole (*Zackeus*,[7] *John*.[6] *Solomon*,[5] *Samuel*,[4] *Samuel*,[3] *John*,[2] *Thomas*[1]). The second son of Zackeus and Annis (Harlow) Cole, was born in Westminster, Vermont, June 16, 1825, and died there December 2, 1879. He married Hattie Cluff in Boston, Massachusetts, where he lived most of his life. He left no children.

233

Daniel Read[8] Cole (*Asa*,[7] *John*,[6] *Solomon*,[5] *Samuel*,[4] *Samuel*,[3] *John*,[2] *Thomas*[1]). The second son of Asa and Sarah (Pitts) Cole was born in Gilsum, Cheshire county, New Hampshire, December 20, 1835. He married November 23, 1858, Adeliza, daughter of Gilman and Eliza (Towne) Jones, who was born in Marlow, New Hampshire, January 3, 1838. He now resides at Keene, New Hampshire, engaged in the grain and feed business, with mills at Marlboro. He is a prominent man in the place, and has been for years one of the city assessors.

His children are:

372. i. Frank A., b. in Keene, Sept. 18, 1861; now engaged in business with his father.

ii. Hattie E., b. July 24, 1870.

235

WARREN MIGHILL[8] COLE (*David M.,*[7] *Manley H.,*[6] *Simeon,*[5] *Samuel,*[4] *Samuel,*[3] *John,*[2] *Thomas*[1]). The only child of David H. and Eunice (Chadwick) Cole was born in Boxford, Massachusetts, —— —, 185–. He married Anna Richardson, a native of Sackville, N. B., in December, 1886. He is one of the leading and active young men of Boxford, and holds the office of collector and treasurer of the town.

236

WILLIAM H. A.[8] COLE (*Caleb M.,*[7] *Manley H.,*[6] *Simeon,*[5] *Samuel,*[4] *Samuel,*[3] *John,*[2] *Thomas*[1]). The youngest child and only son of Caleb M. and Louisa (Jenness) Cole was born in Boxford, Massachusetts, May 9, 1865.

237

SERENUS[9] COLE (*Tisdale S.,*[8] *Jonathan,*[7] *Jonathan,*[6] *Jonathan,*[5] *Jonathan,*[4] *John,*[3] *John,*[2] *Thomas*[1]). The eldest child of Tisdale S. and Laurency (Hallock) Cole, of River Falls, Wisconsin, was born —— ——.

238

GEORGE[9] COLE (*Tisdale S.,*[8] *Jonathan,*[7] *Jonathan,*[6] *Jonathan,*[5] *Jonathan,*[4] *John,*[3] *John,*[2] *Thomas*[1]). The second son of Tisdale S. and Laurency (Hallock) Cole, of River Falls, Wisconsin, was born —— ——.

239

MYRON SMITH[9] COLE (*Horace C.*,[8] *Jonathan*,[7] *Jonathan*,[6] *Jonathan*,[5] *Jonathan*,[4] *John*,[3] *John*,[2] *Thomas*[1]). The first child of Horace C. and Delinda (Smith) Cole, was born in Madrid, St. Lawrence county, New York, January 18, 1826. We quote from his letter:

"I moved with my parents to Hopkinton, St. Lawrence county, New York, in 1832, and thence to West Stockholm, same county, in 1837, where I have lived ever since. I still own the place my father bought in 1838. I worked with my father at the carpenter and joiners' trade, and at farming part of the time till he went west in 1854, attending district school from two to three months in the winter, till I was twenty years of age, aspiring and hoping for something better in the line of education. About that time I became satisfied that I could not study on occount of a heart difficulty, which has troubled me ever since. So it has been work, work. After my father went west I continued to work at my trade till 1860, when I was married to Malinda Averill, of Shelburne, Vermont, after which I worked at farming till 1862, when I enlisted in the army for three years, or during the war. I was wounded in July, 1864, and served in the hospital for five months, when I returned to my regiment, the One Hundred and Sixth New York Volunteers. Was discharged in June, 1865. Since then I have been a farmer.

"Had I followed my own inclination I should have granted your request and sent back your note to me; for I consider my life a very unimportant one. But you can do as you like about publishing what I have written. I will say in closing that here I am at the age of sixty, having a comfortable home. I am out of debt, have the needful things of life, and am hoping for and expecting something better in another world. Yours respectfully, "MYRON S. COLE."

His only child was:

i. Arthur Benjamin, b. July 2, 1869.

240

OSCAR C.[9] COLE (*Horace C.*,[8] *Jonathan*,[7] *Jonathan*,[6] *Jonathan*,[5] *Jonathan*,[4] *John*,[3] *John*,[2] *Thomas*[1]). The fourth child of Horace and Delinda (Smith) Cole was born in West Stockholm, New York, June 25, 1840. He married Angie Libby, of Sanford, York county, Maine, June 17, 1867. He was United States postal clerk for four years, and is now the editor and proprietor of

Oscar Cole.

the Iowa Postal Card, a newspaper published at Fayette, Fayette county, Iowa.

They have two children:

i. Lyle Leverne, b. 1875.
ii. Emma Elvise, b. 1879.

241

Lucius O.[9] Cole (*Osmand R.*,[8] *Jonathan*,[7] *Jonathan*,[6] *Jonathan*,[5] *Jonathan*,[4] *John*,[3] *John*,[2] *Thomas*[1]). The eldest son of Osmand R. and Betsy (Boswick) Cole was born in Chittenden county, Vermont, January 5, 1834. Married three times. Has six children. Served in army. In Libby prison. Minister in Pottsdam, New York.

242

Cyrus Jonathan[9] Cole (*Osmand R.*,[8] *Jonathan*,[7] *Jonathan*,[6] *Jonathan*,[5] *Jonathan*,[4] *John*,[3] *John*,[2] *Thomas*[1]). The sixth child of Osmand R. and Betsy (Boswick) Cole, was born in St. Lawrence county, New York, September 26, 1844; married Susan Wilson, April, 1866. Resides in Elgin, Illinois. Has no children.

243

Charles Wesley[9] Cole (*Osmand R.*,[8] *Jonathan*,[7] *Jonathan*,[6] *Jonathan*,[5] *Jonathan*,[4] *John*,[3] *John*,[2] *Thomas*[1]). The eighth child of Osmand R. and Betsy (Boswick) Cole, was born in St. Lawrence county, New York, March 8, 1846; married Ellen Stiles, April 27, 1869. Resides in Elgin, Illinois.

Their children are:

- i. Henry Luther, b. June 7, 1870.
- ii. Julia Ellen, b. Nov. 26, 1871; d. Aug. 21, 1873.
- iii. Osman Fred., b. Aug. 10, 1873.
- iv. William Charles, b. March 31, 1875; d. Nov. 22, 1877.
- v. Edna Frances, b. April 17, 1878.
- vi. Lizzie Carrie, b. Sept. 6, 1879.

244

MARTIN E.[9] COLE (*Clement C.,*[8] *Jonathan,*[7] *Jonathan,*[6] *Jonathan,*[5] *Jonathan,*[4] *John,*[3] *John,*[2] *Thomas*[1]). The eldest son of Clement C. and Fidelia (Myers) Cole, born November 27, 1840; married Mary E. Chamberlain. Real estate agent in Chicago, Illinois.

Children:

- i. Florence C., b. Oct. 27, 1880.

245

FRANK[9] COLE (*Clement C.,*[8] *Jonathan,*[7] *Jonathan,*[6] *Jonathan,*[5] *Jonathan,*[4] *John,*[3] *John,*[2] *Thomas*[1]). The youngest child of Clement C. and Fidelia (Myers) Cole, born ——— ——. He married a Miss Charles, who died leaving no children.

246

FRED. E.[9] COLE (*Abel Barton,*[8] *Abel,*[7] *Jonathan,*[6] *Jonathan,*[5] *Jonathan,*[4] *John,*[3] *John,*[2] *Thomas*[1]). Son of Abel B. and Maria (Miller) Cole, was born in Westmoreland, New Hampshire, October 14, 1854. He married (1) Adele L. Proctor, February 6, 1886, who was born October 8, 1862, and died November 17, 1884. He is a farmer in Westmoreland, owning the old home farm. On November 23, 1886, he married (2) Nellie E. Chase, of Westmoreland.

247

Frank W.[9] Cole (*Abel B.,*[8] *Abel,*[7] *Jonathan,*[6] *Jonathan,*[5] *Jonathan,*[4] *John,*[3] *John,*[2] *Thomas*[1]). The youngest son of Abel Barton and Maria (Miller) Cole, was born in Westmoreland, New Hampshire, September 9, 1864. He married Alice Shippy, of Bellows Falls, Vermont, September 1, 1886. He was a book-keeper in Bellows Falls, Vermont, and died there February 7, 1887. He was a young man of great energy and ambition, of excellent habits and disposition, and his early death removed a promising and useful citizen.

248

Dan Warren[9] Cole (*Anson,*[8] *Abel,*[7] *Jonathan,*[6] *Jonathan,*[5] *Jonathan,*[4] *John,*[3] *John,*[2] *Thomas*[1]). The third child of Anson and Harriet (Warren) Cole, was born in Westmoreland, New Hampshire, May 10, 1851. He was a clerk in his father's store in Westmoreland for many years, and is now engaged in that capacity in Ashuelot, New Hampshire. He married (1) Ellen M. Burnham, of Westmoreland, September 16, 1874. She was born September 28, 1852, and died May 7, 1881.

Their children were:

i. Lee, b. Feb. 5, 1877; and an infant.

Mr. Cole then married (2) Fannie Cowdery, of Westmoreland, November 9, 1881.

249

Fred. Anson[9] Cole (*Anson,*[8] *Abel,*[7] *Jonathan,*[6] *Jonathan,*[5] *Jonathan,*[4] *John,*[3] *John,*[2] *Thomas*[1]). The fifth and youngest child of Anson and Harriet (Warren) Cole, was born in Westmoreland,

New Hampshire, March 17, 1853. He married Mary Wellington, daughter of Eli Wellington, of Westmoreland, November 20, 1884.

250

WILLIAM A.[9] COLE (*George H.*,[8] *Abel*,[7] *Jonathan*,[6] *Jonathan*,[5] *Jonathan*,[4] *John*,[3] *John*,[2] *Thomas*[1]). The third child of George and Elizabeth (Stratton) Cole, was born November 6, 1857. He is unmarried, and is in partnership with his father in the American House, Fitchburg, Massachusetts.

251

WALTER S.[9] COLE (*George H.*,[8] *Abel*,[7] *Jonathan*,[6] *Jonathan*,[5] *Jonathan*,[4] *John*,[3] *John*,[2] *Thomas*[1]). The fourth child of George H. and Elizabeth (Stratton) Cole, was born September 26, 1859. He is unmarried, and lives in Leominster, Massachusetts.

252

CHARLES AUGUSTUS[9] COLE (*Curtis A.*,[8] *Abijah*,[7] *Jonathan*,[6] *Jonathan*,[5] *Jonathan*,[4] *John*,[3] *John*,[2] *Thomas*[1]). The eldest son of Curtis A. and Olive (Murphy) Cole was born May 14, 1843. He resides in Sherman City, Isabel county, Michigan. He has one son and two daughters.

253

EUGENE[9] COLE (*Curtis A.*,[8] *Abijah*,[7] *Jonathan*,[6] *Jonathan*,[5] *Jonathan*,[4] *John*,[3] *John*,[2] *Thomas*[1]). The fourth son of Curtis A. and Olive (Murphy) Cole was born September 10, 1847. He resides in Breckenridge, Summit county, Colorado, and has one son and two daughters.

254

CARLISLE R.[9] COLE (*Curtis A.*,[8] *Abijah*,[7] *Jonathan*,[6] *Jonathan*,[5] *Jonathan*,[4] *John*,[3] *John*,[2] *Thomas*[1]). The second child of Curtis A. and Harriet (Miller) Cole was born February 7, 1853. He is a carpenter, residing in Diamond Dale, Eaton county, Michigan, and has two sons.

255

WILLIAM H.[9] COLE (*Curtis A.*,[8] *Abijah*,[7] *Jonathan*,[6] *Jonathan*,[5] *Jonathan*,[4] *John*,[3] *John*,[2] *Thomas*[1]). The fifth child of Curtis A. and Harriet (Miller) Cole was born October 11, 1863. He is a farmer and unmarried. He lives with his father in St. Louis, Gratiot county, Michigan.

262

ADELBERT H.[9] COLE (*Edwin A.*,[8] *Asa*,[7] *Abijah*,[6] *Abijah*,[5] *Jonathan*,[4] *John*,[3] *John*,[2] *Thomas*[1]). The eldest son of Edwin A. and Delia (Moore) Cole, was born in Prospect Harbor, Hancock county, Maine, April 28, 1857.

263

FRANK W.[9] COLE (*Edwin A.*,[8] *Asa*,[7] *Abijah*,[6] *Abijah*,[5] *Jonathan*,[4] *John*,[3] *John*,[2] *Thomas*[1]). The youngest son and seventh child of Edwin A. and Delia (Moore) Cole, was born in Prospect Harbor, Maine, July 9, 1868.

264

JOHN R.[9] COLE (*David G.*,[8] *Asa*,[7] *Abijah*,[6] *Abijah*,[5] *Jonathan*,[4] *John*,[3] *John*,[2] *Thomas*[1]). The eldest son of Captain David G. and Sarah (Allen) Cole was born in Prospect Harbor, Maine, June 31, 1861. He married November 17, 1883, Jennie M. Hamilton.

His children are:

i. Ernest, b. Apr. 30, 1885.

265

LOUIS P.[9] COLE (*David G.*,[8] *Asa*,[7] *Abijah*,[6] *Abijah*,[5] *Jonathan*,[4] *John*,[3] *John*,[2] *Thomas*[1]). The younger son of Captain David G. and Sarah (Allen) Cole, was born in Prospect Harbor, Maine, February 8, 1863.

266

EVERARD G.[9] COLE (*Buckman*,[8] *Asa*,[7] *Abijah*,[6] *Abijah*,[5] *Jonathan*,[4] *John*,[3] *John*,[2] *Thomas*[1]). The first child of Captain Buckman and Marion (Allen) Cole, was born in Prospect Harbor, Maine, May 23, 1858.

267

HENRY M.[9] COLE (*Buckman,*[8] *Asa,*[7] *Abijah,*[6] *Abijah,*[5] *Jonathan,*[4] *John,*[3] *John,*[2] *Thomas*[1]). The second child of Captain Buckman and Marion (Allen) Cole, was born in Prospect Harbor, Maine, May 2, 1860. He lives at Sebago Lake, Maine.

268

NATHAN[9] COLE (*Buckman,*[8] *Asa,*[7] *Abijah,*[6] *Abijah,*[5] *Jonathan,*[4] *John,*[3] *John,*[2] *Thomas*[1]). The third child of Captain Buckman and Marion (Allen) Cole was born in Prospect Harbor, Maine, March 8, 1862. He married January 10, 1885, Edith B. Coombs, and lives in Prospect Harbor.

279

HENRY MERWIN[9] COLE (*Asa,*[8] *Asa,*[7] *Asa,*[6] *Abijah,*[5] *Jonathan,*[4] *John,*[3] *John,*[2] *Thomas*[1]). The first child of Asa and Sarah (Merwin) Cole, was born June 11, 1849. He married Louisa M. Temple, of West Medway, Massachusetts, and resides in South Abington, Massachusetts.

His children are:

- i. Two who died in infancy.
- iii. Frederick Richardson, b. May 3, 1874.
- iv. Virginia Merwin, b. May 8, 1875.
- v. Jesse Murry, b. Jan. 1, 1877.
- vi. Mary Elizabeth, b. April 17, 1885.

289

CARSON V.[9] COLE (*Gilbert L.,*[8] *Levi,*[7] *Levi,*[6] *John,*[5] *Jonathan,*[4] *John,*[3] *John,*[2] *Thomas*[1]). The eldest child of Gilbert L. and

Frederika (Wantzchmitt) Cole was born at Adrian, Michigan, May 10, 1856. He grew to manhood in Iowa, and was educated at the State University of Nebraska. In 1878, when the family removed from Iowa to Beatrice, Nebraska, he accompanied them, and is now one of the editors of the Beatrice *Daily Express*. He is unmarried.

290

FRANK W.[9] COLE (*Gilbert L.*,[8] *Levi*,[7] *Levi*,[6] *John*,[5] *Jonathan*,[4] *John*,[3] *John*,[2] *Thomas*[1]). The second son of Gilbert L. and Frederika (Wantzschmitt) Cole was born in Sidney, Iowa, July 21, 1859. He is now a professor of music in Beatrice, Nebraska.

291

GEORGE M.[9] COLE (*Gilbert L.*,[8] *Levi*,[7] *Levi*,[6] *John*,[5] *Jonathan*,[4] *John*,[3] *John*,[2] *Thomas*[1]). The third child of Gilbert L. and Frederika Cole, was born in Sidney, Iowa, September 10, 1861. He is a locomotive engineer on the Burlington & Missouri River railroad, and resides in Hastings, Nebraska.

292

WILLIAM S.[9] COLE (*Gilbert L.*,[8] *Levi*,[7] *Levi*,[6] *John*,[5] *Jonathan*,[4] *John*,[3] *John*,[2] *Thomas*[1]). The fourth son of Gilbert L. and Frederika Cole, was born at Jefferson Barracks, Missouri, April 28, 1864. He is now a jeweler in Beatrice, Nebraska.

293

Edward K.[9] Cole (*Gilbert L.,*[8] *Levi,*[7] *Levi,*[6] *John,*[5] *Jonathan,*[4] *John,*[3] *John,*[2] *Thomas*[1]). The fifth son of Gilbert L. and Frederika Cole, was born in Sidney, Iowa, September 22, 1866. He is now manager of the Telephone and Electric Light Company of Beatrice, Nebraska.

304

Salmon[9] Cole (*Williard,*[8] *Salmon,*[7] *Salmon,*[6] *John,*[5] *Jonathan,*[4] *John,*[3] *John,*[2] *Thomas*[1]). The first child of Williard and Jane (Bothwell) Cole, of Hawksbury, Prescott county, Quebec, was born February 4, 1861.

305

James[9] Cole (*Williard,*[8] *Salmon,*[7] *Salmon,*[6] *John,*[5] *Jonathan,*[4] *John,*[3] *John,*[2] *Thomas*[1]). The second son of Williard and Jane (Bothwell) Cole, was born March 31, 1865.

309

Frederick[9] Cole (*Oris,*[8] *Oris,*[7] *Salmon,*[6] *John,*[5] *Jonathan,*[4] *John,*[3] *John,*[2] *Thomas*[1]). The first child of Oris and Phena (Pollard) Cole, was born ——— ——, 1858. He is married, and lives in Cloyne, Ontario.

310

Edwin[9] Cole (*Oris,*[8] *Oris,*[7] *Salmon,*[6] *John,*[5] *Jonathan,*[4] *John,*[3] *John,*[2] *Thomas*[1]). The fourth child and second son of Oris and Phena (Pollard) Cole, was born in Cloyne, Ontario, in 1863. He is now in British Columbia.

328

FAYETTE ALONZO[9] COLE (*Aljamen A.*,[8] *Daniel M.*,[7] *Laban*,[6] *John*,[5] *Jonathan*,[4] *John*,[3] *John*,[2] *Thomas*[1]). The eldest son and third child of Dr. A. A. and Allyna A. (Sanders) Cole, was born in Marion, Wisconsin, May 12, 1856. In 1880 he married Rebecca Starr, who died about six months after their marriage. He has married a second time, and resides near Elcho Station, Lincoln county, Wisconsin.

329

ALBERT EUGENE[9] COLE (*Aljaman A.*,[8] *Daniel M.*,[7] *Laban*,[6] *John*,[5] *Jonathan*,[4] *John*,[3] *John*,[2] *Thomas*[1]). The fourth son of Dr. A. A. and Allyna A. (Sanders) Cole, born in Marion, Wisconsin, July 19, 1865. He is now an engineer in Shinkley, Minnesota.

332

ALJAMAN E.[9] COLE (*Seymore*,[8] *Daniel M.*,[7] *Laban*,[6] *John*,[5] *Jonathan*,[4] *John*,[3] *John*,[2] *Thomas*[1]). The only son of Seymore and Matilda (Slocum) Cole, was born September 11, 1853. He married December 6, 1876, Nellie Wainwright, of Woodstock, Illinois. He is a farmer in Hayti, Hamlin county, Nebraska.

334

JABEZ DANIEL[9] COLE (*Vernon*,[8] *Daniel M.*,[7] *Laban*,[6] *John*,[5] *Jonathan*,[4] *John*,[3] *John*,[2] *Thomas*[1]). The first child of Vernon and Sarah (Kellogg) Cole, was born in Marion township, Waushara county, Wisconsin, May 21, 1852. He lives in Maple Valley, Wisconsin, and is a widower with one daughter.

335

CLARENCE DE POISTER[9] COLE (*Vernon,*[8] *Daniel M.,*[7] *Laban,*[6] *John,*[5] *Jonathan,*[4] *John,*[3] *John,*[2] *Thomas*[1]). The second son of Vernon and Sarah (Kellogg) Cole, was born in Marion township, Waushara county, Wisconsin, December 22, 1853.

APPENDIX.

York County, Maine.

William Cole. He came to the Massachusetts Bay colony early, and January 23, 1637, two acres were granted to him at Mt. Wallaston. He married Elizabeth, a daughter of Francis Doughty, a merchant of Bristol, England. Her brother, the Rev. Francis Doughty, also came to the colony. He was in Taunton in 1639, and subsequently went to Rhode Island and thence to Long Island, where he was very roughly handled by the Dutch. He finally went to Virginia.

In 1640 Mrs. Cole sued her brother for defrauding her of her marriage portion. There is a letter from Rev. Francis Doughty to Governor Winthrop asking about the case. This is the case in which Mr. Thomas Lechford, the earliest lawyer in the colony, was retained, and to which he refers in "Plain Dealing."

I suspect that Mr. Cole was a follower of Wheelwright, for he removed to Exeter, and was in 1639 a witness to a true deed from the Indians to Wheelwright, and in 1640 removed with him to Wells, Maine, where he was constable in 1645.

He submitted with his sons John and Nicholas to the Massachusetts Jurisdiction, and took the oath at Wells, July 5, 1653. He moved back to Hampton, and died there May 16, 1662, in his eighty-second year.

His children were:

2. i. John.
3. ii. Nicholas, b. 1636.
4. iii. William,
And probably others.

2

Nicholas[2] Cole (*William*[1]). Born —— ——, 1636. He probably went to Wells with his father about 1640. He was a signer of the petition of certain inhabitants of Maine to Cromwell in 1656. He was constable there in 1658. He was appointed ferryman on Cape Porpoise River in 1664, in place of John Sanders, who had removed to Cape Porpoise. He was to keep the ferry seven years. He is mentioned aged 30 in 1666.

His children were:

5. i. Nicholas. b. —— ——. He was killed by the Indians May 11, 1704.

ii. Jane, b. —— ——. She m. Joseph Littlefield, and after his death John Heard, of Dover, N. H., July, 1698. They lived in Kittery, but the record is in Exeter, N. H. Their children are:

(i.) Jane, b. June 18, 1699; m. Nov. 15, 1719, Tristram Coffin, of Dover, and had nine children.

(ii.) Mary, b. Aug. 24, 1700; m. July 1, 1722, Henry Baxter.

(iii.) Abijah, b. Apr. 15, 1702; m. —— Hubbard.

iii. (?) Ann, who was m. to Nicholas Badcock, in 1686, by Justice Barefoote, in Portsmouth or vicinity.

3

John[2] Cole (*William*[1]). He first came to Wells and then settled at Cape Porpoise, where he was living when the people of Maine submitted to the Massachusetts Jurisdiction, he having signed the petition of 1672.

On July 5, 1653, he and eleven others of Cape Porpoise appeared before the Court at Wells, took the oath, and were incorporated as the fifth township in Maine.

At the time of the Indian troubles at the close of the century and the beginning of the next, the people of this region suffered severely. When the troops of Governor Andrus withdrew in 1690, most of the people of Cape Porpoise withdrew to Wells or to Portsmouth. In August, 1703, the few that had ventured back were again driven out, and all improvements destroyed. The town was not resettled till 1714.

John Cole probably lived at Cleaves Cove and there three of his children resided after the town was resettled. He is recorded as on the Grand Jury and as licensed to keep a public house, July, 1674. Savage says he died 1661, as his invoice is produced on April 20 of that year.

His children were, but not in this order:

6. i. Isaac.
7. ii. John.
8. iii. Phillip.
9. iv. Edward.
10. v. Joseph.
11. vi. Benjamin.

4

WILLIAM[2] COLE (*John*[1]). Among those who signed the petition to Massachusetts, of May 18, 1672, requesting them to extend jurisdiction over the province of Maine, was William Cole, of Sheepcoate. He was probably a son of William[1].

5

NICHOLAS[3] COLE (*Nicholas*,[2] *William*[1]). Son of Nicholas and (————) Cole, born —— ——, and killed by the Indians May 11, 1704. See *Boston News Letter*, May 15, 1704. (Reg. Vol. XIII, p. 238).

6

Isaac[3] Cole (*John*,[2] *William*[1]). Son of Isaac and (———) Cole. After the town of Cape Porpoise was resettled in 1714, he lived at Cleaves Cove. He had received a grant from the town in 1681.

[Can he be the Isaac of Exeter, a mill-wright, who sold part of a mill to —— ——, in 1671?]

He may have been the Isaac Cole of Piscataqua, who was killed by the Indians while attending a wedding at Wells, Maine. See *Boston News-Letter*, September 15, 1712. [Reg. Vol. XII, p. 138].

7

John[3] Cole (*John*,[2] *William*[1]). One of the sons of John and (———) Cole, born —— ——. He returned to Cape Porpoise in 1714. He died about 1740.

8

Phillip[3] Cole (*John*,[2] *William*[1]). Son of John and (———) Cole, born —— ——. He returned to Cape Porpoise in 1714, and died about 1725. His widow Mary survived him many years, and lived near Cleaves Cove.

9

Edward[3] Cole (*John*,[2] *William*[1]). I think he was the eldest son of John and (———) Cole, as he signs the oath with his father on July 22, 1674. Nothing further is known of him.

10

Joseph[3] Cole (*John,*[2] *William*[1]). Son of John and (———) Cole, born —— ——. He is mentioned in Bradbury's, Kennepunkport, as living in 1740. There was a Joseph at York in 1680, but the name is spelled Coole, and was probably another man.

11

Benjamin[3] Cole (*John,*[2] *William*[1]). Son of John and (———) Cole, born —— ——. He was living in Manchester in 1734, says Bradbury.

[This fragment is inserted here that it may perchance be of service to some other worker in this field.]

Bridgewater.

[Note. — I think this family belongs to the Plymouth family.]

Joseph Cole. Born probably in Plympton, Massachusetts, early in the eighteenth century. He was a private in Captain Perkins' company in the expedition against Louisburg. He with others being ordered home before the expedition returned, gave the following order in regard to their share of the profits of that expedition:

"Louisburg, September 19, 1745.

"We, the subscribers, select Captain Thomas Perkins to receive our part of the plunder that is comming to us by virtue of our being soldiers at Cape Breton."
[Hist. Gen. Reg., XXV, 251.]

He had previously married Mary ———. He removed to Bridgewater, Massachusetts, where he died.

His children were:

2. i. Samuel, b. —— ——; m. Nov. 16, 1762, to Sarah Packard, of Bridgewater.
3. ii. Ephraim, b. ———; m. ———, Hannah Randall.
4. iii. Joseph, b. —— ——; m. Dec. 8, 1757, to Betty Southworth.
iv. Mary, b. —— ——; m. June 8, 1758, Col. Frederick Pope (b. May 15, 1733; d. Aug. 20, 1812), of Stoughton, Mass., son of Dr. Ralph and Rebecca (Stubbs) Pope, of Stoughton. She had eight children, of whom Frederick, b. Aug. 20, 1772, m. Molly Pierce, of Dorchester, April 13, 1796, and d. in Mechias, Me., Dec. 16, 1826, and William, m. Sarah Pierce, a sister of Molly's, June 19, 1799, was a merchant of Boston, and d. in Dorchester, May 20, 1860, aged 85.
v. Susanna, b. —— ——; m. —— ——, ——— Niles.
vi. Catherine, b. —— ——; m. Feb. 11, 1762, Daniel Littlefield.
vii. Elizabeth, b. —— ——; m. Feb. 11, 1762, Solomon Smith, of East Bridgewater.
5. viii. Eleazer, b. —— 1747; m. July 11, 1769, Lucy Shurtliff, and moved to Maine.
ix. Sarah, b. —— 1749; m. —— ——, —— Withington.
x. Silence, b. —— 1755; d. young.

2

SAMUEL[2] COLE (*Joseph*[1]). Son of Joseph and Mary Cole, born —— ——. He married November 16, 1752, Sarah, daughter of Seth Packard.

His children were:

6. i. William, b. ——, 1753; m. ——, 1773, Molly Lazell.
ii. Rebecca, b. ———, 1755; m. Sept. 8, 1775, Amaziah Cole.
7. iii. Samuel, b. ——, 1761; m. —— ———. He moved West.

3

EPHRAIM[2] COLE (*Joseph*[1]). Second son of Joseph and Mary Cole, born —— ——. He married —— —— Hannah Randall.

Their children were:

i. Zilpha, b. ——, 1754; m. May 7, 1772, Edward Bartlett.

8. ii. Ephraim, b. ———, 1756; m. Dec. 18, 1777, Silence Webb.

iii. Hannah, b. ——, 1759; m. Isaac Keith, and after his death Capt. Seth Keith.

iv. Molly, b. ——, 1764; m. ——, 1782, John Drake.

v. Rachael, b. ———, 1768; m. ———, 1786, Ichabod Packard.

4

JOSEPH[2] COLE (*Joseph*[1]). Third son of Joseph and Mary Cole, born ——— ———. He married Elizabeth, daughter of Constant Southworth, December 8, 1757.

Their children were:

i. Desire, b. —— ——; m. Sept. 25, 1777, Noah Pratt. They removed to Vermont.

9. ii. Joseph, b. —— ——. He moved West.

5

ELEAZER[2] COLE (*Joseph*[1]). Fourth son of Joseph and Mary Cole, born ——, 1747. He married July 11, 1769, Lucy Shurtliff, and moved to Maine.

8

EPHRAIM[3] COLE (*Ephraim,[2] Joseph[1]*). First son of Ephraim and Hannah (Randall) Cole, born ——, 1756, in Bridgewater; married December 18, 1777, Silence Webb. Lived in Bridgewater.

His children were:

i. Ephraim, b. —— ——; m. ——, 1808, Susanna Packard, and had a daughter Susanna, born the same year.
ii. Thomas, b. —— ——; m. ——, 1810, Silence Thayer.
iii. Zibion, b. —— ——; m. ——, 1819, Mary, daughter of Bartlett Field.
iv. Osman, b. —— ——; m. —— ——, Lucy, daughter of Perez Southworth.
v. Alvan, b. —— ——; m. ——, 1823, Eliza, daughter of David French.
vi. Hannah, b. —— ——; m. ——, 1800, Silas Snow.

FREETOWN.

ABIAL COLE. Born about 1735. He was a sergeant in Captain Benjamin Pratt's company of Colonel Thomas Doty's regiment, in service 1758, and also in the company of Captain Levi Rounsevell, of Freetown, minute men of April 19, 1776 (Lexington). He also served one month and seven days in Captain Manasseh Kempton's company of Colonel Carpenter's regiment, in the campaign of 1777, in Rhode Island. He married Annie Pierce, of Middleboro, June 23, 1757. He owned a farm in Freetown, on the line between that town and Middleboro. He moved with his large family to Shutesbury, and died there about 1781, leaving his family in destitute circumstances. Mrs. Cole's brother, Captain Job Pierce, brought them back to Freetown, where she married

Colonel Thomas Rounsevell. They had no children. Colonel Rounsevell died January 31, 1826, aged eighty, and she died in September, 1806.

The children of Abial and Anna (Pierce) Cole were:

i. Abial, b. ——, 1758; enlisted as a soldier in the Revolutionary army, and never returned; is supposed to have perished in the service.

2. ii. John, b. —— ——.

3. iii. Joseph, b. —— ——.

iv. Lydia, b. Nov. 8, 1763; m. Samuel Pickens, of Middleboro, who died Feb. 7, 1823, aged 66. She died May 10, 1843. One daughter, Adelene, m. Lynde Valentine, a prominent man of Freetown, between 1821 and 1855; another, Martha, m. Silas Tenny, of Freetown, and a third, Melancy, m. Capt. John V. Pratt, of Freetown.

v. Betsy, b. —— ——; m. —— ——. Joseph Smith.

vi. Hannah, —— ——.

vii. Phebe, b. —— ——; m. —— —— Benjamin Hix, of Westport.

4. viii. Mercy, b. —— ——; m. Phillip[4] Rounsevell, of Freetown.

ix. Polly, b. —— ——.

5. x. Phineas, b. —— ——.

xi. Anna, b. —— ——; m. Nathaniel Fuller, of Sherburn, Vt., Feb. 5, 1807.

4

MERCY[2] COLE (*Abial*[1]). The eighth child of Abial and Anna (Pierce) Cole, was born —— ——. She married Phillip, the oldest son of Phillip[3] Rounsevell of Freetown.

They had twelve children, viz:

i. Gamaliel Rounsevell, b. Oct. 12, 1776; d. 185–; m. in 1824 Freelove Thompson, of Middleboro. He was a very prominent man in his locality.

ii. Phillip Rounsevell, b. Feb. 7, 1779; d. unmarried.

iii. Abial Rounsevell, b. Sept. 6, 1780; m. July 20, 1803, Betsy Ashley, of Freetown.

iv. Hannah Rounsevell, b. April 12, 1783; m. Bradford Rounsevell, of Freetown.
v. Ebenezer Rounsevell, b. Sept. 27, 1785; m. in 1808, Sally Rounsevell, of Freetown.
vi. Lydia Rounsevell, b. Dec. 3, 1787; never married.
vii. Phebe Rounsevell, b. —— ——; never married.
viii. Benjamin Rounsevell, b. Nov. 29, 1789; m. in 1815, Ann Gifford, of Rochester.
ix. Joseph Rounsevell, b. March 25, 1792; d. July 15, 1821; m. Delia Lawrence, of Freetown.
x. Philena Rounsevell, b. Aug. 12, 1794; m. Jonathan Washburn, of Dartmouth, June 10, 1814.
xi. Alden Rounsevell, b. Oct. 26, 1797; m. in 1822 Cornelia Ashley, of Freetown. He lived in Rochester.
xii. Robert G. Rounsevell, b. —— ——; m. in 1827, Mrs. Delia Rounsevell, widow of his brohter Joseph.

ROCKLAND, ME.

[From Eaton's Thomaston and Rockland, Me. Vol. II, P. 181].

CAPT. WILLIAM COLE. Born August 18, 1791 (in Virginia?). Came from Nashville, Tennessee, to Thomaston, Maine, and commenced trade at Mill River. He married Mary G. Dodge (daughter of Dr. Ezekiel Goddard Dodge, M. D., and Susannah [Winslow] Dodge, of Thomaston), born December 23, 1801, January 20, 1825. Removed his business to Rockland, where he died April 22, 1849.

Children:

i. Mary E., b. Dec. 1, 1826; d. May 5, 1851.
ii. Winslow, b. Aug. 3, 1829; d. Aug. 5, 1829.
iii. Rebecca W., b. Nov. 1 and d. Nov. 2, 1830.
iv. Susan W., b. Sept. 20, 1831; m. Captain Artemus Watts, and resided in Thomaston.
v. Sarah F., b. July 29, 1833; d. Mar. 10, 1852.
vi. Wm. J., b. Aug. 16, 1835; resided in Thomaston; removed to California.

vii. Eveline W., b. Apr. 30, 1857; resided in Thomaston.
viii. Garnet G., b. May 30, d. in June, 1838.
ix. Caroline, b. Dec. 20, 1839; resided in Thomaston, and died October 13, 1861.
x. Harriet A., b. July 18, 1841; d. Aug. 26, 1842.
xi. Henrietta, b. Aug. 23. d. Aug. 30, 1842.
xii. Randall, b. 1846; d. Aug. 12, 1852.

JOHN P. COLE (brother of William), b. in Virginia in 1801. Came from Nashville to Thomaston a few years later; traded at same place. Married July 1, 1828, Lavina Southworth, oldest child of William Southworth, from Duxbury, Massachusetts, and Lucy (Wheaton) Southworth, of Thomaston, born 1805. Removed to Illinois, but returned in 1856; resided in Thomaston; a merchant; removed in 1862 to Massachusetts.

Children:

i. Lavina S., b. Jan. 4, 1829; m. Benj. Avery, of Boston; resided in Thomaston.
ii. Adelia F., b. May 23, 1832; m. J. Augustus Hersey, of Wiscasset, Sept. 3, 1855.
iii. John W., b. Apr. 20, 1834; resided in Thomaston; clerk; removed to California in 1861.
iv. James D., b. Aug. 1, 1836; resided in Thomaston; clerk; enlisted in cavalry; removed to Mass.
v. Adelaide, b. Sept. 4, 1840; m. Lysander Hill, Esq., of Alexandria, Va.

JOHN F. COLE. Born in Waldoborough, Maine, 1799; came to Thomaston; carried on marble manufacturing; married November 6, 1825, Clementina Bryant, daughter of Joseph and Sally (Vose) Bryant, of Thomaston, born October 15, 1804. (Joseph was a son of Charles B., an Englishman.) Resided in Thomaston, and died November 6, 1831. He had a sister, Sarah, born 1793, who married Charles Starrett, of Thomaston, son of Thomas, of Warren (who was born 1793), September 30, 1815, tailor in Thomaston; died January 25, 1857, and had children:

i. Sarah W., b. Oct. 24, 1816; m. Isaac Hodgman, of Thomaston; d. Aug. 2, 1839.
ii. Mary C., b. Mar. 13, 1818; m. Tileston H. Smith, of Thomaston; d. July 3, 1856.
iii. Chas. T., b. May 30, 1820; m. Sarah S. Healey, of Thomaston; removed to Deadham, Mass.
iv. John C., b. Apr. 11, 1823; d. July 17, 1832.
v. David J., b. June 5, 1825; m. Martha Ann Harrington, Nov. 14, 1849; bookseller, teacher, inventor.

Children of John F.:

i. John J., b. Aug. 6, and d. Sept. 4, 1826.
ii. Sarah Clementina, b. July 20, 1827.
iii. John Andrew, b. Oct. 16, 1829; removed to Cal. with his mother and the family.
iv. Mary Catherine, b. Oct. 8, 1831.

[The following are notes of some of the early settlers and their children whom I have not been able to connect with the previous families.]

ELIZABETH. There sailed for New England, August 11, 1635, in the Bachelor de Lo, Thomas Webb, master, one Elizabeth Cole, aged twenty-three, a maid servant to Lyon Gardner. She had a certificate of conformity from the rector of her parish. [Reg. XIV, 322.]

In 1661 the proprietors of the undivided land of Salem petitioned for a proprietors' meeting. Among them was Elizabeth Cole, who signed with a mark.

JOHN, of Gloucester, Massachusetts. Wife Mehitable. Son Daniel, born May 14, 1669. [Reg. IV, 361.]

CLEMENT COLE, born 1605. He came in the Susan and Ellen from London, aged thirty. He had a certificate of conformity, and that he was no subsidy man. He probably had wife and children, as September 30, 1639, he had a lot for seven heads granted at the Mt. Wollaston (Braintree). The record of that allowance says that he had served with Captain Robert Keayne four years.

ALEXANDER. A Scot, from Dunbarton. In 1684 he was admitted as a member of the Scotch Charitable Society of Boston. The next year he was at Salem. He married Bethia Pitman, widow of John Silsbee, of Salem, and died in 1687, his will being dated June 24, and probated August 24 of that year. His will mentions two maiden sisters, Ann and Jeanette, as living in Dunbarton. He had one son, Alexander.

ARTHUR. He died in Cambridge, September 4, 1676. Arthur had married November 27, 1673, Lydia ———, who, after his death, married William Eager, April 13, 1680.

His children were:

i. Arthur, b. Dec. 10, 1674.
ii. Daniel, b. March 7, 1676.

FRANCIS. Boston. Wife's name Sarah. Had child:

i. Sarah, b. April 29, 1689.

GREGORY. A freeman of Portsmouth, Rhode Island, 1655.

JOHN. John Cole, aged forty, was a passenger in the ship Confidence, John Jobson, master, from London, April 11, 1638.

There was a John Cole at Salisbury from 1640 to 1650. Savage says he died 1682. On December 25, 1650, he was rated for 8s. 6d., and on May 18, 1652, for 4s. 10d. for half a year. [Reg. III, 55.] I am inclined to think this was John[2] (*James*[1]) of Hartford.

MATHEW. At Northampton 1663. He married, 1663, Susannah Cunliff, born March 15, 1645, only child of Henry Cunliff, who had removed from Dorchester to Northampton in 1659. He was killed by lightning April 28, 1665. On December 12 of that year the widow married John Webb, jr., of Northampton. On July 8, 1666, one Lydia Cole, of Northampton, died. It is possible that she was his daughter.

JOHN COLE. Early settler of Reading and South Reading, 1640–1700. [H. G. Reg., Vol. II, p. 46.]

EDWARD COLES. Passenger for Virginia in the Thomas and John, January 6, 1635; age twenty. [Reg., Vol. II, p. 374.]

THOMAS COLES. Passenger for Virginia in the Transport (age thirty-two) of London, Edward Walker, master, July 4, 1635. Certificate of conformity from minister of Gravesend. [Reg., Vol. III, p. 389.]

THOMAS COWLES. A seaman of Badminster, Somersetshire, England, 1759. Reference to in Memoirs of Sir Martin Forbisher. [Reg., Vol. III., p. 14.]

ROBERT. Boston. His wife was Ann (Staines?) daughter of Richard of Boston, born January 29, 1664.

His children were:

i. Staines, (dau.) b. Jan 19. 1681.
ii. Staines, (son), b. Dec. 10, 1682.
iii. Richard, b. Jan. 21, 1685.

SAMPSON. Boston, 1673, in which year he married Elizabeth, daughter of Edward and Elizabeth [Cole] (*Samuel*[1]) Werden.

His children were:

i. Elizabeth, b. June 7, 1674; d. young.
ii. Elizabeth, b, Nov. 19, 1679.
iii. David, b. Dec. 21, 1683.
iv. Jonathan, b. Sept. 2, 1686.

GEORGE COLE. Was at Lynn, 1637. Removed to Sandwich. The Plymouth records show that on April 16, 1640, one acre of land was to be granted to George Cole, and that the matter would be considered further when he brought in his estate. Probably went back to Lynn and died there about 1653, as an inventory of such a person is found of June 28 of that year. Another of that name, perhaps his son, was one of Captain Lathrop's company, known as the "Flower of Essex," that was so nearly annihilated in the battle of Bloodybrook, September 18, 1675. He was probably badly wounded, and died later, as his will is dated November 8. [See Essex Inst. Pub. II, p. 183].

HENRY. Was on jury from Sandwich, 1643, June 6. Savage thinks he went to Connecticut; if so see Henry, of Middletown. On list of men able to bear arms in Sandwich, 1643. Of Barnstable. Indicted for pilfering from Lieut. Mathew Fuller, March 7, 1654. Respited March 2, 1668-9. Sued Joseph Holly, administrator of Tristram Hull, late of Barnstable, damages for a colt bought by Hull and not paid for. He recovered a verdict of £9 and costs.

About 1660 he sued Tristram Coffin, of Nantucket, for value of a boat sold to Coffin. He recovered a verdict of £5 and costs.

EUNICE COLE. [Drake's Annals of Witchcraft, 100-3]. Of Hampton, N. H. Accused of witchcraft, 1656. She was wife of William Cole, who died in 1662. From his will made a few days before his death the inference is drawn that he is much younger than his wife. After the death of her husband she was detained as a prisoner some years, and was so held in October, 1668, and again the record of June 8, 1668, shows a payment for her maintenance. She seems to have been alternately at large and in prison. She was feared as a witch, and yet persecuted by the boys and hated by the ignorant. As late as 1680 she was tried as a witch, but "no full proof" appearing, she was put in prison during the pleasure of the Court. She died in a little hut, alone, in the rear of the present academy.

I present here letters giving some account of two families. The first is probably a branch of the Plymouth family, but the other seems to be from a different ancestor from any of the other families:

WINOOSKI, VT., April 26, 1886.

Frank T. Cole, Esq., Columbus, Ohio:

DEAR SIR—Yours of the 31st ult. in relation to the Cole family came duly to hand. I am informed by James H. Cole, an uncle now about eighty years old, that he thinks my great-grandfather's name was Archippus; that he lived in Taunton, Massachusetts; was proprietor of iron works. He had two sons only that grew to manhood, Thomas and Archippus. Archippus was a seaman, and died at about the age of seventy-five years, leaving no male issue.

My grandfather, Thomas Cole, was born in Taunton, Massachusetts, March 22, 1767, and died in Calias, Vermont, June 24, 1849. He had three sons that grew to manhood, Thomas, James H., and Ira. Ira died October 25, 1833, aged twenty-two years, and unmarried.

James H. is now living, aged about eighty years. He has no living children; has one grand-daughter only of his descendants.

Thomas Cole, my father, was born in Montpelier, Vermont, March 26, 1805, and died at Defiance, Ohio, in 1871. He had two sons that grew to manhood, myself the older; have one child, a daughter.

My brother, A. K. Cole, has three sons. One, Charles K., is married, and has one child, a daughter. The other two sons are unmarried.

I have thus traced my ancestors from my great-grandfather, and all his male issue now living are:

	AGE.		AGE.
James H. Cole.............	80	C. K. Cole.................	23
Ormand Cole..............	56	Walter Cole..........	20
A. K. Cole................	51	Harry Cole................	10

It seems that I am not of the family that you supposed it might be.

Your work is highly interesting, and shall be pleased to hear from you hereafter.

Respectfully, ORMAND COLE.

MINNEAPOLIS, MINN., April 6, 1874.

Mr. F. T. Cole:

MY DEAR SIR—Your letter of the 30th of last January was duly received, but my brother in Illinois having all of the old family papers, I was obliged to delay my answer until I could hear from him. I enclose the paper he sent me, and will herewith add what I can, hoping you may be able to glean something to your purpose. I make no apology for the illiteracy of my family, because in the common course of things there seems to be little or no help for it.

My father and mother and their children were born in the State of Virginia, in the midst of the most stupendous monster, human slavery, and its history is too well understood in its baneful tendencies to require elaboration in this connection. It was impossible for poor people to become educated in Virginia at that period, and although my father removed to Illinois soon after the birth of his youngest child still we were so poor that all of us arrived to manhood and womanhood before an education could be obtained even in a free State. To read and write to a very limited degree is about the extent to which the education of my father's family attained, *with one single exception*, and of that I must speak with as much modesty as the facts will allow.

My beloved wife, who was well educated, died April 16, 1857, leaving me two small children, one of which is since dead; the other still lives.

In September, 1858, I entered the preparatory class at Shurtliff College at Upper Alton, Illinois, and literally worked my way through a seven years' course, receiving my literary diploma and degree of P. B. in 1862, and my theological diploma in 1866. I then prosecuted my ministerial profession with considerable success until I lost my health, in 1871, since which time I have preached only occasionally. I was chaplain of the Minnesota Senate during 1869–70. Have since been invited to several important pulpits, but ill health has prevented acceptance. I am the only one of the name, so far as I have ever heard, who ever attended a college — all my ancestors, so far as I know, living and dying in illiteracy.

My father naturally was a man of broad and generous feelings, comprehensive views, and of the most reliable character, his word always being equal to a sealed bond. Although born and brought up in the country and principles of slavery, he instinctively scorned the doctrines of bondage, and plead and labored to the extent of his natural powers for freedom in church and State. He was a natural leader, and had he been educated, without doubt would have been felt widely in public, as he always was in private. My mother was naturally gifted also, and both together stood at the head of a remarkable family in many natural respects. Industry, integrity, and perseverance characterized the family to the extent of my acquaintance. But for want of culture we have been obliged to live in comparative obscurity.

It takes generations to destroy the cursed influence of human slavery, and if any of us have maintained an honorable standing in the community where we have lived, we will give all the glory to God, where it belongs.

Politically, then, we believe in freedom, and religiously we are Baptists, with few exceptions. "To the law and to the testimony," both in church and State, is the motto of our family. By that we are willing to live and die.

Some of my brothers had more or less connection with the late war, but I am unable to state definitely, we being so scattered up and down the country.

My father and my oldest brother both held the office of justice of the peace in the early days of Illinois, but of no consequence this.

R. S. Cole, my oldest brother, is a Baptist preacher.

Tradition says that three brothers by the name of Cole came from England to this country in an early day, one settling in the East, one in the South, the other I know not where. I have no doubt whatever that the one settling in the South was my great-grandfather.

I give first my father's family record, as I find it in the old family Bible, the only relic I have, and second my own family record:

FIRST.

William Cole and Ellen Samuel, married December 23, 1811.

BIRTHS.

William Cole, } father and mother { July 18, 1788.
Ellen Samuel, } father and mother { July 27, 1789.

Catherine Ann Cole, January 15, 1814.
Rebecca Jane Cole, April 16, 1815.
Mary Ellen Cole, July 18, 1816.
Richard Samuel Cole, December 22, 1817.
Robert Cole, January 22, 1819.
William Whitehead Cole, M. D., June 26, 1820.
Eliza Frances Cole, November 30, 1821.
James Albert Cole, December 30, 1822.
Daniel Johnson Cole, May 5, 1824.
Sarah Ann Elizabeth Cole, October 20, 1825.
Churchill Gordon Cole, May 18, 1827.
Thornton Mason Cole, January 11, 1829.
Addison Lewis Cole, February 9, 1831.
George Cumberland Cole, February 7, 1833.

SECOND.

Addison Lewis Cole and Mary Middleton Sewall (born July 13, 1835; died April 16, 1857). Married October 1, 1853.

CHILDREN.

Lewis Bingham Cole, January 1, 1856.
Adoniram Judson Cole, April 2, 1856.

The occupation of our family has for several years been farming, as a rule. My father owned fourteen hundred acres of land in Cass county, Illinois, and divided the same equally among his sons at the majority of the youngest, giving the daughters their portion in money, and reserving a small competency for himself while he and mother lived. Two of my brothers have acquired considerable property, but most of the family who remain alive have not acquired much. Honest toil, with little of the speculative, characterize the name so far as I know. I spent all I had and all I could make meantime upon my education, and graduated after the most severe sacrifice and self-denial, at the age of thirty-five, and in the struggle injured my constitution perhaps beyond full recovery.

The whole family lived in Illinois for years in poverty, and when we had acquired a little means the shame of age kept us from education. The privations of a frontier life are necessarily beyond the comprehension of those without experience, but to those who have gone through it, it is a reality far beyond envy. In our case, as in multitudes of others, human slavery was a curse whose effects will not be effaced for generations to come. The prejudices and jealousies it engendered retain their hold through blood, and it is only through the most uncompromising effort that I have been able to sustain my convictions of the necessity of culture, against the denial of many of my relatives. Very truly,

ADDISON LEWIS COLE.

[Extract from the Letter of Rev. R. S. Cole.]

Moses Samuel, our grandfather, was born in Holland, and came to America at the age of eighteen. He was a Jew, and remained strictly in that faith till his death. He died in Culpepper county, Virginia, September 25, 1830, aged eighty years, and was buried in Richmond, Virginia. His wife was Roseland Zemerman, who was born of German parents, in Madison county, Virginia. She died October 15, 1830, aged seventy-one.

Great-grandfather Cole is believed to have come from England. His son Daniel, my grandfather, was born in Prince William county, Virginia, and died there, aged eighty-six. He served in the War of 1812. He was twice married, and had twenty-one children, sixteen of whom grew to maturity.

He was a farmer and carpenter, and owned slaves. His family was scattered by removal or death, and his last years were spent alone among his slaves.

My father was born in Prince William county, and my mother, Ellen Samuel, in Madison county. One of Grandfather's brothers, Richard Cole, was a Baptist minister.

We moved to Illinois in the fall of 1833.

I have father's and mother's church letter, given them by the Mt. Poney Baptist Church, September 14, 1833. We started for Illinois a few days later, and were fifty-two days on the road. We settled in Morgan county, Illinois.

Grandfather's name was Daniel. His children were William, Daniel, Fanny, Eliza, and two other daughters by his first wife, and Henry, Samuel, Thomas, Richard, Betsy (married Rev. Henry Davis), Adeline, and one other daughter.

Carrollton, Illinois. R. S. Cole.

LIST OF SUBSCRIBERS.

NAME.	RESIDENCE.	NO. COPIES.
Batcheldor, Charles	Bloomfield, Ky	1
Benson, Lewis E	Arwell, Vt	1
Broadbent, Mrs. Lina	Bloomfield, Ky	1
Cass, Mrs. Helen A	Erving, Mass	1
Cole, Addison	Minneapolis, Minn	1
" A. W	Hyde Park, Ill	3
" Albert M	Howard, R. I	1
" Asa	West Medway, Mass	1
" Benj. J	Lake Village, N. H	8
" Chas. A	Sherman City, Mich	1
" Chas. H.	West Medway, Mass	1
" David G	Prospect Harbor, Me	1
" Edwin D	Roscoe, Ill	1
" Fred. E	Westmoreland, N. H	1
" George H	Fitchburg, Mass	1
" George	Keene, N. H	1
" Mrs. Harriet W	Westmoreland, N. H	1
" Harrison	Columbus, O	1
" Henderson	Elk Falls, Kan	1
" Henry M	Whitman, Mass	1
" Jefferson K	Peabody, Mass	1
" Jeremiah	Brooklyn, N. Y	1
" John A	Hyde Park, Ill	3
" Mrs. Levilla G	Westmoreland, N. H	1
" Miss Lorrella H	Lewiston, Me	1
" Martin E	Chicago, Ill	1
" Seth B	Nyack, N. Y.	1
" Truman	Sandusky, N. Y	1
" William H	Westminster, Vt	1

NAME.	RESIDENCE.	NO. CO
Cole, William H.	St. Louis, Mich	
" William J.	Monroe Center, Ill	
Cleaves, Mrs. Isabella P.	Prospect Harbor, Me.	
Daggett, Miss Sarah L.	Westmoreland Depot, N. H.	
Deasy, Mrs. Emma L.	Prospect Harbor, Me.	
Deasy, Luere B.	Bar Harbor, Me.	
Denning, S. R.	Sullivan, Me.	
Esty, William C.	Amherst, Mass	
Everett, E. S.	Portland, Me.	
Handy, Dan and Fred	Prospect Harbor, Me.	
Handy, Mrs. M. A.	" " "	
Hoffman, John	Gillett, Wis.	
McDermid, Mrs. Emily	Clintonville, Wis.	
McFarland, Mrs. Harriet	" "	
McLean, Mrs. Mary	" "	
Mahoney, Marcus H.	Portland, Me.	
Moon. Frank D.	Duluth, Minn.	
[illegible]n, Mrs. Martha E.	Royalston, Mass	
[illegible] Mrs. Mary E.	Westmoreland Depot, N. H.	
[illegible], Mrs. Eliza A.	Pembroke, Me.	
Porter, William D.	Indianapolis, Ind.	
Robertson, Mrs. Helen S.	Harrington, Me.	
Sperry, Mrs. J. B.	Fayette, Ia.	
Staples, Mrs. G. S.	Portland, Me.	
Seyffarth, Mrs. Caroline	Rindge, N. H.	
Whitney, Mrs. Emeline C.	Needham, Mass.	

www.ingramcontent.com/pod-product-compliance
Lightning Source LLC
Chambersburg PA
CBHW030912270326
41929CB00008B/672